IDIOT'S GUIDES.
AS EASY AS IT GETS!

Grammar and Style

by Mark Peters, PhD

ALPHA

A member of Penguin Group (USA) Inc.

ALPHA BOOKS

Published by Penguin Group (USA) Inc.

Penguin Group (USA) Inc., 375 Hudson Street, New York, New York 10014, USA • Penguin Group (Canada), 90 Eglinton Avenue East, Suite 700, Toronto, Ontario M4P 2Y3, Canada (a division of Pearson Penguin Canada Inc.) • Penguin Books Ltd., 80 Strand, London WC2R 0RL, England • Penguin Ireland, 25 St. Stephen's Green, Dublin 2, Ireland (a division of Penguin Books Ltd.) • Penguin Group (Australia), 250 Camberwell Road, Camberwell, Victoria 3124, Australia (a division of Pearson Australia Group Pty. Ltd.) • Penguin Books India Pvt. Ltd., 11 Community Centre, Panchsheel Park, New Delhi—110 017, India • Penguin Group (NZ), 67 Apollo Drive, Rosedale, North Shore, Auckland 1311, New Zealand (a division of Pearson New Zealand Ltd.) • Penguin Books (South Africa) (Pty.) Ltd., 24 Sturdee Avenue, Rosebank, Johannesburg 2196, South Africa • Penguin Books Ltd., Registered Offices: 80 Strand, London WC2R 0RL, England

International Standard Book Number: 978-1-61564-440-7
Library of Congress Catalog Card Number: 2013947931

16 15 14   8 7 6 5 4 3 2 1

Interpretation of the printing code: The rightmost number of the first series of numbers is the year of the book's printing; the rightmost number of the second series of numbers is the number of the book's printing. For example, a printing code of 14-1 shows that the first printing occurred in 2014.

Printed in the United States of America

Note: This publication contains the opinions and ideas of its author. It is intended to provide helpful and informative material on the subject matter covered. It is sold with the understanding that the author and publisher are not engaged in rendering professional services in the book. If the reader requires personal assistance or advice, a competent professional should be consulted. The author and publisher specifically disclaim any responsibility for any liability, loss, or risk, personal or otherwise, which is incurred as a consequence, directly or indirectly, of the use and application of any of the contents of this book.

Most Alpha books are available at special quantity discounts for bulk purchases for sales promotions, premiums, fundraising, or educational use. Special books, or book excerpts, can also be created to fit specific needs. For details, write: Special Markets, Alpha Books, 375 Hudson Street, New York, NY 10014.

Publisher: *Mike Sanders*
Executive Managing Editor: *Billy Fields*
Executive Acquisitions Editor: *Lori Cates Hand*
Development Editor: *John Etchison*
Senior Production Editor: *Janette Lynn*

Cover Designer: *Laura Merriman*
Book Designer: *William Thomas*
Indexer: *Angie Bess Martin*
Layout: *Ayanna Lacey*
Proofreader: *Cate Schwenk*

To Ed and Janet Peters.

Contents

8 Wrapping Up Action with Complements 131

9 Using Phrases 141

Appendixes

Introduction

Welcome to *Idiot's Guides: Grammar and Style*!

What brings you here?

If I had to guess, I'd assume one of the following descriptions applies to you:

- You're a student of some sort. You might be in middle school, high school, college, or even graduate school, but you've realized you need some extra help with grammar and style.

- English is not your first language, and you're struggling to get a handle on English grammar.

- You've received an unexpected opportunity to write something important—like a business report or an article—and you want to brush up on your grammar and improve your style.

- Your supervisor at work (or maybe a kind colleague) suggested you work on the basics of writing so you can present yourself better in emails and other written communication.

- You're a curious person who likes language and wants to spend a little more time learning how it works.

Do you fit in one of those categories? If so, welcome aboard.

If not, welcome aboard anyway. As long as you have a desire to learn about the nuts and bolts of grammar and the rules of thumb for style—or just a desire to improve your writing—this book should be educational.

What You Will Learn in This Book

Part 1, Introduction to Grammar and Style, provides a look at some of the reasons why grammar and style are important. I'll discuss different usage levels and the importance of writing at the appropriate level, whether you're writing a text message, short story, newspaper article, or dissertation. I'll also discuss literary devices, which aren't just for fiction writers and poets.

Part 2, Grammar Basics, looks at the parts of speech: nouns, verbs, adjectives, adverbs, prepositions, conjunctions, and interjections. I'll introduce you to concepts and terminology that will be important throughout the book, including the different sentence types.

Part 3, Using the Parts of Speech to Build Sentences, will help you utilize some of the building blocks and components of grammar that have already been introduced. In particular, you'll learn about nouns and verbs, which become subjects and predicates in sentences.

Part 4, Writing with Style, looks at various ways you can make your writing not only grammatically correct, but enjoyable to read. Sentence variety is one important aspect of writing with style, and I'll discuss many other ways to make your writing lively and readable. I'll also suggest ways to keep your writing inoffensive and bias-free.

Part 5, Fine-Tuning the Mechanics, will help you with some of the smaller details of writing, especially spelling, capitalization, and punctuation. You'll learn the various uses of commas, which can be very confusing. I'll also discuss parentheses, colons, question marks, exclamation marks, and semicolons. Hint: there are only two uses for semicolons.

After that, you'll also find a glossary of key terms and a list of resources for further reading.

Grammar and Style Supplements and Tidbits

Warnings, tips, definitions, and assorted bits of advice will be sprinkled throughout the book to enrich your growing knowledge of English grammar.

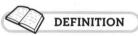 **DEFINITION**

In definition sidebars, I explain specialized grammar and style terms.

USAGE TIDBIT

These sidebars feature an extra morsel of usage advice or an interesting fact.

 PRACTICAL POINT

These sidebars present an extra bit of grammar or style advice.

 DANGER ZONE

When there's a danger of overapplying a rule or just an additional rule to share, it is discussed in one of these sidebars.

Acknowledgments

I'd like to thank my parents, Edward and Janet.

Thanks to all my writing students over the years. Whether you knew it or not, you helped me learn, too.

I'd also like to thank my dog, Monkey. He has excellent grammar for a dog.

Special Thanks to the Technical Reviewer

Idiot's Guides: Grammar and Style was reviewed by an expert who double-checked the accuracy of what you'll learn here, to help us ensure this book gives you everything you need to know about grammar and style. Special thanks are extended to Joy Dean Lee.

Trademarks

All terms mentioned in this book that are known to be or are suspected of being trademarks or service marks have been appropriately capitalized. Alpha Books and Penguin Group (USA) Inc. cannot attest to the accuracy of this information. Use of a term in this book should not be regarded as affecting the validity of any trademark or service mark.

Introduction to Grammar and Style

Even NASCAR drivers can't go from 0 to 200 miles per hour instantly. They have to gradually work their way up to the high speeds. In grammar you have to start slowly, too. This part will help you begin to learn the parts of speech and elements of grammar that will be crucial throughout the book—and in your future as a writer.

Motivation is also helpful when learning anything new. Maybe you already have strong reasons for learning about grammar and style, but in these chapters, you'll learn many reasons why grammar and style are important.

I'll introduce a lot of rules and conventions throughout this book, but this section will discuss the purpose of the rules and conventions. You'll learn some linguistic concepts such as syntax and morphology, as well as usage levels. Every type of writing is at a certain usage level, and it's important to know what level is appropriate. You wouldn't want to write at the Twitter level for a résumé.

I'll also discuss some aspects of style, including the use of literary techniques such as allusion, alliteration, and metaphor. Even if you don't want to write fiction or poetry, knowing about the creative potential of English can enrich your writing and make it much more enjoyable to read. Even the driest forms of writing have some art to them.

Rules and Conventions

As you set out on your journey to master English grammar and related topics, the first and most pressing question you might ask is: Why do I have to know this stuff? I'm not going to major in English or become a novelist. How is grammar going to help me?

That's understandable. After all, if you can read this book, engage in coherent discourse, and keep in touch via texting, email, Skype, and other digital media, you might wonder why you need to follow a bunch of apparently arbitrary rules.

This chapter answers those questions and more, as it brings you up to speed on what grammar, usage, and mechanics are all about and why they matter. I think you'll find there's a lot more to grammar and style than you think, and that they can help you not only in school and at work, but in how you present yourself throughout your life.

In This Chapter

- Understanding grammar, usage, and mechanics
- Recognizing different usage levels
- Following conventions
- Appreciating why this stuff matters

Brushing Up on Three Key Concepts

One of the keys to good writing is to define your terms, so the reader knows what you're talking about. The following list identifies and defines the three key terms discussed in this chapter:

- *Grammar* is the structure of a language that governs how words are formed and arranged to build phrases, clauses, and sentences.

- *Usage* is the customary way people express themselves in words; for example, formally or informally.

- *Mechanics* are the minutiae of writing, including spelling, capitalization, and punctuation.

Understanding Grammar

Grammar has two branches: *morphology*, which applies to the formation of words, and *syntax*, which applies to the arrangement of words to form phrases, clauses, and sentences. The following sections dig deeper into these two branches of grammar to give you a general understanding of what it's all about.

> **PRACTICAL POINT**
>
> Grammar is both *descriptive* and *prescriptive*. Linguists approach grammar as *descriptive*; they analyze and describe the way native speakers actually use a language. English teachers, on the other hand, tend to treat grammar as *prescriptive*—a set of rules that must be followed. We like to think of grammar, usage, and mechanics as both prescriptive and descriptive, because we all need to agree on some rules in order to communicate effectively with one another while recognizing the fact that language evolves over time. In other words, we need to follow rules, but those rules are subject to change.

Morphology: Words

Morphology is the study of *morphemes*—the smallest recognizable units in a language. For example, the word *cats* is comprised of two morphemes—the root word *cat* and the *–s* that makes it plural. The word *inconceivable* contains three morphemes: the root word *conceive*, the prefix *in–* and the suffix *–able*. The word *earring* is a *compound word* (a word made up of two or more words) consisting of two morphemes—*ear* and *ring*. Knowing something about morphology can help you spell words correctly and determine their meaning without having to crack open a dictionary.

Morphology also applies to the roles that words play in sentences—whether a word functions as a noun, verb, adjective, adverb, or one of the other eight parts of speech described in Chapter 3.

Of course, you can know much more about morphology, including the distinctions between roots, stems, and affixes (such as prefixes and suffixes); free and bound morphemes; and inflectional and derivational morphemes. But such information is of interest only to those working toward a degree in English or linguistics. For the rest of us, knowing about root words, compound words, prefixes, suffixes, and parts of speech is sufficient.

Practice

How many morphemes are in each of the following words?

1. class
2. unknown
3. infrequently
4. boots
5. failsafe
6. indefatigable
7. unsmiling
8. spider
9. fortunate
10. precooked
11. synergy
12. changing
13. rearranging
14. totally
15. spatula

Answers:

1. class: 1 morpheme (class)

2. unknown: 2 morphemes (un + known)

3. infrequently: 3 morphemes (in + frequent + ly)

4. boots: 2 morphemes (boot + s)

5. failsafe: 2 morphemes (fail + safe)

6. indefatigable: 4 morphemes (in + de + fatigue + able)

7. unsmiling: 3 morphemes (un + smil + ing)

8. spider: 1 morphemes (spider)

9. fortunate: 2 morphemes (fortune + ate)

10. precooked: 3 morphemes (pre + cook + ed)

11. synergy: 1 morpheme (synergy)

12. changing: 2 morphemes (change + ing)

13. rearranging: 3 morphemes (re + arrange + ing)

14. totally: 2 morphemes (total + ly)

15. spatula: 1 morpheme (spatula)

DANGER ZONE

Make sure you don't identify morphemes that aren't there. For example, *spider* may look like it contains the suffix *-er*, but it does not; *spider* is a morpheme with a complete meaning of its own.

Syntax: Word Order

Syntax applies to the way words are arranged to form phrases, clauses, and sentences. For example, most sentences in English start with a subject (noun or pronoun) followed by a verb with something at the end to complete the thought:

Molly	ran	down the hill.
subject	**verb**	**prepositional phrase**
		as adverb describing *ran*

Syntax also relates to the placement of adjectives (usually before the noun they modify) and adverbs (usually after the verb they modify); the arrangement of words in a prepositional phrase (preposition followed by the object of the preposition); the structure of relative clauses, such as those that start with *who, which,* or *where;* and so on. You'll find out more about syntax throughout Parts 1 through 3 of this book.

Choosing a Usage Level

Usage is the conventional use of a language in any given context. You probably change usage levels without ever realizing it; for example, you may talk one way to your parents and another way to your friends. You probably write in an entirely different way when writing an article or essay.

All types of writing vary in usage level. A text message to a friend will be extremely informal (and possibly sloppy). A peer-reviewed research article will be impeccably researched and written in an objective, scientific style. A newspaper editorial and a personal essay will both be subjective and opinionated but might vary wildly in terms of tone and purpose. An email to a friend will be much more informal than an email applying for a job. Depending on the audience and purpose, you'll have to write at many different usage levels, adjusting your tone, style, and diction.

The term *usage* also refers to the acceptable way of using certain words and phrases. For example, some people tend to confuse the terms *number of* (items) and *amount of* (substance). Instead of saying that fans purchased "a record *amount of* tickets" (wrong) you should say they purchased "a record *number of* tickets" (correct).

 USAGE TIDBIT

Computers and smart phones have introduced an entirely new level of usage for informal emails, texting, tweeting, and other casual online communication in which abbreviations are common and correct spelling is sometimes rare. This book contains very little coverage of these areas. The only recommendation we offer is to remain sensitive to what's considered acceptable and unacceptable to your audience. When in doubt, opt for more formal language until you have a better feel for what's considered acceptable.

Adhering to Conventions

Given the fact that most writing these days is typed, you don't need to dot your i's and cross your t's, but you still need to pay attention to *mechanics,* including the following items:

Spelling: A good spellchecker catches most typos, but it may not catch the use of wrong words, such as *their* instead of *there* and *its* (possessive of *it*) instead of *it's* (short for *it is*). You still need to proofread your prose and know how to spell and use a dictionary.

Capitalization: Capitalization is a convention that helps readers identify names, titles, headings, beginnings of sentences, and so on.

Punctuation: Knowing when to use periods, colons, semicolons, commas, dashes, quotation marks, and so on is essential to cueing your readers on when to pause and to helping them move through your writing smoothly.

Abbreviations: Abbreviations, including e.g. (for example), i.e. (that is), and etc. (etcetera), serve as a form of shorthand. Conventions for forming and using abbreviations ensure that readers know what each abbreviation stands for.

Numbers: Conventions regarding numbers cover everything from whether to use a comma to mark the thousands place to whether you use numerals or words for 1 (one) to 10 (ten).

Appreciating the Purpose of Rules and Conventions

People sometimes argue that grammar, usage, and mechanics don't matter as long as you're able to communicate clearly. The flaw in that argument is that clear communication requires adherence to conventions. Grammar, usage, and mechanics guidelines serve as the rules of the road. As long as everyone follows them, communication proceeds smoothly. Break the rules, and clarity suffers: readers must work harder to figure out exactly what you're trying to express, and they may simply give up or misinterpret your intended meaning.

The following sections highlight a few rules and conventions for communicating effectively in English. These sections also provide examples to show how breaking the rules can muddle communication.

Place the Subject First

In English, syntax is very flexible, but people generally expect sentences to follow certain patterns: they expect sentences to begin with a subject followed by a verb. When you stray from conventional syntax, you run counter to the listener's or reader's expectations, placing an added burden on your audience to decipher your intended meaning. Following are a few examples of sentences with syntax issues:

Sailing he was to the shores of Iceland.

The *Titanic* an iceberg sank.

To Natalie my tennis racket I gave.

Reading the sentences, you probably figured out their intended meaning, but your job would have been much easier if they followed conventional subject-verb syntax:

He was sailing to the shores of Iceland.

An iceberg sank the *Titanic*.

I gave Natalie my tennis racket.

PRACTICAL POINT

If you're writing poetry (verse), you have much greater freedom to experiment with syntax in order to develop rhythm and rhyme, but when writing prose, stick with more conventional word order.

Watch Where You Place Phrases and Clauses

A misplaced phrase or clause may result in ambiguity, as in the following example:

The couple returned from their Caribbean cruise which they had thoroughly enjoyed in a limousine.

Again, you can probably figure out the intended meaning, but at first reading, it sounds as though the couple had their Caribbean cruise in a limousine. You could fix this either by moving the phrase *in a limousine* closer to the verb it describes (*returned*) or by setting off the relative clause (*which* …) with commas:

The couple returned in a limousine from their Caribbean cruise, which they had thoroughly enjoyed.

The couple returned from their Caribbean cruise, which they had thoroughly enjoyed, in a limousine.

Read more on phrases and clauses in Chapters 9 and 10.

Avoid Awkward Shifts in Verb Tense

Verb tense conveys an action's time zone: past, present, future, and so on. Rules that govern tense help ensure that whenever someone relates a series of events, they do so in a way that's consistent with the actual chronology of the events. Just imagine how confusing a passage would be if verb tenses were used willy-nilly:

> All employees <u>will review</u> the safety policies and procedures before the accident <u>occurred</u>, but no one at the scene of the accident <u>were following</u> procedures.

Consistent use of tense clarifies the timeline, indicating when each action occurred in relation to the other actions:

> All employees <u>had reviewed</u> the safety policies and procedures before the accident <u>occurred</u>, but no one at the scene of the accident <u>followed</u> the procedures.

> Read more on verbs in Chapter 6.

Avoid Dangling Modifiers

A *dangling modifier* is a word or phrase that's in the wrong place. As a result, the misplaced modifier unintentionally describes the wrong word, as in the following example:

> <u>Having read the book</u>, the movie disappointed me.

In this example, "having read the book" describes "the movie," which doesn't make sense. By placing the modifier before the word it should describe, the sentence becomes much clearer:

> <u>Having read the book</u>, <u>I</u> found the movie disappointing.

> Read more on dangling modifiers in Chapter 15.

Beware of Misplaced and Omitted Commas

The comma is one of the most diminutive of punctuation marks, but an omitted or misplaced comma can cause considerable confusion. Here's an example of how a comma can completely change the meaning of a sentence:

> Let's bake, Grandma!

> Let's bake Grandma!

A missing *serial comma* (the comma before the last item in a series) can also confuse the reader, though less dramatically. For example, suppose you're emailing a friend to say that you invited four people over for dinner—your neighbors Joe and Tammy Smith and your friends Jan and Bob. You write:

> We invited the Smiths, Jan and Bob.

Without the serial comma, this could mean that you invited only Jan and Bob, whose last name is Smith, over for dinner. By using the serial comma, you clarify what you really mean:

> We invited the Smiths, Jan, and Bob.

Read more on commas in Chapter 17.

Use Parallel Constructions

Parallel construction results when two or more related phrases are in the same grammatical form; for example, they're all nouns, they're all verbs, or they're all *gerunds* (verbs ending in *–ing* that act as nouns). When items aren't parallel, a sentence sounds awkward, as in the following example:

> The company rewarded its employees for their <u>hard work</u>, expertise, and <u>paying attention to detail</u>.

Even to the untrained ear, something sounds a little off about that sentence. The terms *hard work* and *expertise* are standard nouns, but the last item, *paying attention to detail*, is a gerund. Parallelism clarifies the meaning and improves the sound of the sentence:

> The company rewarded its employees for their <u>hard work</u>, <u>expertise</u>, and <u>attention to detail</u>.

Read more on parallelism in Chapter 13.

Practice

Each of the following sentences contains errors or poor choices in grammar, usage, or mechanics. Rewrite each sentence to fix anything that doesn't seem right. If you can't spot or correct the error, don't beat yourself up. Instead, use this practice session to figure out where you need the most help. The answers that follow this exercise reference the chapters in this book where you can find additional information about the relevant rule and how to avoid making the same or similar mistakes.

1. Plant trees is what the Arbor Day Foundation encourages people to do.

    _____

2. The artist, Pablo Picasso, is one of my favorites.

    _____

3. Over my house the jet flew.

    _____

4. Jill's passions included hiking, skiing, and to write.

    _____

5. Halle's car was in the shop for three weeks but none of the mechanics had
    time to service it.

    _____

6. Parrots tend to nest in hollowed-out trees, which are generally not nest builders.

    _____

7. Their heading to the stadium to watch the game.

    _____

8. Because the restaurant was so drafty patrons complained of being cold.

    _____

9. The pen, which Mark borrowed from Lisa, leaked inside his shirt pocket.

    _____

10. After winning the game, the fans celebrated right along with the team.

    _____

Answers:

1. The Arbor Day Foundation encourages people to plant trees. (See Chapter 14 for more about syntax.)

2. The artist Pablo Picasso is one of my favorites. (Or "Pablo Picasso is one of my favorite artists." See Chapter 17 for more about comma usage.)

3. The jet flew over my house. (Learn more about syntax in Chapter 14.)

4. Jill's passions included hiking, skiing, and writing. (See Chapter 13 to learn about parallel constructions.)

5. Halle's car was in the shop for three weeks, but none of the mechanics had time to service it. (Chapter 14 discusses various ways to connect sentences.)

6. Parrots, which are generally not nest builders, tend to nest in hollowed-out trees. (See Chapter 10 for additional guidance on using and positioning relative clauses.)

7. They're heading to the stadium to watch the game. (Chapter 20 covers common spelling mistakes.)

8. Because the restaurant was so drafty, patrons complained of being cold. (See Chapter 17 for more about comma usage.)

9. The pen that Mark borrowed from Lisa leaked inside his shirt pocket. (Chapter 10 covers restrictive and nonrestrictive clauses and how to punctuate each.)

10. After winning the game, the team celebrated right along with its fans. (See Chapter 15 to find out more about dangling modifiers and how to purge them from your writing.)

The Least You Need to Know

- Grammar is the structure of a language according to which words are formed and arranged to build phrases, clauses, and sentences.
- Usage is the conventional use of a language in any given context or situation.
- Standard informal English is acceptable and appropriate for most types of written and oral communication.
- Mechanics consists of the conventions governing spelling, capitalization, punctuation, abbreviations, and numbers.
- The ultimate goal of learning grammar, usage, and mechanics is to be able to communicate effectively and efficiently.

Beyond the Rules: Writing with Style

A parent or teacher who only says "Don't do that!" and "Cut that out!" won't be very effective. Telling people what not to do doesn't help them figure out what to do—and why.

Similarly, expressing yourself effectively through language isn't only about following rules and avoiding mistakes; it also involves learning the craft of writing, so you know how to hook readers and compel them to continue reading.

While grammar, usage, and mechanics are about rules and conventions and what you should and shouldn't do, style is about what you can do. Style encompasses the infinite possibilities and potential of the English language.

Because style is about unlocking possibilities, it's more subjective than grammar. Pinning down exactly what it is and how to develop a distinctive style is difficult, if not impossible. This chapter is my attempt to bring you up to speed on style basics.

In This Chapter

- Understanding what style is
- Beginning with a few style guidelines
- Techniques for improving your writing style
- Waxing poetic with figurative language
- Getting specific with style guides

Defining Style

Style is the manner in which a writer chooses to present content to an audience in order to achieve the desired effect. While some experts define style as a writer's distinctive form of expression—or voice—style goes beyond that. A writer can change styles depending on the nature of the publication, the audience, the topic, the goal that the writer seeks to achieve, and a host of other variables. Journalists and technical writers, for example, usually make a conscious effort to keep their personality out of their writing in order to establish an objective viewpoint. Copywriters want to sell something and may try to do so by evoking an emotional response from their audience.

Style shouldn't be a mechanical structure superimposed on the content. Style should develop organically along with the content so the final written product serves whatever purpose the author has in mind. The style you use should help you convey information, describe a character, report a story, persuade readers to think or act a certain way, or achieve some other purpose.

Feel the pace shift within the following paragraph from Jack London's short story "A Piece of Steak," as the description transitions from Sandel, a spirited young boxer, to his opponent, Tom King, who's more experienced and methodical:

> Sandel was in and out, here, there, and everywhere, light-footed and eager-hearted, a living wonder of white flesh and stinging muscle that wove itself into a dazzling fabric of attack, slipping and leaping like a flying shuttle from action to action through a thousand actions, all of them centred upon the destruction of Tom King, who stood between him and fortune. And Tom King patiently endured. He knew his business, and he knew Youth now that Youth was no longer his. There was nothing to do till the other lost some of his steam, was his thought, and he grinned to himself as he deliberately ducked so as to receive a heavy blow on the top of his head. It was a wicked thing to do, yet eminently fair according to the rules of the boxing game. A man was supposed to take care of his own knuckles, and, if he insisted on hitting an opponent on the top of the head, he did so at his own peril.

While your goal may not be to write a short story or a novel, you still need to be sensitive to the subtle messages that different styles convey. If you're writing a letter of complaint to a company, for example, you want the tone to be assertive but respectful. If you were writing a letter of apology to a customer, on the other hand, you'd want to sound courteous and accommodating.

Some Different Styles

Every type of writing or genre has a certain style. Here are brief descriptions of some common writing genres and their styles:

News articles. These are written in an objective, presentational style by journalists. The writer tries to be invisible. As they say, this is a "just the facts" type of writing.

Column. This form of journalism expresses an opinion and is usually written in a personal style that highlights the wit of the writer. In a newspaper, you should be able to read the facts in news articles, then read someone's opinions of the facts in columns.

Editorials. Columns are sometimes called editorials, but an editorial is also a specific type of opinion piece that's usually written by the editor and represents the opinion of the entire paper. This kind of editorial usually doesn't list an author, since it is meant to represent the paper as a whole (and may be the work of a few editors). An editorial has a less personal voice than a column.

Magazine articles. There is a wide range of magazine articles, but generally they are examples of in-depth reporting that dig deeply into a topic or a person's life. Magazine writers have more leeway for creativity (such as humor and extended description) than writers of news articles.

Essay writing. This category overlaps quite a bit with magazine writing. However, essays are often more personal than magazine articles. Often, essays fall in the category of creative nonfiction, a type of writing that uses the literary devices of fiction to write about true events.

Scholarly journal articles. These are scientific articles that present and discuss research. Scholarly articles are written in all the sciences, from the hard (physical) sciences to the soft (social) sciences. This type of writing is written in an extremely objective, detached style with a meticulous eye for detail.

Research papers for school. These mimic scholarly journal articles but are quite different. The main difference is that the student almost never does any original research except for reading articles, so a research paper is almost always the equivalent of a literature review. Research papers are assigned to help students improve as writers and thinkers. They are usually written with a strong thesis statement: a sentence that captures the argument of the paper.

Advertising copy. This can range from a single slogan ("I'm lovin' it!") to the entire script of a commercial. One of the best examples of a clever advertising campaign is Dos Equis' "The Most Interesting Man in the World" character, perhaps the most roguish, charming beer pitchman in history. Ad copy is often humorous, and it should catch people's attention. This is writing with a simple purpose: get people to buy your product. A secondary goal would be to help people remember your product and have good associations with it. That process is known as branding.

Creative writing. This is a broad category that could include dramatic writing, humor writing, and advertising copy, but it most commonly refers to poetry and fiction. The simplest definitions of poetry and fiction might be that poetry expresses emotions and fiction tells stories, but those are extremely simplistic definitions that only apply in a very broad sense. Poetry and fiction are both huge categories full of variety, and you should seek out a book on either to learn more.

> **PRACTICAL POINT**
>
> Good style is engaging, clear, and direct. Bad style is dull, muddled, and unclear.

Theatrical writing. This includes writing for the stage or video, such as playwriting and screen-writing. Theatrical (also called dramatic) writing is just as creative as poetry and fiction, but there's a big difference: playwrights and screen writers write for actors to perform their words. Theatrical writing also includes writing for television and internet videos, as well as dramatic forms such as the one-act play, 10-minute play, and sketch, a comedic form made famous by *Saturday Night Live*.

Comedy writing. Like ad copy, comedy writing has a simple purpose: make people laugh (and often, think). Comedy writing includes scripts for TV and movies, jokes for standup comedians and the internet, and humor pieces, which are comedic essays. One of the best sources of humor pieces is *The New Yorker*'s Shouts & Murmurs section.

Business writing. This includes a variety of professional writing, including business reports, memos, PowerPoint presentations, letters, and even job materials such as a résumé. Business writing is brief and to the point: it should communicate as simply and directly as possible (though business writing is often full of jargon, which you'll learn more about in Chapter 12).

Grant writing. This is a very specific type of writing aimed at securing funding from agencies and organizations that give grants (money) to businesses and individuals. Grant-writing is dry, technical, and precise (and also lucrative if you know how to do it well).

Blog post. Blogging is one of the most difficult types of writing to sum up; the range of blog styles will make you dizzy. A blog could be a series of pictures of your cat, a disconnected bunch of rants on politics, a group of posts about your vacation to Greece, or a forum for serious discussions of feminism—or any other topic. The credentials of bloggers vary wildly. Any person in the world can blog, from your weird neighbor to a linguistics professor. To judge the value of a blog, consider the quality of the writing, the purpose of the blog, and the credentials of the blogger. For your own blog, think about whether you'd like your blog to be a fun hobby or a potential asset to your career. It could be either.

Tweet. A message for the popular social network and microblogging service Twitter, the key feature of a tweet is that it must be 140 characters or fewer. Despite the seeming triviality of the form, many writers—of humor and more serious matters—have used tweeting to build an audience that has led to paying work, such as writing books or TV shows. How you tweet is entirely up to you. Reposting someone else's tweet—which is like quoting it—is retweeting.

Text message. This is probably the most informal type of writing. However, like anything else, some people take texting more seriously than others. The purpose of many texts is to have a conversation or to pass on information such as "I'm running late" or "My gate at the airport changed."

You should also know that writing genres are not uniform types of writing: everyone writing in a genre doesn't write the same way. If you want to learn more about the style of one of these types of writing, you should pick up a book geared toward that type of writing.

When it comes to writing, there is variation within variation within variation. Each publication has its own style, but each writer also has a style. When writing in a specific genre, you should find a balance between your own style and that of the genre.

The following section is more general: it describes elements of good style that will usually help you communicate effectively and economically in words.

Style Guidelines

Although style varies and what constitutes a good writing style is somewhat subjective, the following guidelines can help you write with style:

Keep it simple. Writing doesn't have to be complicated to be good. It needs to be clear and direct. Unless you have a reason to do otherwise, stick with relatively short sentences and paragraphs.

Establish a smooth and logical flow. Good writing flows smoothly from word to word, sentence to sentence, and paragraph to paragraph. A smooth and logical flow is often the product of a clear idea, the right structure, and meticulous organization. When writing has a strong central idea, heavy-handed transition words—such as *although, therefore,* and *in conclusion*—aren't needed as much to transition from one sentence or paragraph to the next.

USAGE TIDBIT

You can often create subtle transitions by repeating a key word from a sentence or paragraph in the sentence or paragraph that follows it. These transitions can help your writing hold together for the reader, kind of like how I just repeated *transitions*.

Develop an attitude. Be conscious of the tone you're setting. Do you want to come across as serious or playful, intimate or detached, angry or conciliatory, tough or tender?

Start most sentences with a subject-verb combo. The subject is the person, place, or thing that's acting or being. The verb is the action or condition. Starting with a subject-verb combo helps you avoid many common flaws in style.

Vary your sentence structure. Although you should start most sentences with a subject-verb combo, you can combine sentences, add phrases and clauses, and experiment with syntax to establish an engaging rhythm and pace.

Write mostly in the active voice. Active voice makes the subject of the sentence clear. Passive voice omits or hides the subject. Check out these examples:

> **Active:** NASA launched the satellite into orbit.

> **Passive:** The satellite was launched into orbit.

Although passive voice is suitable in certain situations when you want to gloss over the subject, you should usually write in the active voice, which is much clearer and easier to read.

Write with concrete nouns and action verbs. By choosing vivid nouns and strong verbs, you won't need as many adjectives, adverbs, and phrases.

Choose precise words. You can often reduce wordiness and increase the impact of a message by taking time to choose the right words. Use a thesaurus to scope out your options and a dictionary to narrow your options to the word with just the right meaning.

Trim the fat. Terse expressions have greater impact.

 DANGER ZONE

Remain sensitive to a word's *denotation* (literal meaning) and *connotation* (idea or emotion that people commonly associate with the word). Certain words have a positive or negative connotation. Compare the words *miserly* and *frugal*. Both words mean to spend money sparingly, but *miserly* carries the negative connotation of being stingy, whereas *frugal* carries the positive connotation of managing money wisely.

Sharpen Your Style

One way to develop a good writing style is to consciously strive to follow the guidelines described in the previous section. The following are additional ways to develop a mastery of style:

Write with a purpose. Is your purpose to entertain, inform, instruct, persuade, or do something else? Writing with a clear purpose will help you gauge your writing's effectiveness as you draft and revise. If your writing fails to meet your objective, you have more work to do.

Don't procrastinate or be a perfectionist. Beginners often agonize about the quality of their writing so much that they're unable to get any writing done. Just start writing, even if you don't feel ready. You can always fine-tune it later, but there will be nothing to fine-tune if you don't start.

Write more or less in the manner you normally speak. Some writers try so hard to sound educated that the message gets lost in tortured prose. Write as you speak and then revise and reorganize as needed to make your message crystal clear.

Keep your audience in mind. When writing to an individual, keeping your audience in mind is easy. If you're writing to a larger audience, try to single out one individual and imagine yourself speaking to him or her.

Read good writing. You can find good writing in everything from classic novels to quality newspapers and magazines, including *Rolling Stone* magazine, *Vanity Fair, The Wall Street Journal,* and *Sports Illustrated.* Try reading a few pieces aloud to tune your ear to good writing.

Emulate a writing style you like. While you don't want to write just like someone else, exercises in emulating a certain writing style make you more conscious of style and allow that style to influence your own.

Read your own writing aloud. If you're tripping over your own words, your readers will have an even harder time maintaining their balance. Reading aloud often reveals problems that need fixing. Eventually, you'll be able to read aloud in your head.

Distance yourself from what you wrote. Write a rough draft and then set it aside for a few hours or (even better) a day or two. Now read it again. This technique gives you a more objective view of the text and often reveals areas that require fine-tuning.

Request feedback. Have someone else read what you wrote and tell you what they think. You don't have to take their feedback, but someone looking at a paper with fresh eyes can help you learn the strengths and weaknesses of your writing.

PRACTICAL POINT

In business, technical, and internet writing, compose short paragraphs and use headings and lists to break up the text into easily digestible snippets. This approach makes the content more accessible and easier to skim. It also lessens the need for you to transition between sentences and paragraphs.

Enhance Your Prose with Literary Devices

Literary devices are techniques that writers have developed to take language beyond its literal meaning and appeal to the senses. Although you're more likely to encounter literary devices in fictional works and poetry, you can use them in other types of writing to drive home a point, clarify an idea, or punch up your prose. The following sections cover literary devices commonly used in writing prose.

Paint a Picture with Figurative Language

Figurative language uses words to engage the senses, memories, and imagination of the reader through a variety of literary devices, including the following:

- *Simile* is a comparison using *like* or *as:*

  Sonny Liston jabbed like a jackhammer.

- *Metaphor* is a comparison not using *like* or *as*:

  The public defender was buried beneath his caseload.

- *Personification* is the attribution of human qualities to a nonhuman being or object:

  The tornado ravaged the city like an angry mob.

- *Paradox* is the juxtaposition of two apparently contradictory ideas:

  A baby is a new life; for parents, it's also the end of their old life.

- *Hyperbole* is an exaggeration used to drive home a point:

  Mark lived life at a 100 miles an hour.

- *Allusion* is a reference to something outside of the text that the audience probably knows about:

  The adrenaline rush infused onlookers with Herculean strength, enabling them to lift the car off of the injured driver.

- *Idiom* is a common expression whose meaning has little or no connection with its literal meaning. For example, the phrase "keep your nose to the grindstone" doesn't literally mean to do so, it means to focus on your work. A word of caution: use idiomatic expressions sparingly, if at all, in formal writing.

Tune In to the Sounds of Language

Although this book isn't about writing poetry or song lyrics, you should still be sensitive to the way language sounds and know something about the literary devices at your disposal to produce sound effects:

- *Alliteration* is the repetition of the same first consonant sound in adjacent or nearby words:

  <u>S</u>nakes <u>s</u>lithered <u>s</u>oftly through the grass.

- *Assonance* is the repetition of vowel sounds in nearby words:

  We heard the s<u>ou</u>nd of p<u>ou</u>nding from the apartment d<u>ow</u>n the hall.

- *Consonance* is the repetition of consonant sounds in nearby words, not necessarily at the beginning of each word:

  Jack <u>m</u>u<u>m</u>bled du<u>m</u>bly.

- *Onomatopoeia* is the formation of a word that sounds like what it means; for example, *boom, pop, growl*, and *buzz*.

- *Rhythm* is any recognizable pattern of sound that helps the text flow smoothly. Sentence length and variety, word choice, and punctuation all contribute to the rhythm of a sentence. The following example contains a long sentence followed by a very short one, producing an abrupt shift in rhythm:

  The show presented a magnificent array of music, dance, acrobatics, drama, and humor, all carefully choreographed and meticulously performed to engage and entertain. Unfortunately, the audience was not impressed.

 DANGER ZONE

Don't overuse literary devices. Indulging in too much of a good thing may distract readers from the point you're trying to make. Use literary devices sparingly and strategically to hook your readers, keep them reading, and leave a lasting impression.

Practice

On the line following each sentence below, write the name of the literary device used in the sentence.

1. Following King Solomon's lead, the judge threatened to split the car in two and give each owner half.

2. Nothing had prepared Patty for Paul's perpetual palaver.

3. The homeowners were underwater on their mortgage and facing the possibility of foreclosure.

4. Don't loan your coat to Joan.

5. I'm thirsty enough to drink Niagara Falls.

6. After splashing water on his face, Dylan felt refreshed.

7. None of the senators would even utter the phrase "balanced budget," because it was such a political hot potato.

8. To some people, plants are like pets.

9. Hail smacked the metal roof like a cacophony of cats.

10. Earth is a doctor that heals herself.

Answers:

1. Allusion to King Solomon

2. Alliteration—repetition of "p"

3. Metaphor comparing the state of being behind on one's mortgage to drowning

4. Assonance—repetition of long "o" vowel sound

5. Hyperbole—nobody can actually drink Niagara Falls

6. Onomatopoeia—the word *splashing*

7. Idiom—*hot potato*

8. Simile comparing plants to pets

9. Consonance—repetition of the hard "c" sound

10. Personification comparing the Earth to a doctor

Consult Style Guides

For additional guidance on how to write clear, error-free prose, consult one or more *style guides,* which come in two types:

General purpose style guides cover the fundamentals of good writing regardless of what you're writing. Strunk and White's *The Elements of Style* is a classic, popular style guide. For a more up-to-date look at style and writing improvement, try a book such as Ben Yagoda's amusingly titled *How to Not Write Bad.*

Specialized style guides serve as collections of rules and best practices to follow when writing for specific publications (for example, if you're writing an article for the *Journal of Clinical Psychiatry,* you'll probably be required to follow American Psychological Association (APA) style guidelines). Popular specialized style guides include the following:

> *The Chicago Manual of Style*
>
> *MLA (Modern Language Association) Handbook for Writers of Research Papers*
>
> *The Publication Manual of the American Psychological Association*
>
> *The Associated Press Stylebook*
>
> *The New York Times Manual of Style and Usage*

If you're writing or editing an article for a magazine, newspaper, or journal, ask which style guidelines to follow.

DEFINITION

The term **style guide** is a bit of a misnomer. Style guides rarely cover style in any depth. A more appropriate name for them would be *usage and mechanics guides,* and I should have covered them in Chapter 1, where I discuss usage and mechanics. However, since everyone else in the business refers to these publications as style guides, I'll follow their lead.

The Least You Need to Know

- Style is the manner in which a writer chooses to write.
- Style varies according to genre and publication, as well as individual.
- A good writing style uses words to engage and communicate effectively and efficiently.
- To hone your writing style, write with a purpose, say what you mean, and keep your audience in mind.
- Use figurative language, when appropriate, to engage your readers' senses.
- Consult style guides for grammar, usage, and mechanics guidelines, especially if you're writing or editing for publication.

PART 2

Grammar Basics

What are the parts of speech? What is a sentence? How do the parts of a sentence work together? I'll answer these basic issues of grammar in these chapters. The meat and potatoes of this book will be served.

This section of the book is very word-oriented. I'll discuss nouns, verbs, adjectives, adverbs, prepositions, conjunctions, and interjections. Also, I'll go beyond the types of words to discuss what they can do grammatically. This is especially important when discussing how nouns become subjects and verbs become predicates. I'll include many quizzes to help you test yourself on the information.

I'll also introduce you to the types of sentences, which will be essential later when the focus shifts to style. There can be no style without grammar, and you can't use grammar without having some type of style. The twin topics of this book are always intertwined, even when one is in the spotlight.

If you have a test on grammar and style in one hour and need to cram, these are the chapters you should focus on. I'll introduce you to the terminology and concepts that will be expanded on later. These sections will lay the foundation for becoming a true student of English grammar.

Brushing Up on Parts of Speech

Parts of speech are the categories used to group words by the roles they play in sentences, kind of like how actors play lead and supporting roles on stage and in TV and movies.

Some words name a thing, others express an action, some modify other words, several join words and clauses, and a few simply utter short exclamations.

You don't have to be able to name or define the parts of speech in order to pen punchy prose, but you do need to have a working knowledge of them, so you know what I'm talking about when I mention them in other chapters.

The good news is that the English language has only eight parts of speech: nouns, pronouns, verbs, adjectives, adverbs, conjunctions, prepositions, and interjections. The bad news is that working with some of these parts of speech can get pretty involved. This chapter brings you up to speed on the parts of speech and their nuances.

In This Chapter

- Getting to know the different parts of speech
- Telling the difference between a noun and a pronoun
- Recognizing the three verb types
- Connecting words with conjunctions and prepositions
- Straddling the lines that define the parts of speech

Meeting the Actors: Nouns and Pronouns

Nouns and *pronouns* represent beings: people, places, and things, including abstract things such as love and freedom. In any given sentence, they're the ones doing the action or on the receiving end of the action. The following sections explain the difference between nouns and pronouns and provide additional relevant details for dealing with them.

The Lead Actors: Nouns

Nouns conjure up images of creatures, locations, or objects—*dog, tornado, neighbor, Popeye, Australia.* Anything that can act, be acted upon, or just plain *be* has a noun that names it. Nouns come in four basic types:

Common: Your average everyday nouns that represent a class of objects as opposed to a particular individual. Words such as *car, cat, toe, tree, idea,* and *location* are all common nouns.

Proper: Names of individuals and places. Proper nouns always start with a capital letter; for example, *Aunt Mary, Patrick, Bora Bora, Fido,* and the *Hope Diamond.*

Compound: When two or more words represent a single being or entity, you're looking at a compound noun: *mother-in-law, baseball, toothbrush,* and *tennis shoe* are all compound nouns. Note that some are one word, some are hyphenated, and some are two or more words separated by spaces. Sometimes more than one spelling is correct, and the accepted spelling can change over time. For example, *base-ball* was once correct, but it would look weird today if you hyphenated *baseball.*

Collective: Collective nouns are those that represent a group, such as *team, herd, crew, flock, gang,* and *troupe.* Although it is representing a group, the noun itself can be treated as singular or plural.

> **PRACTICAL POINT**
>
> Some nouns are born from verbs. Collectively referred to as *verbals, gerunds* (verb forms ending in *-ing*) and *infinitives* (for example, *to jump*) function as nouns, as in the following example:
>
> *Jumping rope* is my favorite exercise.

The Supporting Cast: Pronouns

Just as nouns represent classes of objects or individual persons, places, or things, pronouns represent nouns. The English language provides you with pronouns so you don't have to keep repeating the noun, which can become quite annoying. Most pronouns have an *antecedent*—a noun that the pronoun represents, as in the following example:

<u>Sally</u> always traveled with <u>her</u> dog.

Sally is the antecedent (a proper noun, by the way), and *her* is the pronoun that refers back to *Sally*. While nouns tend to change form only in the possessive (*Sally's* instead of *Sally*), pronouns take on many forms to reflect their function. Keep reading to find out more about the different pronoun forms.

Personal pronouns represent a specific person, place, or thing. They come in two types: subjective and objective, which play different roles in a sentence.

Subjective personal pronouns:

	Singular	**Plural**
First person	I	we
Second person	you	you
Third person	he, she, it	they

Objective personal pronouns:

	Singular	**Plural**
First person	me	us
Second person	you	you
Third person	him, her, it	them

For more about how subjective and objective pronouns function in a sentence, see "Changing Case" later in this chapter.

Possessive pronouns signify ownership:

	Singular	**Plural**
First person	my, mine	our, ours
Second person	your, yours	your, yours
Third person	his, hers, its	their, theirs

 DANGER ZONE

Although you typically show possession by adding –*'s* to the end of a word, *its*, the possessive form of *it* without the apostrophe before the *s*, is the exception. The word *it's* is a contraction meaning *it is*.

Reflexive pronouns reflect action performed on oneself:

	Singular	**Plural**
First person	myself	ourselves
Second person	yourself	yourselves
Third person	himself, herself, itself	themselves

Intensive pronouns emphasize the doer of the action. They're identical to the reflexive pronouns, but the action isn't performed on the actor. The following two examples demonstrate the difference:

Reflexive: Sally slapped <u>herself</u> silly.

Intensive: Sally cooked the meal <u>herself</u>.

Demonstrative pronouns point things out or demonstrate them. *This, that, these,* and *those* are all demonstrative pronouns.

Relative pronouns—*that, where, which, who, whom,* and *whose*—enable you to add information about the noun you just mentioned. Here are a couple examples:

The delivery truck, <u>which</u> was already late, slammed into the loading dock.

This summer, we're traveling to Bora Bora, <u>where</u> we vacationed three years ago.

Interrogative pronouns ask a lot of questions (five, to be precise):

- *What … ?*

- *Which … ?*

- *Who … ?*

- *Whom … ?*

- *Whose … ?*

Indefinite pronouns can't make up their mind whom or what they refer to. The following lists some of the indefinite pronouns and distinguishes the singulars from the plurals and those that can go either way.

The Indefinite Pronouns

Singular	Plural	Singular or Plural
another	both	all
anybody	few	any
anyone	many	more
anything	several	none
each		most
either		some
everybody		
everyone		
everything		
neither		
no one		
nobody		
nothing		
one		
somebody		
someone		
something		

Reciprocal pronouns, such as *each other* and *one another,* belong to the mutual admiration society. These pronouns are used to show that two or more entities have an equal relationship. Here are a couple examples of the reciprocal pronouns in action:

> The crew members respected <u>one another</u>.

> Family members tend to like <u>each other</u>.

Differences in Noun and Pronoun Behavior

With nouns and pronouns, you're likely to observe an inequality: pronouns come in nine flavors, but nouns have only four. Why? Because nouns change form only to become plural or possessive, whereas pronouns change to become personal, possessive, reflexive, intensive, demonstrative, and so on, all in the singular and plural.

Check it out. Regardless of the role it plays, a noun remains fairly constant:

> **Personal:** <u>Sally</u> drives a truck.
>
> **Possessive:** <u>Sally's</u> truck barreled past the exit.
>
> **Reflexive:** <u>Sally</u> drove <u>Sally</u> to the depot. (Now you know why we have reflexive pronouns.)
>
> **Interrogative:** <u>Sally</u> drove to the depot?

You get the idea. Now observe how versatile a pronoun is, changing form based on the role it plays:

> **Personal:** <u>She</u> drives a truck.
>
> **Possessive:** <u>Her</u> truck barreled past the exit.
>
> **Reflexive:** Sally drove <u>herself</u> to the depot.
>
> **Interrogative:** <u>Who</u> drove to the depot?

Changing Case

Nouns and pronouns may change *case* depending on the role they play in a sentence. English has three cases:

Subjective: The noun or pronoun serves as the subject of the sentence—the person, place, or thing doing the action or existing in some state or quality of being.

Objective: The noun or pronoun is on the receiving end of the action, typically as a *direct object* (the object being acted upon) or the *indirect object* (the object receiving the direct object). For example, if I pay *you $25*, the $25 is the direct object, because that's what I'm handing you, and you're the indirect object, because you're receiving the money.

Possessive: Nouns and pronouns in the possessive *case* own something. To show ownership, you add *-'s* to the end of a noun or just an apostrophe to plural nouns ending in *-s*. Pronouns show ownership much differently, as explained next.

> **DEFINITION**
>
> **Case** is the form of a pronoun that reflects how the pronoun functions in a sentence.

When nouns change case, you barely notice because all they do is tack on –'s to form the possessive. When pronouns change case, they morph into entirely different beings. Here's just a small sample for comparison purposes:

	Subjective	**Objective**	**Possessive**
Singular Noun	hamster	hamster	hamster's
Pronoun			
1st person	I	me	mine, ours
2nd person	you	you	yours
3rd person	he, she, it	him, her, it	hers, his, its

To find out more about how pronouns change case, check out the earlier section that focuses solely on pronouns.

Practice

Fill in the blank with the correct form of the pronoun that refers back to its antecedent.

1. All of us decided to visit the art museum; _____ wanted to see Picasso's painting *The Old Guitarist.*

2. They drove _____ to the museum instead of taking the light rail.

3. The train, _____ was running ahead of schedule, showed up earlier than they had anticipated.

4. _____ Harry and Sally wanted to get married, but _____ was willing to commit to a specific date.

5. The flock of Canadian geese migrated south when _____ food supply started to run short.

6. Aurora couldn't think of _____ to buy her father for his birthday.

7. Connor _____ made the pizza from scratch.

8. Seasonal allergies _____ may not be responsible for all of your symptoms.

9. When I listen to heavy metal music, I can barely hear _____ think.

10. Although the two lovers certainly admired _____, they rarely demonstrated _____ affection in public.

Answers:

1. All of us decided to visit the art museum; <u>we</u> wanted to see Picasso's painting *The Old Guitarist.*

2. They drove <u>themselves</u> to the museum instead of taking the light rail.

3. The train, <u>which</u> was running ahead of schedule, showed up earlier than they had anticipated.

4. <u>Both</u> Harry and Sally wanted to get married, but <u>neither</u> was willing to commit to a specific date.

5. The flock of Canadian geese migrated south when <u>its</u> food supply started to run short.

6. Aurora couldn't think of <u>anything</u> to buy her father for his birthday.

7. Connor <u>himself</u> made the pizza from scratch.

8. Seasonal allergies <u>themselves</u> may not be responsible for all of your symptoms.

9. When I listen to heavy metal music, I can barely hear <u>myself</u> think.

10. Although the two lovers certainly admired <u>each other</u>, they rarely demonstrated <u>their</u> affection in public.

Taking Action with Verbs

Verbs are words that express an action, state of being, or relationship between two things. They tell the reader what the *subject* (actor) in a sentence does or is or is being. Verbs come in three types: action, linking, and helping, as described in the following sections.

PRACTICAL POINT

Both nouns and verbs can be *inflected*; that is, you can add letters to the base of a noun or verb to change its syntactic function without changing its fundamental form. You can inflect most nouns by adding *-s* or dropping the *y* and adding *-ies* to form the plural. You can inflect a verb to change its tense or mood or make it agree with the subject of the sentence in person and number; for example, *I holler* (present tense using the verb's base) becomes *I hollered* (past tense with the base plus the inflection, *holler + ed*). To find out a whole lot more about inflecting verbs, turn to Chapter 6.

Action Verbs

Action verbs are the movers and shakers of the English language; they *build* and *demolish, love* and *despise, hope* and *despair.* They *cower* in the corner of one sentence and *emerge* triumphant at the end of another. Action verbs fuel your writing, so make them your go-to verbs instead of making them sit it out on the sidelines.

> **USAGE TIDBIT**
>
> In chess, players have come up with standard relative values of the chess pieces. For example, a pawn is worth 1, bishops and knights are worth 3 apiece, a rook is worth 5, and a queen is worth 9. In writing, action verbs are queens, helping verbs are bishops, and linking verbs are pawns. Use as many queens as possible and as few pawns as necessary.

Linking Verbs

Compared to action verbs, linking verbs *are* lazy. Instead of action, they express a state or condition, connecting the subject of a sentence with a *subject complement*—a noun, pronoun, or adjective in the form of a single word or a phrase that identifies or describes the subject. Following are examples of linking verbs on the job:

> You <u>seem</u> terribly curious. (The adjective phrase *terribly curious* serves as the subject complement.)
>
> Cecie <u>is</u> the girl with the crying-heart tattoo. (Here the linking verb identifies Cecie as the girl with the crying-heart tattoo, a noun phrase serving as the subject complement.)
>
> Ted <u>isn't</u> himself when he has a migraine headache. (Here the linking verb *isn't* connects Ted to the reflexive pronoun *himself.*)

Common linking verbs are all forms of *be,* including:

am	been	was
are	being	were
be is		

Linking verbs also include verb phrases ending in *be, being, or been,* including *can be, was being,* and *could have been.*

Additional linking verbs to add to your stock include the following:

appear	remain
become	seem
feel	smell
get	sound
grow	stay
look	taste
prove	

Some of these linking verbs double as action verbs, as you can see in the following two examples:

Action verb: The chef <u>smelled</u> the escargot before serving it.

Linking verb: The chef <u>smells</u> like escargot.

> **USAGE TIDBIT**
>
> To determine whether a verb is serving as an action verb or linking verb, try substituting the verb *seem*. If the sentence still sort of makes sense, you're looking at a linking verb. If the sentence sounds terrible, you're looking at an action verb; for example, something seems off in the sentence "The chef <u>seemed</u> the escargot before serving it."

Helping Verbs

Helping verbs pitch in when other verbs need their services, as in the following examples (the helping verbs are bold italic, while the main verb is italic):

The building ***will be*** *demolished* later this year.

Everyone ***could have*** *finished* dinner if we had arrived 30 minutes earlier.

Crew members ***have*** *delighted* cruise ship passengers for years with their zany antics.

Just so you know, separating the helping verb from the main verb is okay and more effective at times, as long as the separation doesn't risk confusing the reader. Here are a few examples:

I ***have*** always *preferred* cupcakes over muffins.

I ***am*** not *going* to put up with this much longer.

Did you *wonder* where I'd been?

Transitive and Intransitive Verbs

Grammarians also classify verbs as transitive and intransitive:

Transitive verbs require an object; for example, "The jar <u>contains ...</u>" is an incomplete thought that leaves the reader wondering what the jar contains ... jam, beets, lightning bugs?

Intransitive verbs, on the other hand, *don't* take a direct object; for example, in the sentence "Everyone <u>laughed</u>." the word *laughed* is intransitive. Now, if everyone *laughed off the practical joke,* the verb would be transitive.

Most verbs can function as either transitive or intransitive depending on the context:

> **Transitive:** The accountant <u>balanced</u> the books.

> **Intransitive:** The account <u>balanced</u>.

USAGE TIDBIT

To find out whether a verb is transitive or intransitive or both, look it up in a dictionary. Dictionaries typically group meanings and tag each group as *v.i.* (verb intransitive) and *v.t.* (verb transitive) or *used with an object* and *used without an object.*

Infinitives

The *infinitive* form of a verb (see Chapter 6), is *to + verb;* for example, *to forgive, to forget, to imagine.* Infinitives are tricky little buggers. Although they're forms of verbs, they don't act as verbs; instead, they play the role of nouns, adjectives, and adverbs, as in these examples:

> <u>To admit</u> my limitations would convey a lack of confidence. (Infinitive serving as a noun, the subject of the sentence.)

> After careful deliberation, I decided <u>to admit</u> my limitations after all. (Infinitive serving as an adverb modifying the verb *decided.*)

> I have a responsibility <u>to admit</u> my limitations to other team members. (Infinitive serving as an adjective describing the noun *responsibility.*)

Adjectives and adverbs are covered later in this chapter.

Practice

In each of the following sentences, underline the verbs. If a helping verb accompanies an action verb, be sure to underline the helping verb as well.

1. Nobody knows how many guests will be coming to the party.

2. Journalists question everything; as a rule, they are a very inquisitive bunch.

3. Now that Mark was feeling much better, his doctors agreed to release him from the hospital.

4. Patrons are not allowed to use cell phones in our restaurant.

5. You have two 15-minute breaks, during which time you are not to leave the building.

Answers:

1. Nobody <u>knows</u> how many guests <u>will be coming</u> to the party.

2. Journalists <u>question</u> everything; as a rule, they <u>are</u> a very inquisitive bunch.

3. Now that Mark <u>was feeling</u> much better, his doctors <u>agreed</u> to release him from the hospital. (If you underlined *to release*, that's incorrect, because <u>to release</u> serves as an adverb modifying the verb *agreed*.)

4. Patrons <u>are</u> not <u>allowed</u> to use cell phones in our restaurant. (If you underlined *to use*, that's incorrect, because <u>to use</u> serves as an adverb modifying the verb *allowed*.)

5. You <u>have</u> two 15-minute breaks during which time you <u>are</u> not <u>allowed</u> to leave the building. (Again, underlining *to leave* would be wrong, because it's an adverb modifying the verb *allowed*.)

Getting Descriptive with Adjectives and Adverbs

Adjectives and adverbs are commonly referred to as *modifiers*, because they narrow the meaning of nouns, verbs, and sometimes other adjectives and adverbs. The following sections introduce these descriptive words and reveal their similarities and differences.

Adjectives and Articles

Adjectives modify nouns and pronouns by answering any of the following four questions:

- **What kind?**

  the *nosy* neighbors, the *sparkling* jewels

- **How much?** or **How many?**

  numerous compliments, *countless* nights

- **Which one?**

  this finger, *that* house

- **Whose is it?**

  my money, *their* home, *her* child (The possessive adjectives or possessive determiners are *my, your, her, his, its, our,* and *their.*)

You usually place an adjective directly before the word it modifies, except in the following two situations:

- When using the adjective as a *predicate adjective* following a linking verb:

  The evening grew <u>dark</u>.

- When you want to have the adjective after the noun for some good reason:

  The players, <u>worn out</u> from the long trip, appeared listless on the field.

The most basic and popular adjectives are the articles: *a, an,* and *the.* If English is your first language, you instinctively choose the right article by ear. If English is your second or third language, you may need to brush up on the rules for choosing the correct article:

- Use *a* or *an* (*indefinite articles*) to introduce a nonspecific member of a group for the first time; for example, *<u>A</u> slug is a lousy choice for a pet.* Use *a* before words that start with a consonant sound and *an* before words that start with a vowel sound.

- Use *a* or *an* to indicate membership to a group; for example, *Barbara is <u>a</u> Buddhist.*

- Use *the* (*definite article*) to introduce a specific person, place, or thing or one or more specific members of a group; for example, *Ethiopia has plans to dam <u>the</u> Blue Nile* (a specific body of water). *Young George Washington chopped down <u>the</u> cherry tree* (referring to a specific cherry tree).

- Use *a* or *an* to introduce a specific instance of a specific thing; for example, you'd normally introduce *sun* with *the*, but you might use the indefinite article instead in a sentence such as <u>*A* cruel sun scorched the fields.</u>

- Use *the* to emphasize the importance or singularity of a person, place, or thing, as in the sentence *California is <u>the</u> place to go for avid surfers.*

Omit the article:

- When discussing people, places, or things in general; for example, <u>*Movies* are my favorite form of entertainment.</u>

- Before mass nouns when mentioning them generally. A *mass noun* (sometimes referred to as a noncount noun) is one that can't have a number before it; for example, *coffee* and *electricity*. Here's an example of a mass noun in a sentence: <u>*Rice* is a staple in most Asian countries.</u>

- When mentioning a sport, as in the sentence *Sandy loves to watch <u>football</u>*.

- Before the names of most countries, unless they contain the words *kingdom, republic, state,* or *union* (as in <u>*the*</u> *Soviet Union*) or when referring to multiple areas (as in <u>*the*</u> *Bahamas*).

USAGE TIDBIT

Frequently, you use an indefinite article before a noun the first time you mention it. After the reader knows which member of the group you're referring to, you use the definite article before the noun, because the noun is no longer general but specific. Here's an example:

Melissa has two pets: <u>a</u> gerbil and <u>a</u> ferret. <u>The</u> ferret is friendly; <u>the</u> gerbil is not.

For more about adjectives, head to Chapter 7.

Adverbs

Adverbs play several roles, modifying verbs, adjectives, and other adverbs. Most adverbs end in *–ly*; for example, *carefully, expeditiously,* and *scornfully*. But many don't end in *–ly*, especially the adverbs that designate a location where the action took place, such as *here, there,* and *everywhere*. To further complicate their usage, nouns can double as adverbs; for example, *today, tomorrow,* and *north*.

When modifying verbs, adverbs commonly answer the following questions:

- **How?**

  steps *gingerly*, dances *enthusiastically*

- **When?**

  arrives *early*, leaves *late*

- **Where?**

  travels *abroad*, tunnels *underground*

- **To what degree?**

  nearly completed, *almost* won

You may also use adverbs to modify adjectives and other adverbs, as in the following examples:

> **Adverb modifying an adjective:** *Jimbo has established himself as an <u>incredibly</u> talented musician.* (The adverb *incredibly* modifies the adjective *talented*.)

> **Adverb modifying another adverb:** *He will <u>probably</u> never sacrifice his practice time.* (The adverb *probably* modifies the adverb *never*.)

In this section, you merely dipped your big toe in the sea of adverbs. To fully immerse yourself, dive in to Chapter 7.

Practice

In each of the following sentences, underline all adjectives and adverbs. Do not underline articles.

1. My steak was perfectly seasoned.

2. Sandy and Pete, both well-educated engineers, patented their own mini digital camera.

3. The shuttle bus was intended only to transport shoppers from the train to the strip mall.

4. The sycamore trees nearly bent in half in the face of wind gusts of up to 85 miles an hour.

5. The soccer team exited the stadium ecstatic over its incredible comeback victory.

Answers:

1. <u>My</u> steak was <u>perfectly</u> seasoned.

2. Sandy and Pete, both <u>well-educated</u> engineers, patented <u>their</u> <u>own</u> <u>mini digital</u> camera.

3. The <u>shuttle</u> bus was intended <u>only</u> to transport shoppers from the train to the <u>strip</u> mall.

4. The <u>sycamore</u> trees <u>nearly</u> bent in half in the face of <u>wind</u> gusts of <u>up to</u> <u>85</u> miles an hour.

5. The soccer team exited the stadium <u>ecstatic</u> over <u>its</u> <u>incredible</u> <u>comeback</u> victory.

Making the Right Connections with Conjunctions

Conjunctions enable words and *phrases* to reach across the aisle and hold hands. English has three types of conjunctions: *coordinating, subordinating,* and *correlative.* To find out more about each type, read on.

Coordinating Conjunctions

A *coordinating conjunction* connects words, phrases, or clauses of pretty much equal rank. They are: *and, but, or, for, nor.* Use them to join a pair of items, several items in a series, or two or more phrases or coordinate clauses, as in the following examples:

Stan ate Polish sausage, pierogi, <u>and</u> golumpki. (Connecting items in a series.)

He felt full, <u>but</u> he decided to order dessert anyway. (Connecting two coordinate clauses.)

The desserts, printed on the menu <u>and</u> arranged on the dessert tray, all looked delicious. (Connecting two phrases.)

Stan deliberated over whether to order babka <u>or</u> budyn. (Connecting two items, both nouns.)

> **DEFINITION**
>
> A **phrase** is a group of words functioning as a conceptual unit that doesn't qualify as a clause, because it doesn't have a subject (actor) and a predicate (action). A **clause** is sort of a sentence within a sentence, in that it has a subject and a predicate, but it's part of another sentence. Clauses come in two flavors: coordinate and subordinate. A **coordinate clause** is the same rank as the main clause and could stand alone. A **subordinate clause** embellishes the main clause and can't stand alone. A **sentence** is a combination of a subject and predicate that can stand on its own two feet; that is, it expresses a complete thought.

Subordinating Conjunctions

Subordinating conjunctions introduce subordinate clauses, which might not make sense yet. After you meet the subordinating conjunctions and see them used in examples, you'll have a better idea of what they are and their purpose in life. So, without further ado, here are the most commonly used subordinating conjunctions:

after	even though	that
although	how	though
as	if	till
as long as	in order that	unless
as much as	inasmuch as	until
as soon as	now that	when
as though	provided	whenever
because	since	where
before	so that	wherever
even if	than	while

Here are some examples of subordinating conjunctions in action. Note that the entire subordinating clause is underlined and notice the position of each clause—at the beginning or end of the sentence.

Provided that I receive your check this week, I will send you the car's title in the mail.

Wherever it ultimately decides to move, the company will offer its employees jobs and relocation packages.

Please proceed to the waiting room after you have completed and submitted your forms.

The herd of antelope migrated north because the drought had turned the grasslands to desert.

Correlative Conjunctions

Correlative conjunctions come in pairs, with the second conjunction of the pair being a coordinating conjunction:

both …	and …
either …	or …

neither ...   nor ...

not only ...   but (also) ...

whether ...   or ...

To understand the function of correlative conjunctions, you need to know what *correlate* means. Basically, it means that the pair of words forming the correlative conjunction connect two equal grammatical terms, as in the following examples:

<u>Neither</u> Charles <u>nor</u> Andrea knows about the party.

You can <u>either</u> wash the windows or <u>mop</u> the floors.

This project gives you <u>not only</u> an opportunity to experiment, <u>but also</u> a chance to earn some big bucks.

PRACTICAL POINT

Correlative conjunctions are tricky when you're trying to decide whether the subject of the sentence is singular or plural (see Chapter 5) or trying to maintain parallelism (covered in Chapter 13), but don't concern yourself with those issues just yet.

Practice

In each of the following sentences, underline the conjunction(s) and write *Coordinating, Subordinating,* or *Correlative* in the blank to indicate the type of conjunction it is.

1. Molly and Cyrus fully enjoyed the rock concert. _____

2. Although the animals seemed content, the shelter was overcrowded.

   _____

3. Tim accomplished what he had set out to do and was now eager for a new challenge.

   _____

4. I can't decide whether to stay in this line or move to the shorter one.

   _____

5. Susan seems content wherever she happens to live. _____

Answers:

1. Molly <u>and</u> Cyrus fully enjoyed the rock concert. <u>Coordinating</u>

2. <u>Although</u> the animals seemed content, the shelter was overcrowded. <u>Subordinating</u>

3. Tim accomplished what he had set out to do <u>and</u> was now eager for a new challenge. <u>Coordinating</u>

4. I can't decide <u>whether</u> to stay in this line <u>or</u> move to the shorter one. <u>Correlative</u>

5. Susan seems content <u>wherever</u> she happens to live. <u>Subordinating</u>

Building Relationships with Prepositions

Prepositions establish a relationship between a noun or pronoun and another word in a clause. For example, if you climb under a table, the preposition *under* describes your relation to the noun *table.*

In most cases, prepositions are accompanied by other words to form a *prepositional phrase,* usually consisting of the preposition followed by an article and a noun that serves as the *object of the preposition.* The following paragraph contains two examples of prepositional phrases with the prepositional phrase in italics and the preposition underlined:

> Spelunkers climbed <u>*down*</u> *a cable ladder* lowered <u>*into*</u> *the cavern* to rescue Ms. Fitzgerald's cat. (Preposition *down* establishes the relationship between the spelunkers and the cable ladder, and *into* reveals the relationship between the cable ladder and the cavern.)

Every *prepositional phrase* includes a preposition and *object of the preposition,* which usually comes after the preposition.

Here are some commonly used single-word prepositions:

about	by	outside
above	concerning	over
across	down	past
after	during	since
against	except	than
along	excluding	through
amid	following	to
among	for	toward

around	from	under
at	in	underneath
before	inside	unlike
behind	into	until
below	like	up
beneath	near	upon
beside	of	versus
besides	off	via
between	on	with
beyond	onto	within
but (meaning "except")	opposite	without

Some prepositions are made up of two or more words:

according to	close to	instead of
ahead of	due to	near to
all over	except for	next to
as early as	in back of	on top of
as late as	in between	other than
as much/many as	in front of	out of
as of	in keeping with	similar to
as often as	in place of	up to
away from	in spite of	with regard to
because of	in view of	with respect to
close by		

Practice

In each of the following sentences, underline every prepositional phrase, including the preposition and the object of the preposition.

1. Into the night, Gary proceeded to search.

2. The marina was on the far side of the lake.

3. The giddy swimmers were unaware of the white sharks swimming beneath them.

4. Dandelions tend to sprout along the edges of the lawn.

5. Fighter jets can fly circles around jetliners in flight.

Answers:

1. <u>Into the night</u>, Gary proceeded to search.

2. The marina was <u>on the far side</u> <u>of the lake</u>.

3. The giddy swimmers were unaware <u>of the white sharks</u> swimming <u>beneath them</u>.

4. Dandelions tend to sprout <u>along the edges</u> <u>of a lawn</u>.

5. Fighter jets can fly circles <u>around jetliners</u> <u>in flight</u>.

Dealing with Interjections: Yay!

An *interjection* is an exclamatory remark that typically expresses emotion and is grammatically unrelated to any other words in the sentence in which it appears. In fact, interjections often stand on their own, complete with their own punctuation, as in "Ouch!" Here's a short list of interjections:

Ahh	Gee	Ouch
Ahem	Gosh	Shoot
Alas	Hey	Ugh
Alrighty	Hmmm	Uh
Argh	Huh?	Whoa
Awww	Mmm	Whoops

Boo	Nah	Wow
Darn	Ooh	Yay
Duh	Oops	Yikes

USAGE TIDBIT

Writers often use interjections in dialogue to make it sound more realistic.

Blurring the Lines That Define Parts of Speech

Many words in the English language defy attempts to categorize them as a particular part of speech. Often, the only way to really tell which role a word or phrase plays in a sentence is to examine it carefully in context. Here are a couple examples of words functioning as different parts of speech:

Merely thinking of <u>jogging</u> <u>jogged</u> his memory. (The word jog is used first as a noun and then as a verb.)

With his can of <u>oil</u>, Ed <u>oiled</u> the hinges on the door, being careful not to get any on the <u>oil</u> painting hanging on the nearby wall. (Here, *oil* is first a noun, then a verb, and finally an adjective.)

The Least You Need to Know

- Nouns name a person, place, or thing; pronouns usually reference a previously mentioned noun.
- Verbs express action or being and come in three types: action, linking, and helping.
- Adjectives modify nouns and pronouns; adverbs modify verbs, adjectives, and other adverbs.
- Coordinating conjunctions connect grammatical elements of equal rank; subordinating conjunctions introduce grammatical elements of lesser rank.
- Prepositions establish a relationship between a noun or pronoun and another word in a clause.
- Interjections are exclamatory remarks that show emotion and are unrelated, grammatically, to any other words in a sentence.

Recognizing the Parts of a Sentence

Chances are you know people who have a bad habit of not finishing their sentences. They start strong and then fade out at the end, assuming you'll catch their drift. Needless to say, those incomplete sentences are annoying, especially if you have no idea what the person is trying to say.

Of course, we all kind of stumble along when we're speaking, and the standards for talking aren't nearly as strict as they are for writing. But some people bring the incompleteness and chaos of speech into writing, and that can cause problems for readers.

If you happen to be one of those people, this chapter can cure you of that foible. Here you'll discover the difference between sentences, phrases, and clauses; the various ways to end and embellish sentences; and a variety of sentence structures.

By learning more about the rules for making sentences, you'll learn something more: how to communicate as clearly as possible.

In This Chapter

- Understanding what makes a sentence a sentence
- Complementing your actions
- Tacking on phrases
- Recognizing the two main types of clauses
- Sampling sentence structures

What Exactly Is a Sentence?

A *sentence* is a collection of words containing a noun (or pronoun) and a verb that expresses a complete thought, statement, question, or command. Here's an example of a sentence in its simplest form:

<u>Martha</u>   <u>paces</u>.
Noun   **Verb**

Grammarians use more precise language to describe the two parts of a sentence:

Subject: The person, place, or thing that the sentence is about along with all the words that modify that person, place, or thing.

Predicate: The verb that animates the subject and all words that modify that verb.

> **DEFINITION**
>
> A **sentence** is a group of words that express a complete thought, usually consisting of a subject and predicate. A sentence can be a statement, question, or command.

Although the subject usually comes first, you can invert the order, placing the predicate first. Here are a few examples of subjects and predicates forming sentences:

<u>Natalie</u>   <u>chuckled</u>.
Subject   **Predicate**

<u>Here comes</u>   <u>the sun</u>.
Predicate   **Subject**

<u>Dylan, realizing he was late,</u>   <u>hurried home</u>.
Subject   **Predicate**

<u>At the end of the path stood</u>   <u>Larry</u>.
Predicate   **Subject**

The following sections describe the subject and predicate in greater detail and give instructions on how to identify each in a sentence.

Part 1: Subject

The *subject* of a sentence can be simple or complete. A *simple subject* consists solely of a noun or pronoun. A *complete subject* consists of the noun or pronoun and any words or phrases that modify (describe) it. Here's an example:

> A premature baby with medical issues requires considerable attention and care to remain healthy.

Here, *A premature baby with medical issues* is the complete subject; *baby* is the simple subject.

Part 2: Predicate

Just as a subject can be simple or complete, so too can a *predicate*. A *simple predicate* is the main verb (or verb phrase) in a sentence. A *complete predicate* consists of the verb and any words or phrases that describe the verb, such a phrase describing how the action was performed. Here's an example:

> Management decided to offer the company's employees a cafeteria plan.

Here, *decided to offer the company's employees a cafeteria plan* is the complete predicate; *decided* is the simple predicate.

> **DEFINITION**
>
> The **subject** of a sentence is the person, place, or thing the sentence is about. The **predicate** is the action that the subject performs or the subject's state of being.

Sentences with Compound Subjects and Verbs

Compound subjects consist of two or more nouns. *Compound verbs* consist of two or more verbs. When you have a sentence with a compound subject, be careful to choose the right verb form: singular if only one of the subjects performs the action or plural if two or more perform the action. For example:

> The <u>elephant</u>, <u>giraffe</u>, and <u>hippopotamus</u> *live* in the jungle.

> The <u>elephant</u>, <u>giraffe</u>, or <u>hippopotamus</u> *lives* down the street.

With a compound verb, the subject performs more than one action; for example:

> This morning, Sam <u>scrambled</u> the eggs and <u>fried</u> the bacon.

> **DANGER ZONE**
>
> When you have a compound verb consisting of only two verbs, avoid the temptation to separate them with a comma:
>
> **Right:** Nancy hit a homer and circled the bases.
>
> **Wrong:** Nancy hit a homer, and circled the bases.
>
> Use the comma only when separating two complete sentences—also known as independent clauses—as shown here:
>
> **Right:** Nancy hit a homer, and the crowd cheered.

Identifying the Subject

Knowing who or what the sentence is about is important for two reasons: First, whether the subject is singular or plural determines whether the verb needs to be singular or plural. Second, knowing what the subject is helps you write more concisely and directly using nouns and verbs instead of phrases such as *there are, it is,* and *here are* (more about that in a minute).

Unfortunately, picking subjects out a sentence can be nearly as difficult as finding a lost kid at an amusement park. The following are some tricks of the trade for pinpointing subjects:

Find the action first, then ask, "Who or what is doing this?" For example, suppose the sentence is "Outside the perimeter of our fence live wild animals." The verb is *live,* so you ask "Who or what lives?" The answer: *animals.*

Ignore any prepositional phrases. For example, suppose the sentence is "Beyond the river breeds a colony of seagulls." The verb is *breeds,* so you ask "Who or what breeds?" Of course, the seagulls are actually doing the breeding, but *of seagulls* is a prepositional phrase modifying *colony,* so you must disregard it according to this rule. When you do, you discover the true subject of the sentence: *colony.*

Proceed with caution when sentences begin with *there are, here are,* or similar word combinations. These combos usually include a false subject (*here* or *there*). The true subject appears later in the sentence. For example, in the sentence "There are numerous options," *There* is the false subject; the true subject is *options*—the options are numerous.

Assume that *you* is the subject in commands and requests. For example, in the sentence "Forge ahead!" the subject *you* is understood, not stated. In a request, such as "Please pass the porridge," again, *you* is understood or assumed; it doesn't appear in the sentence.

To find the subject in a question, rephrase the question as a statement. For example, if the question is "When is the train scheduled to arrive?" the statement is "The train is scheduled to arrive when …." Now identifying the subject is a snap: *train.*

Keep in mind that certain forms of verbs function as nouns. *Gerunds* (verbs ending in *–ing*) and *infinitives* (*to + verb*) function as nouns. In the sentence "Jogging around the park reinvigorates me," the simple subject is *Jogging* (a gerund), because jogging is doing the reinvigorating, even though I'm the one doing the jogging.

> **USAGE TIDBIT**
>
> Write sentences with strong nouns and verbs. Avoid starting a sentence with a wimpy word combo such as *There are ...* or *It is ....*

Practice

Underline the simple subject in each of the following sentences, keeping in mind that more than one noun may comprise the subject.

1. The prospects for peace improved only slightly with the prime minister's visit to the region.

2. Where is the company headed?

3. The sky burst into color with the arrival of the butterflies.

4. There are dozens of hostels along the Pilgrim route of the Camino Santiago in Galicia, Spain.

5. Barry, along with the rest of his family, planned to arrive early to get better seats.

6. Please share your story with us.

7. Toward the finish line sprinted Jessie.

8. Cassie and her co-workers were delighted with the big bonuses they received.

9. On his way to work, Jerry stopped for a cappuccino.

10. Getting lost in a big city isn't my idea of a good time.

Answers:

1. The <u>prospects</u> for peace improved only slightly with the prime minister's visit to the region.

2. Where is the <u>company</u> headed?

3. The <u>sky</u> burst into color with the arrival of the butterflies.

4. There are <u>dozens of hostels</u> along the Pilgrim route of the Camino Santiago in Galicia, Spain.

5. <u>Barry</u>, along with the rest of his family, planned to arrive early to get better seats.

6. Please share your story with us. (<u>You</u> is understood.)

7. Toward the finish line sprinted <u>Jessie</u>.

8. <u>Cassie</u> and her <u>co-workers</u> were delighted with the big bonuses they received.

9. On his way to work, <u>Jerry</u> stopped for a cappuccino.

10. <u>Getting lost</u> in a big city isn't my idea of a good time.

Completing Actions with Complements

A *complement* is a noun, verb, or adjective (any of which can be a single word or a phrase) that's part of the predicate and that completes the action. Following are a few examples of complements in action (the complement is underlined):

> Glenn quickly became <u>irritated</u>.
>
> The poodle learned <u>to jump</u> through hoops.
>
> Voters elected Obama <u>president</u>.
>
> The bank teller handed Wanda her <u>cash</u>.

Complements come in different forms, depending on the function they perform in a sentence. The following sections describe the different forms and provide examples.

Direct and Indirect Objects

Direct and *indirect objects* are on the receiving end of the action (verb):

Direct object: The person, place, or thing that receives the action of the verb. For example, if you're launching a spaceship to Mars, *spaceship* is the direct object, because that's what's being launched.

Indirect object: The person, place, or thing *to which/whom* or *for which/whom* the action is performed. The indirect object always precedes the direct object. In the sentence "Canada sends Mali humanitarian aid," *Mali* is the indirect object, and *aid* is the direct object.

The tricky part about indirect objects is that if you put the word *to* or *for* before the object, you're no longer looking at an indirect object; you're looking at a prepositional phrase. Reword the previous example sentence as "Canada sends humanitarian aid to Mali," and now *Mali* is no longer an indirect object; it's the object of the preposition *to*. (For more about objects of prepositions, see Chapter 3.)

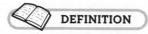 **DEFINITION**

A **direct object** is a noun or pronoun that the action touches. An **indirect object** is a noun or pronoun to whom or for whom the direct object has been acted upon.

Object Complements

An *object complement* is a noun or adjective that comes after a direct object and explains what the direct object has become. Once you see some examples, you'll have a better idea of what object complements are:

The Thortons painted their house <u>yellow</u>.

Committee members voted Halloway <u>chairperson</u>.

The landscapers kept the branches <u>pruned back</u>.

In each of these examples, the direct object (*house, Halloway,* and *branches*) becomes something (*yellow, chairperson,* and *pruned*). What the direct object becomes is an object complement.

Why does this matter? Because proper placement of the word is important for expressing your intended meaning. For example, if instead of painting their *house yellow,* the Thortons painted their *yellow house,* you'd still be wondering what color they painted it. By moving the word *yellow* before *house* instead of placing it after *house,* you transform the word *yellow* from an object complement into an adjective, and it performs an entirely different function with a totally different meaning.

Subject Complements

A *subject complement* is a noun or adjective that follows a linking verb and describes the subject of the sentence. Subject complements come in two types:

Predicate nominative: A noun or pronoun that follows a linking verb and modifies the subject; for example:

Michael is a licensed <u>beautician</u>.

Predicate adjective: An adjective that follows a linking verb and modifies the subject; for example:

Our new neighbors seem <u>amicable</u> and <u>fascinating</u>.

Practice

In each of the following sentences, underline the complements and write the type of complement in the space provided—use the abbreviations d.o. (direct object), i.o. (indirect object), o.c. (object complement), and s.c. (subject complement). In the case of subject complements, you can identify whether it's a predicate nominative (p.n.) or predicate adjective (p.a.) to earn extra credit.

1. Your dog seems more affectionate than mine. _____

2. Friends and family sent Michelle flowers to congratulate her on her promotion. _____

3. Readers of the newspaper overwhelmingly named Mel's Diner their favorite restaurant in Memphis. _____

4. Lilly sent Florence an email message confirming their plans. _____

5. Mel sent the cigars to me as a gift. _____

Answers:

1. Your dog seems more <u>affectionate</u> than mine. <u>s.c., p.a.</u>

2. Friends and family sent <u>Michelle</u> <u>flowers</u> to congratulate her on her promotion. <u>i.o., d.o.</u>

3. Readers of the newspaper overwhelmingly named <u>Mel's Diner</u> their favorite <u>restaurant</u> in Memphis. <u>d.o., o.c.</u>

4. Lilly sent <u>Florence</u> an email <u>message</u> confirming their plans. <u>i.o., d.o.</u>

5. Mel sent the <u>cigars</u> to me as a gift. <u>d.o.</u>

Accentuating Sentences with Phrases

A *phrase* is a group of words that doesn't include a subject-verb pair that functions as a unit—a subject, verb, object, adjective, or adverb. (If the group of words were to contain a subject-verb pair, it would qualify as a clause, not a phrase.) The English language has several different kinds of phrases that vary according to their composition and function in a sentence. The following sections introduce the different kinds of phrases and show them in action.

DEFINITION

A **phrase** is a group of words that functions as a unit but doesn't contain a subject-verb combo.

Verb Phrases

Verb phrases, not to be confused with verbal phrases discussed later in this chapter, are typically comprised of one or more helping verbs and an action verb that together express a single action; for example:

> has investigated
>
> will be visiting
>
> had been completed

Technically speaking, these groups of words qualify as phrases, because 1) they're a group of words that act as a unit and 2) they don't have a subject-verb pair (only verbs). In this book, we prefer to treat verb phrases simply as verbs, whether the verb consists of one word or more (see Chapter 6).

Prepositional

The mother of most (not all) phrases is the *prepositional phrase*—a grammatical unit that begins with a preposition, ends with an object of the preposition, and almost always functions either as an adjective or adverb. Examples of prepositional phrases used as nouns are rare. (For more about prepositions, including a list of common prepositions, flip back to Chapter 3.) Here are a few examples of prepositional phrases with the prepositions underlined:

> <u>in</u> the yard
>
> <u>from</u> Nebraska
>
> <u>behind</u> the cemetery
>
> <u>inside</u> the perimeter
>
> <u>of</u> wombats

When working as an adjective, a prepositional phrase modifies a noun, as in these examples:

> The compost pile <u>in the yard</u> smelled rancid. (modifies *pile*)
>
> We met our new neighbors <u>from Nebraska</u>. (modifies *neighbors*)
>
> There is a woods <u>behind the cemetery</u>. (modifies *woods*)
>
> He passed to the guard <u>inside the perimeter</u>. (modifies *guard*)
>
> A noteworthy characteristic <u>of wombats</u> is their backward pouch. (modifies *characteristic*)

When filling in as an adverb, a prepositional phrase modifies a verb, adjective, or another adverb, as in these examples:

The swim team practiced <u>in the Gulf</u>. (modifies the verb *practiced*)

The coach seemed oblivious <u>to the risks</u>. (modifies the adjective *oblivious*)

Jellyfish bobbed furtively <u>through the water</u>. (modifies the adverb *furtively*)

And here's something you're unlikely to bump into—a prepositional phrase functioning as a noun:

<u>Inside of 10 minutes</u> is too little time.

Appositives

An *appositive* is a noun or pronoun (single word or phrase) that modifies another noun or pronoun and appears right after the word or just before the word it modifies. The following examples give you a glimpse of appositives at work:

<u>A highly venomous snake</u>, the king cobra can deliver enough venom in a single bite to kill 20 people.

Embry and Tonya, <u>sisters and skilled equestrians</u>, excelled in every competition.

The boat, <u>a 20-foot roundabout with a diving platform and a 150 horsepower engine</u>, was for sale at the marina.

> **DANGER ZONE**
>
> Not every phrase that comes before or after a noun and modifies it is an appositive. An appositive must be a noun or pronoun. For example, in the sentence "Tim, wondering who had called, checked caller ID," the phrase *wondering who had called* is a verbal phrase, not an appositive.

Verbals

A *verbal* is a verb that functions as a noun, adjective, or adverb in a sentence. A *verbal phrase* is a group of words containing a verbal that, as a unit, functions as a noun, adjective, or adverb in a sentence. Take a look at the following examples:

<u>Skipping rope</u> is a great cardiovascular workout. (*Skipping* is a verb used as a noun. *Skipping rope* is the verbal phrase.)

<u>Elated</u>, the fans jumped for joy. (The verb *elated* is used as an adjective to modify *fans*.)

People take vacations <u>to relax</u>. (The infinitive form of the verb *relax* is used as an adverb to modify the verb *take*.)

Verbals come in four forms: gerunds, infinitives, and present and past participles.

> **📖 DEFINITION**
>
> A **verbal** is a verb that functions as a noun, adjective, or adverb in a sentence.

A *gerund* is a verb form ending in *–ing* that functions as a noun; for example, "<u>Flying</u> is exhilarating." A gerund phrase is the gerund along with any associated words; for example, "<u>Flying over Pittsburgh</u> is wonderful!" Like its first cousin, the noun, a gerund can serve different roles in a sentence:

Subject: <u>Fishing</u> is a popular sport.

Direct object: I hate <u>waiting</u> in line.

Object of a preposition: Our employees became more efficient by <u>working</u> smarter.

Subject complement: Pat's favorite hobby is <u>gardening</u>.

An *infinitive* is a verb form, typically consisting of *to* + verb, that functions as a noun, adjective, or adverb; for example, in the sentence "Ellen loves <u>to ski</u>," *to ski* functions as a direct object. An infinitive phrase is the infinitive along with any associated words; for example, "Ellen loves <u>to ski on lakes and rivers</u>." Following are examples of infinitives functioning as different parts of speech:

<u>To sleep</u> through the night would be a welcome relief. (*to sleep* functions as a noun, the subject of the sentence)

The tourists decided <u>to dock</u> at Key West. (*to dock* functions as a direct object)

The diver's purpose was <u>to discover</u> sunken treasure. (*to discover* functions as the predicate nominative describing the subject *purpose*)

Dr. Miller had the foresight <u>to patent</u> the innovative new medical procedure. (*to patent* functions as an adjective modifying the noun *foresight*)

We live <u>to love</u>. (*to love* functions as an adverb modifying the verb *live*)

Although the infinitive form of a verb includes the word *to*, in some cases, the *to* is dropped, creating what's commonly called a *bare infinitive*, as in these examples:

> I let her <u>buy</u> me a drink.

> You had better <u>call</u> home.

> Help them <u>decide</u>.

A *participle* is a verb form that, when used without a helping verb such as *is* or *has been*, functions as an adjective, as in the following examples:

> The <u>darkening</u> skies indicated that a storm was brewing.

> <u>Blurred</u> vision may be a symptom of cataracts or macular degeneration.

Participles come in two varieties:

Present participle: Like the gerund, the present participle is the verb form ending in *–ing*. (But remember that gerunds are nouns, whereas present participles are adjectives.)

Past participle: Past participles of regular verbs (see Chapter 6) end in *–ed*. Past participles of irregular verbs end in *–d, –e, –g, –t, –en*, or *–n*; for example, *paid, done, sung, sent, spoken,* and *grown*.

 DANGER ZONE

> Don't confuse a participle that functions as an adjective with a participle that's part of a verb phrase expressing action. For example, in the sentence "The president was willing to compromise," *was willing* is a verb phrase, the predicate of the sentence, not an adjective.

Past and present participles can team up with other words to form *participial phrases,* as in the following examples:

> <u>Concerned about his growing debt</u>, Gary consulted a financial advisor. (In this example, a past and a present participle, *concerned* and *growing,* both play a role in the participial phrase.)

> The ship, <u>sailing to Bermuda</u>, disappeared in the area <u>known as the Bermuda Triangle</u>. (This example contains two participial phrases: the first starting with the present participle *sailing,* and the second with a past participle *known.*)

Practice

In each of the following sentences, a phrase appears underlined. On the blank line next to each sentence, write down the phrase type: prepositional, appositive, gerund, infinitive, present participle, or past participle. If the phrase modifies another word, also write down the word it modifies.

1. Bill and Melinda Gates, <u>well-known philanthropists</u>, manage a multibillion dollar trust fund. _____

2. <u>Blessed with abundant rich farmland</u>, the United States plays a key role in combating world hunger. _____

3. <u>To avoid problems</u>, the hikers chose a longer route with fewer obstacles. _____

4. The crew was scheduled to reach its destination <u>within six days</u>. _____

5. On summer mornings, Melissa loved <u>tending to her flower garden</u>. _____

6. <u>Named Employee of the Month</u>, Stu was allowed to park in the space nearest to the front entrance. _____

7. <u>Against all odds</u>, the sockeye salmon survived their 900-mile trek up three rivers, climbing 6,500 feet. _____

8. <u>To audition for the play</u> had always been his dream. _____

9. <u>Disillusioned by politics</u>, Samantha decided to return to business. _____

10. The parent-teacher organization let Steve <u>lead its fundraising efforts</u>. _____

Answers:

1. <u>appositive acting as a noun to modify *Bill and Melinda Gates*</u>

2. <u>past participle acting as an adjective to modify *the United States*</u>

3. <u>infinitive acting as an adverb to modify the verb *chose*</u> (why they chose a longer route)

4. <u>prepositional acting as an adverb to modify the verb *scheduled*</u> (when the crew was scheduled)

5. <u>gerund</u>

6. <u>past participle serving as an adjective to describe *Stu*</u>

7. <u>prepositional phrase used as an adverb to modify the verb *survived*</u>

8. <u>infinitive used as a noun, the subject of the sentence</u>

9. <u>past participle used as an adjective to describe *Samantha*</u>

10. <u>bare infinitive</u>

Grasping the Basics of Clauses

A *clause* is a group of words containing a subject and a predicate. Grammarians distinguish between two types of clauses: independent and dependent. Dependent clauses are further categorized according to the role they play in the sentence—noun, adjective, or adverb. For additional details, read on.

DEFINITION

A **clause** is a group of words containing a subject and a predicate.

Independent Clauses

An *independent clause* can stand on its own two feet; if you pull it out of a sentence, capitalize the first letter of the first word, and stick a dot at the end, you have a sentence—probably a short sentence, but a sentence nevertheless. Following are examples of independent clauses appearing along with either independent or dependent clauses:

<u>Police evacuated the city</u> as the storm approached.

<u>The magician performed amazing feats of prestidigitation</u>, but <u>the crowd was not impressed</u>.

Wherever they moved, <u>good fortune followed</u>.

When combining independent clauses in a sentence, connect them with coordinating conjunctions: *and, but, or, for, nor*. For more about coordinating conjunctions, jump back to Chapter 3.

Dependent (Subordinate) Clauses

A *dependent* (*subordinate*) clause has a subject and verb but doesn't express a complete thought and therefore is not a sentence. A subordinate clause almost always begins with a word or two that signal the clause's dependency and establishes a relationship between the clause and the rest of the sentence. Here are some words that clue you into the fact that you're probably looking at a subordinate clause:

after	even though	until
although	if	whatever
as	in order that	when
as if	provided that	whenever
as long as	since	where
as though	so that	whereas
because	than	wherever
before	though	whether
even if	unless	while

In a sentence, a dependent clause may play the role of a noun, adjective, or adverb.

A *noun clause* is a dependent clause that functions as a noun in a sentence. Here are a few examples:

> Whoever steps up to the challenge will receive a commendation. (subject)
>
> I doubt whatever he says about Larry. (direct object)
>
> Melinda said that we can sleep over at her house. (direct object)

An *adjective clause* is a dependent clause that modifies a noun, as in the following examples:

> My neighbor, who just won the state lottery, is my friend.
>
> The lake, where I do most of my fishing, is three miles from my house.
>
> They're the times that I love best.

An *adjective clause* often begins with a relative pronoun, such as *which, who* or *whoever, whom* or *whomever,* and *that.* In most cases, the relative pronoun refers back to an *antecedent*—a previously mentioned noun. Relative clauses can be restrictive or nonrestrictive:

Restrictive clauses contain information that's essential to the meaning of the clause, so are not separated from the main clause by a comma; for example, "The person *who has the winning ticket* receives a prize." The relative clause, in this case, restricts the person receiving the prize to only that individual who has the winning ticket.

Nonrestrictive clauses contain supplemental information that the reader doesn't need to determine the identity of the antecedent, so they're separated from the main clause by a comma; for example, "Amanda, whom the CEO appointed department head, is unlikely to micromanage her staff."

An *adverb clause* is a dependent clause that modifies a verb, adjective, or another adverb, as in the following examples:

Amy visits her mother <u>whenever she feels the urge</u>. (adverb modifying *visits*)

This dishwashing detergent is more effective <u>than the other leading brand is</u>. (adverb modifying the adjective *effective*)

Geese migrate farther <u>than ducks do</u>. (adverb modifying another adverb, *farther*)

The *infinitive clause* straddles the line separating phrases and clauses. Technically speaking, an infinitive clause has a subject and a verb, but the verb is in the form of an infinitive, which doesn't function as a bona fide verb. The following examples shed some light on this phrase/clause phenomenon:

The electric company expects <u>its customers to pay their bills</u>.

I invited <u>my friends to visit me</u>.

As you can see, each of these clauses has a subject along with the infinitive form of a verb.

In an *elliptical clause,* one of the key components (the subject or the verb) is implied, not stated directly. Here are a few examples with the omitted (implied) words enclosed in brackets:

Ben likes ice cream more than Joe [likes ice cream].

While [she was] driving to the mall, Jen discovered a shortcut to her doctor's office.

The massage therapist spent more time with my sister than [she spent] with me.

Practice

In each of the following sentences, a clause is underlined. Write the type of clause (independent or dependent) on the line next to the sentence. For dependent clauses, specify whether the clause functions as a noun, adjective, or adverb.

1. Carolyn, <u>whose counsel is so important to me</u>, is well-known for her integrity.

2. Loan officers had suspected fraud all along, <u>but they failed to report it to authorities</u>.

3. <u>Whenever they purchased presents</u>, they donated an equal amount to charity.

4. Scott always maxed out his IRA contributions, <u>so that he would be able to retire in relative comfort</u>.

5. Jolie suspected the entire time <u>that her brother was planning a surprise birthday party for her</u>.

6. Tim golfs <u>whenever he has the opportunity</u>.

7. Although Louise has an active social life, <u>she enjoys her solitude</u>.

8. <u>As businesses begin to harness the marketing power of facial recognition technology</u>, consumers are becoming increasingly concerned about privacy issues.

9. Do you know <u>who is responsible for locking the doors</u>?

10. <u>When my alarm buzzes</u>, I know I need to wake up.

Answers

1. <u>dependent, adjective (modifies Carolyn)</u>

2. <u>independent</u>

3. <u>dependent, adverb (tells when they donated)</u>

4. <u>dependent, adverb (explains why Scott maxed out his IRA contributions)</u>

5. <u>dependent, noun (what Jolie expected)</u>

6. <u>dependent, adverb (specifies when Tim golfs)</u>

7. <u>independent (the clause that wasn't underlined is dependent)</u>

8. <u>dependent, adverb (explains why consumers are becoming concerned)</u>

9. <u>dependent, noun (object of the verb *know*)</u>

10. <u>dependent, adverb (indicates when I know)</u>

Common Sentence Structures

One component of good writing is to vary the sentence structure, as explained in Chapter 14, and one way to vary sentence structure is to combine independent and dependent clauses in different arrangements to form any of the following four sentence types: simple, compound, complex, or compound-complex. The following sections describe each of these sentence types in turn and challenge you to practice forming the different sentence types.

Simple Sentence

A *simple sentence* is comprised of only one subject-predicate combination, as in the following examples:

> Stars shimmer at night.

> Qualified technicians perform all repairs on our customers' computers and related equipment.

As demonstrated in the second example, a simple sentence can be quite long, but it's made up of only one independent clause and contains no dependent clauses.

Compound Sentence

A *compound sentence* contains two or more independent clauses and no dependent clauses, as in the following examples:

> The band's performance was exceptional, but the song selection disappointed fans.

> Joan wanted to take a taxi; John preferred the subway.

> John and Joan disagreed on the mode of travel; nevertheless, they reached a compromise and decided to take a bus.

You have several options for linking the independent clauses that comprise a compound sentence:

Comma and conjunction: Use a comma followed by one of the coordinating conjunctions: *and, but, yet, or, for, nor.*

Semicolon, no conjunction: To subtly indicate that two independent clauses are related, separate them with a semicolon instead of a period.

Semicolon and conjunctive adverb: To more clearly indicate the logical or chronological relationship between two independent clauses, use a semicolon with a conjunctive adverb followed by a comma. Conjunctive adverbs include the following:

accordingly	hence	otherwise
also	however	similarly
besides	incidentally	still
certainly	likewise	then
consequently	meanwhile	therefore
finally	moreover	thus
further	nevertheless	undoubtedly
furthermore		

Complex Sentence

A *complex sentence* contains only one independent clause and one or more dependent clauses. Here are a few examples of complex sentences with the independent clauses underlined and the dependent clauses in italics:

Before Jessie's father would grant his permission, she needed to present him with an itinerary for the evening.

To generate additional revenue, Illinois raised taxes on businesses, *whereas Indiana lowered taxes to attract more businesses.*

The Rocky Mountains, *which were formed 50 to 100 million years ago,* run from southern Colorado to the Canadian border.

Compound-Complex Sentence

A *compound-complex* sentence contains at least two independent clauses and one dependent clause. Following are a couple examples of compound-complex sentences with the independent clauses underlined and the dependent clauses in italics:

Darryl, *who is an incredible accordion player,* joined a Zydeco band; the band plays regularly at venues in and near the French Quarter.

Although Reese pledged her support for the proposal, she secretly doubted *that it would fix the problem*; the proposal failed to address some key issues.

Practice

In the blank to the right of each of the following sentences, identify the sentence type: simple, compound, complex, or compound-complex:

1. Whoever is the last person to leave the building needs to lock all the doors, because burglaries are common in this neighborhood. _____

2. Whenever we have a big storm, the water floods our basement. _____

3. Mandy invited Christy and her friends to the concert, which was scheduled for the following Friday; unfortunately, Christy already had plans. _____

4. Sam returned the defective merchandise and demanded a refund or store credit.
    _____

5. Danny and Scott pretended to be honest business owners, but they both knew that what they were planning was unethical, even though it happened to be legal.
    _____

Answers:

1. complex
2. complex
3. compound-complex

4. simple
5. compound-complex

The Least You Need to Know

- A sentence requires at least one subject-predicate pair.
- A complement is a noun, verb, or adjective (single word or phrase) that's part of the predicate and completes the action.
- A phrase is two or more words that form a grammatical unit but doesn't contain a subject and predicate.
- A verbal is a verb form that functions as another part of speech—a noun, adjective, or adverb.
- A clause contains a subject-verb pair that can stand alone as a sentence (independent clause) or not (dependent clause).
- Structurally, sentences come in four types: simple, compound, complex, and compound-complex.

Using the Parts of Speech to Build Sentences

Now it's time to take the building blocks of writing and combine them into larger forms that you can use when making sentences.

In these chapters, you'll get a closer look at the most important words of all: nouns and verbs. You'll learn how nouns form the subject and object of a sentence, naming all the people, places, things, and conditions that exist. You'll learn how verbs explain what those nouns do and are. Since a subject and verb are needed to make a grammatical sentence—or an independent clause—it's important to understand nouns and verbs thoroughly. Nouns and verbs are to grammar what hydrogen and oxygen are to water: essential, irreplaceable components. There's also a chapter on complements, which adds information to subjects, predicates, and objects.

I'll also go in-depth on adjectives and adverbs: words that modify other words. Those adjectives and adverbs aren't as powerful as nouns and verbs, but you should understand and use them carefully. A well-placed adjective or adverb can make a sentence sound smooth and flowing. An unnecessary or vague adjective or adverb can make a sentence sound clichéd, annoying, or confusing.

In this part, I'll discuss phrases and clauses, which are the largest chunks of language outside of complete sentences. You'll learn the difference between a phrase and a clause and how to move both around a sentence when revising. I'll also look at the different types of phrases and clauses and how to identify them.

Using Nouns and Pronouns as Subjects

Thing is one of the broadest, most general words in English. In a way, everything is a thing. All those things have nouns that represent them, and just as there are varied nouns, there are diverse subjects of sentences.

Every sentence and every clause has a subject, but they don't all have the same type of subject. The subject may be a noun or a pronoun, singular or plural, stated or unstated. If a sentence begins with a pronoun, it probably has an antecedent—a noun it refers back to. In addition, you can start sentences with dummy subjects, such as it and there. In other words, using nouns and pronouns as subjects is much more involved than it sounds.

This chapter takes some of the complexity out of starting sentences with nouns and pronouns and shows you how to use nouns and pronouns properly to identify the subject of the sentence—the person, place, or thing the clause or sentence is about.

In This Chapter

- Recognizing the subject in a sentence
- Making a noun plural or possessive
- Starting a sentence with a pronoun
- Beginning a sentence with *it, they,* or *there*
- Dealing with some commonly confused pronouns

Starting a Sentence with a Noun

Every sentence begins with a noun or pronoun. Starting with a noun is by far the easier of the two options because, as explained in Chapter 3, nouns change form only in the plural and possessive.

The following sections explain how to start sentences with a singular or plural *subject* and explore some variations you're certain to encounter.

> **DEFINITION**
>
> The **subject** of a sentence is the person, place, or thing the sentence is about. The rest of the sentence describes what the subject is doing or being.

Starting with a Singular Subject

A singular subject is a solitary singular noun that the sentence is about, as in the following example:

> Evan capitulates.

One person, *Evan*, performs the action—*capitulates*. Note that when a singular noun performs the action, it calls for a singular verb form, as explained in Chapter 6.

Remember from Chapter 3 that collective nouns are often treated as singular nouns, even though they represent numerous beings:

> A swarm of bees chases Jenny.

Starting with a Plural Subject

A plural subject is a plural noun or two or more nouns that the sentence is about. Here are a couple examples:

> Evan and Sue capitulate. (two nouns functioning as a plural subject)

> The bees chase Jenny. (a plural noun functioning as a plural subject)

When a sentence is about two or more beings, the verb must be in its plural form for *subject-verb agreement,* as explained in Chapter 6 and demonstrated in these examples.

In the second example, notice that even though bees are still chasing Jenny, *bees* is plural (unlike the collective noun *swarm*), so the subject requires the plural form of the verb *chase*.

> **DEFINITION**
>
> According to the principle of **subject-verb agreement,** the subject of a sentence must always agree with its verb in number. In other words, subject-verb agreement means singular subjects need singular verbs and plural subjects need plural verbs.

Inserting the Subject in a Question

When composing questions, putting the subject in the correct place is more challenging, because positioning depends on the type of question:

Subject questions: In a subject question, an interrogative pronoun usually comes first, followed by the verb, and functions as the subject; for example:

<u>Who</u> ate my candy bar?

<u>What</u> happened?

Object questions: In an object question, the subject usually appears in the question sandwiched between a helping verb and an action verb or immediately after the helping verb. Here are a couple examples:

Who do <u>you</u> want to win the contest?

Where did <u>you</u> go?

> **USAGE TIDBIT**
>
> To identify the subject in a question, rephrase the question as a statement. For example, if the question is "Who ate my candy bar?" reword it as "So-and-so ate my candy bar." All the words match up except for *Who* and *So-and-so,* so *Who* serves the same function as *So-and-so*—the subject of the statement. Object questions are even easier. Rephrase "Where did you go?" as the answer to the question, and you get "You went _____. *You* is the subject.

Omitting the Subject in a Command

When issuing a command, you do so in the imperative mood, as explained in Chapter 6, and typically drop the subject, *you,* because *you* is implied:

[You] Take out the trash.

[You] Please help me find my keys.

Using a Verbal as a Subject

As explained in Chapters 3 and 4, certain verb forms—specifically gerunds, infinitives, and participles—can function as nouns. As such, they can also function as subjects in sentences. Following are a few examples of verbals acting as subjects:

<u>Passing</u> on the right is something drivers should never do.

<u>To sit</u> at the hospital all day is exhausting.

<u>Listening</u> may be the more important skill.

With verbals, you still need to watch subject-verb agreement or, in this case, verbal-verb agreement. Although a verbal is almost always singular, you could have two of them acting as a compound subject, as in this example:

<u>Swimming</u> and <u>skiing</u> are my two favorite water sports.

Practice

Underline the subject in each of the following sentences:

1. Inside the walls of the house lived a colony of termites.

2. The saplings arrived just in time for fall planting.

3. Plan to check in at least 15 minutes prior to your scheduled appointment.

4. Playing billiards is one of my favorite pastimes.

5. Which one of the pilots flew your plane?

6. The crew was entrusted by the captain to sail the ship.

7. A gaggle of Canadian geese formed a menacing flotilla.

8. When did management decide to hire an IT specialist?

9. Monitoring computer use is a parent's responsibility.

10. Looking forward to the next game, the coach decided to formulate a new strategy.

Answers:

1. colony

2. saplings

3. you

4. playing

5. which

6. crew

7. gaggle

8. management

9. monitoring

10. coach

Using a Pronoun Instead of a Noun

Not all sentences start with nouns. Some begin with *pronouns,* such as *I, you, we,* or *they.* If you're starting with first- or second-person pronouns (*I, we, you* singular, or *you* plural), you're probably not going to run into any problems, as long as you remember the rule that plural nouns and pronouns require plural verbs. These pronouns are easy, because there's usually no question about who they represent.

Pronoun use becomes more complicated when starting a sentence with a third-person pronoun—*he, she,* or *it* (all singular) or *they* (plural)—because who or what these pronouns represent must be previously established. If, out of the blue, someone tells you, "It was the best meal I ever ate," you have no idea what that person is talking about. For such a sentence to make sense, the pronoun must clearly refer back to an *antecedent*—a noun that the pronoun represents. If the person was talking about eating a steak dinner at Debbie's Diner, and then says, "It was the best meal I ever ate," now you know what *it* stands for—the steak dinner at Debbie's Diner.

In the following sections, you'll find out how to choose the correct pronoun and establish a clear connection between a pronoun and its antecedent.

> **DEFINITION**
>
> A **pronoun** is a word—such as *I, we, you, he,* and *she*—that takes the place of a noun. It refers to a person, place, or thing, but not by name. An **antecedent** is the noun that the pronoun refers to or stands for.

Subjective Pronouns

When using a pronoun as the subject of a sentence, choose the subjective personal pronoun that most accurately refers back to the antecedent or represents the speaker or the person the sentence is about. As explained in Chapter 3, the subjective personal pronouns are:

	Singular	**Plural**
First person	I	we
Second person	you	you
Third person	he, she, it	they

Antecedent-Pronoun Agreement

Regardless of what role a pronoun plays in a sentence, it must agree with its antecedent in person, number, and gender:

Person: The type of individual(s)—for example, whether the pronoun refers to person(s) or thing(s).

Number: The quantity of individual(s)—one (singular) or more than one (plural).

Gender: The sexual identity of the person, place, or thing. In relation to subjective personal pronouns, the three genders relate only to the third-person singular pronouns: *he* (masculine), *she* (feminine), and *it* (neuter). *I, we,* and *you* can be masculine or feminine; *they* can be masculine, feminine, or nongendered.

Clarifying the Antecedent-Pronoun Connection

The biggest issue you face when using subjective third-person personal pronouns is making sure the pronoun clearly refers back to the intended antecedent. An ambiguous connection leaves a sentence open to misinterpretation. Usually when an antecedent-pronoun connection is ambiguous, the ambiguity is caused by one of the following issues:

- The antecedent and pronoun are very far apart, as in the following example:

Linda went to the movie by herself, because her friends Jackie and Stacy were both away on vacation. <u>She</u> loved <u>it</u>.

In the last sentence, the reader has to do a little work to identify what *she* refers to. Figuring out what *it* refers to (*the movie*) is even harder, because the word *vacation* is so near to *it*.

- Two or more nouns precede the antecedent and are in close proximity to one another, as in this example:

When Fred dropped his <u>accordion</u> on the coffee <u>table,</u> <u>it</u> shattered. (Did the accordion or the coffee table shatter?)

When reading, you should assume the pronoun refers to the closest possible candidate to be the antecedent—in this example, *table*. However, if the accordion shattered, then the ambiguity would definitely be misleading. It's best to revise a sentence so it can only be read one way.

- *It* is used as a dummy subject, as in the following sentence:

<u>It</u> was obvious from the look on his face that he was guilty.

This leaves the audience wondering "What was obvious?" Certainly not the antecedent. A clearer way to say this would be:

Obviously, from the look on his face, he was guilty.

To avoid pronoun-antecedent ambiguity, place the pronoun as near to the noun it modifies as possible. If ambiguity still exists, then repeat the noun, as in the following example:

When Fred dropped his <u>accordion</u> on the coffee table, <u>the accordion</u> shattered.

Dealing with Reflexive Actions and Pronouns

You don't use reflexive pronouns to start a sentence, but they're so integral to the subject of a sentence, we thought we should mention them here. To refresh your memory, reflexive pronouns are the *self* and *selves* pronouns: myself, himself, herself, yourselves, themselves, and so on.

As explained in Chapter 3, a reflexive pronoun describes action performed on oneself. Here's another, more practical way to put it: use a reflexive pronoun after a transitive verb when the subject is the same as the direct or indirect object. Here's an example:

I	blame	myself.
subject	**transitive verb**	**direct object**

You're more likely to see certain verbs teaming up with reflexive pronouns. Here are some verbs commonly used with reflexive pronouns:

apply	express	kill
behave	find	lost
blame	help	see
cut	hurt	teach
dry	introduce	wash
enjoy		

Practice

Correct each of the following sentences to ensure pronoun-antecedent agreement and clear up ambiguous references.

1. Each of the teams will have their own captain.

   _____

2. Mia and Alyssa took the bus into town and ate lunch at Dan's Deli, because it was less expensive than taking a taxi.

   _____

3. Jayden invited Olivia to dinner to meet his mom and dad, not realizing he would be away on business.

   _____

4. Despite their ability to survive in freshwater habitats, the bull shark isn't a freshwater species.

   _____

5. Every one of the players blamed themselves for the loss.

   _____

Answers:

1. Each of the teams will have its own captain.

2. Mia and Alyssa took the bus into town, because it was less expensive than taking a taxi, and ate lunch at Dan's Deli.

   OR

   Mia and Alyssa took the bus, which was less expensive than taking a taxi, into town and ate lunch at Dan's Deli.

3. Jayden invited Olivia to dinner to meet his mom and dad, not realizing his dad would be away on business. (meaning his dad would be away on business)

   OR

   Jayden, not realizing he would be away on business, invited Olivia to dinner to meet his mom and dad. (meaning Jayden would be away on business)

4. Despite its ability to survive in freshwater habitats, the bull shark isn't a freshwater species.

5. All of the players blamed themselves for the loss.

   OR

   Every one of the players blamed herself or himself for the loss.

Using Expletive Expressions Sparingly

When you see or hear the word *expletive*, you may think *swear word*, but *expletive* also refers to a generic word that stands in place of a subject or object in anticipation of a word or phrase that defines it more clearly, as in the following examples:

There are few people who shop for groceries on Friday nights.

It wasn't until my 53rd birthday that I started feeling old.

Technically speaking, nothing is wrong with constructions such as these. Stylistically, however, expletives use weak verbs, make sentences wordy, and leave readers wondering what *there* or *it* refers to. Whenever you come across a sentence containing *There are … who …* or *It is … that …* or other sentences that follow that pattern, try to revise the sentence to place the true subject first followed by the verb. Following are revisions of the previous examples:

Few people shop for groceries on Friday nights.

Not until my 53rd birthday did I start feeling old.

Occasionally, *There is/are* … and *Here is/are* … constructions are okay to use, especially if they're introducing an important point or a list. Here are a couple examples:

Here are the three clues to look for: …

There are numerous reasons to exercise. First, exercise improves cardiovascular health. …

 DANGER ZONE

Avoid starting sentences with *It is/was* … or *There are* … unless you're referring to an antecedent or have some other good reason for doing so.

Practice

Reword the following sentences to remove the expletive.

1. There are about three million people who live in Chicago.

   _____

2. It is faster to ride the train than to drive.

   _____

3. There are numerous benefits to owning your own home.

   _____

4. There are several ethnic restaurants that serve delicious cuisine.

   _____

5. It is a fact that a walrus can eat up to 6,000 clams in a single meal.

   _____

Answers:

1. About three million people live in Chicago.

2. Riding the train is faster than driving.

3. Owning your own home has numerous benefits.

4. Several ethnic restaurants serve delicious cuisine.

5. <u>A walrus can eat up to 6,000 clams in a single meal.</u>

OR

<u>That a walrus can eat up to 6,000 clams in a single meal is a fact.</u>

Sorting Out *Who, Which,* and *That*

Choosing between *that, which,* and *who* can be quite a challenge. The following rules offer guidance:

- Use *who* to refer to people or named animals: for example, Rover the dog and Garfield the cat. Place a comma before *who* if the clause is nonrestrictive. (See Chapter 4 for more about the difference between restrictive and nonrestrictive clauses.)

- Use *that* or *which* without a comma before it in restrictive clauses to refer to places, things, and unnamed animals.

- Use *which* with a comma before it in nonrestrictive clauses that refer to places, things, and unnamed animals.

Following are some examples:

The doctor <u>who</u> examined me is from Slovenia. (Use *who* because the doctor is a person; omit the comma because the clause is restrictive—it's required to identify the specific doctor who examined me.)

My doctor, <u>who</u> owns a Lamborghini, is from Slovenia. (Use *who* here again, but set off the relative clause from the rest of the sentence with a pair of commas, because the clause is nonrestrictive; it's not necessary for identifying which doctor the sentence is about.)

The bug <u>that</u> bit Jessie is either a sweat bee or a horse fly. (Use *that* or *which* with no comma before it, because the clause is restrictive; it's talking about the bug that bit Jessie and not some other bug that may have done something else.)

Rhododendrons, <u>which</u> are highly susceptible to root rot, grow poorly, if at all, in clay soils. (Use which, but use a comma before and after the nonrestrictive clause to set it off from the rest of the sentence.)

Knowing When to Use *Who* or *Whom*

No pronouns cause more confusion than *who, whom,* and their close cousins *whoever* and *whomever.* The following rules help you decide which to use:

- Use *who* or *whoever* when the pronoun functions as a subject or predicate nominative:

    <u>Whoever</u> wants the last piece of pizza can have it. (*whoever* as subject)

    Nobody at the party knew <u>who</u> the stranger was. (*who* as predicate nominative; *the stranger* was *who*)

- Use *whom* or *whomever* when the pronoun functions as an object:

    The boy <u>whom</u> Sally took to the dance was quite handsome. (*whom* as direct object—the person Sally asked)

    You can purchase tickets from <u>whomever</u> you choose. (*whomever* as the object of the preposition *from*)

- *Whom* and *whomever* are misused frequently, and both have an old-fashioned, snooty air about them. The best thing to do is write around them, avoiding their use, if possible: both words are likely to disappear from English before long.

USAGE TIDBIT

Drop the pronoun when possible to tighten up your prose. For example, instead of writing "The dog that I adopted has fleas" say "The dog I adopted has fleas." The word "that" is often unnecessary, but also look for occurrences of who, whom, and which that can be cut without confusing the reader.

Practice

In each of the following sentences, circle the correct pronoun.

1. Mason, (who / whom) I gave directions to, had no trouble getting to the airport on time.

2. The mechanic (who / that) worked on my car was certified.

3. Animals (who / that) migrate usually do so to find food, reproduce, or seek out better weather.

4. *Cloud Atlas,* (which / that) didn't win an Oscar in any category, was my favorite movie of the year.

5. Bella's dog, (who / whom / which) she adopted from a shelter, is a full-bred Keeshond.

Answers

1. <u>whom</u>
2. <u>who</u>
3. <u>that</u>
4. <u>which</u>
5. <u>whom</u>

The Least You Need to Know

- A singular noun requires a singular verb; a plural noun requires a plural verb.
- A pronoun must agree with its antecedent in person, number, and gender.
- Use expletive expressions, such as "There are ..." and "It is ..." sparingly if at all.
- Use *who* and *whom* to refer to people or named animals.
- Use that and which to refer to places, things, and unnamed animals.
- Use *who* for subjects and *whom* for objects.

Taking Action with Verbs

Verbs have power. Verbs do things. They make things happen in language. Verbs eat, jump, organize, slash, collect, explode, and explain. Verbs are the athletes of language, and they're definitely multi-sport.

Everyone knows that verbs express action, but they convey much more than that. They also provide subtle clues as to who or what is performing the action; when the action occurs, occurred, or will occur; the attitude of the speaker; and whether the subject of the sentence is on the giving or receiving end of the action.

Sound complicated? It is. However, this chapter breaks everything verb-related into easily digestible, bite-size morsels.

Just as there are many different verbs for consuming food—such as biting, chewing, swallowing, and digesting—there are many steps in the consuming process. If you take verbs one step at a time, you'll have an easier time absorbing their lexical nutrients.

In This Chapter

- Picking verb forms out of a police lineup
- Choosing the right verb tense: timing is everything
- Getting your nouns and verbs to agree in person and number
- Wrapping your brain around the concept of mood
- Opting for the active over the passive voice

Recognizing Verb Forms

Every verb has four forms that, as shown in the following table, you use to create the various tenses—present, past, future, and so on.

Verb Forms

Present/Root	Present Participle	Past	Past Participle
live	(is) living	lived	(have) lived
work	(is) working	worked	(have) worked
swim	(is) swimming	swam	(have) swum

I added *is* and *have* to the present and past participles as a reminder that these require a helping verb; for example, instead of saying "I living in Chicago," you say "I am living in Chicago." As explained in Chapter 3, some of the helping verbs include *am, is, are, was, were, have, has, has been, had,* and *will be.*

In the following sections, I explain how to form the infinitive (easy stuff) and then show you how to form the present participle, past, and past participle of the most common verbs. Once you've mastered these basics, you're well on your way to forming verb tenses.

Forming the Infinitive

A verb's *infinitive* is the action itself without any tense or other accoutrements. To form the infinitive, you simply add *to* to the beginning of the root. So the infinitives of the verbs listed in the preceding table are *to live, to work,* and *to swim.*

You can use infinitives as nouns or parts of noun phrases (for example, "I love *to swim*"), to give a reason for performing another action (as in "I often walk *to clear* my mind"), and to express general or habitual action (as in "To grow flowers, you must plant seeds.") See Chapter 9 for more about using infinitives in phrases.

> **DEFINITION**
>
> An **infinitive** is the base form of a verb, usually preceded by the word *to*, that functions as a noun, adjective, or adverb. An infinitive is used after an auxiliary verb (without the word *to*) to express action or being. For example:
>
> **Used as noun:** Carol loves <u>to drive</u>.
>
> **With an auxiliary verb:** Carol <u>must drive</u>.

Regular Verb Forms

Creating the four verb forms of regular verbs is a snap:

root	verb
present participle	verb + –ing
past	verb + –ed
past participle	verb + –ed

Following are some variations on the theme:

- If the verb ends in *e*, drop the *e* before adding *–ing* or *–ed*, as in *moving, moved*.

- For one-syllable words, double the consonant at the end of the verb before adding *–ing* or *–ed*, as in *beg, begging, begged* and *hop, hopping, hopped*. (Words ending in *w, x, y*, and *z* do not follow this rule.)

- For two-syllable words accented on the second syllable, double the consonant at the end of the verb before adding *–ing* or *–ed*, as in *admit, admitting, admitted*, and *refer, referring, referred*.

Irregular Verb Forms

Irregular verb forms are more difficult to master, because they don't follow the rules for forming the past and past participle. They might …

- Change vowels as in *shrink, shrank, shrunk*.

- Change endings as in *lose, lost, lost*.

- Completely change as in *go, went, gone*.

- Drop a vowel as in *lead, led, led*.

- Change vowels and add an ending as in *fly, flew, flown*.

- Stay the same as in *bet, bet, bet*.

The following table lists some of the most common irregular verbs along with their past and past participle forms. You still form the present participle by adding *–ing* to the base (and dropping the *e* or doubling the consonant at the end of the verb when necessary).

Irregular Verb Forms

Root	Past	Past Participle
be	was/were	been
beat	beat	beaten
become	became	become
begin	began	begun
bend	bent	bent
bet	bet	bet
bid	bid	bid
bite	bit	bitten
blow	blew	blown
break	broke	broken
bring	brought	brought
build	built	built
burn	burned/burnt	burned/burnt
burst	burst	burst
buy	bought	bought
catch	caught	caught
choose	chose	chosen
come	came	come
cost	cost	cost
cut	cut	cut
dig	dug	dug
dive	dove/dived	dived
do	did	done
draw	drew	drawn
dream	dreamed/dreamt	dreamed/dreamt
drink	drank	drunk
drive	drove	driven
eat	ate	eaten
fall	fell	fallen
feel	felt	felt
fight	fought	fought
find	found	found
fly	flew	flown

Root	Past	Past Participle
forget	forgot	forgotten
forgive	forgave	forgiven
freeze	froze	frozen
get	got	got/gotten
give	gave	given
go	went	gone
grow	grew	grown
hang	hung/hanged	hung/hanged
have	had	had
hear	heard	heard
hide	hid	hidden
hit	hit	hit
hold	held	held
hurt	hurt	hurt
keep	kept	kept
know	knew	known
lay	laid	laid
lead	led	led
learn	learned/learnt	learned/learnt
leave	left	left
lend	lent	lent
let	let	let
lie	lay	lain
lose	lost	lost
make	made	made
mean	meant	meant
meet	met	met
pay	paid	paid
prove	proved	proven/proved
put	put	put
read	read	read
ride	rode	ridden
ring	rang	rung
rise	rose	risen

continues

Irregular Verb Forms (continued)

Root	Past	Past Participle
run	ran	run
say	said	said
see	saw	seen
sell	sold	sold
send	sent	sent
set	set	set
show	showed	showed/shown
shut	shut	shut
sing	sang	sung
sit	sat	sat
sleep	slept	slept
speak	spoke	spoken
spend	spent	spent
stand	stood	stood
swim	swam	swum
take	took	taken
teach	taught	taught
tear	tore	torn
tell	told	told
think	thought	thought
throw	threw	thrown
understand	understood	understood
wake	awoke	awoken
wake	woke	woken
wear	wore	worn
win	won	won
write	wrote	written

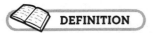 **DEFINITION**

Irregular verbs are those that don't conform to the standard patterns of forming the past and past participle.

Telling Time with Tenses

The verb tense provides a general indication of the action's timing—for example, past, present, or future. The following table lists the 12 tenses and briefly describes when to use each tense.

The 12 Verb Tenses

Tense	Use to Describe	Example
Present	Current or habitual action	*I camp.*
Past	Completed action	*I camped.*
Future	Future action	*I will camp.*
Present progressive	Continuous present action	*I am camping.*
Past progressive	Continuing action completed in the past	*I was camping when the storms moved in.*
Future progressive	Continuing action that is yet to happen	*I will be camping.*
Present perfect	Completed or continuing action	*I have camped in the winter.*
Past perfect	Action completed before another past action	*I had camped before I visited Mount Rushmore.*
Future perfect	Future action or condition completed before another future action or condition	*By next Sunday, I will have camped for two weeks.*
Present perfect progressive	Past action continuing into the present	*I have been camping all month.*
Past perfect progressive	Continuing past action stopped by a past event	*I had been camping for a week before the tornado sirens sounded.*
Future perfect progressive	Continuing future action completed before a future event	*By the time you read my letter, I will have been camping for at least two weeks.*

The following table gives you a bird's-eye view of the 12 tenses and how to form them using the four verb forms discussed in the previous section: root, past, present participle, and past participle.

Forming the 12 Verb Tenses

Tense	Formation	Example
Present	present	*walk*
Past	past	*walked*
Future	will/shall + root	*will walk*
Present progressive	am/is/are + present participle	*is walking*
Present perfect	have/has + past participle	*has walked*
Past perfect	had + past participle	*had walked*
Future perfect	will have + past participle	*will have walked*
Past progressive	was/were + present participle	*was walking*
Future progressive	will/shall + be + present participle	*will be walking*
Present perfect progressive	have/has + been + present participle	*have been walking*
Past perfect progressive	had + been + present participle	*had been walking*
Future perfect progressive	will + have + been + present participle	*will have been walking*

In the following sections I explain the 12 tenses in greater detail, along with some nuances for using each tense and common problems that arise in selecting which tense to use. But first, let's take a look at how to form the tenses of the very irregular verb *to be*.

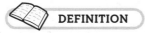 **DEFINITION**

Verb tense indicates the time of the action and whether the action has been completed or is ongoing.

Tensing Up with the Verb *To Be*

The weirdest verb of all irregulars is the verb that expresses being—*to be*. Since *to be* is used to form many of the other tenses, you really need to know how to *conjugate* it; that is, you need to know all of its forms in simple and perfect tenses and in person and number. Person refers to who is doing the action (for example, *I, you,* or *they*); number refers to singular or plural. (For example, *it* is singular and *they* is plural.)

For *to be*, the tricky tenses to conjugate are the present, past, and present perfect tenses and their continuous counterparts:

	Singular	**Plural**
Present		
	I *am*	we *are*
	you *are*	you *are*
	he/she/it *is*	they *are*
Past		
	I *was*	we *were*
	you *were*	you *were*
	he/she/it *was*	they *were*
Present perfect		
	I have *been*	we *have been*
	you have *been*	you *have been*
	he/she/it *has been*	they *have been*
Present progressive		
	I *am being*	we *are being*
	you *are being*	you *are being*
	he/she/it *is being*	they *are being*
Present perfect progressive		
	I *have been being*	we *have been being*
	you *have been being*	you *have been being*
	he/she/it *has been being*	they *have been being*
Past progressive		
	I *was being*	we *were being*
	you *were being*	you *were being*
	he/she/it *was being*	they *were being*

For the remaining tenses, the verb form is identical regardless of person and number:

Past perfect	*had been*
Future	*will be*
Future perfect	*will have been*
Past perfect progressive	*had been being*
Future progressive	*will be being*
Future perfect progressive	*will have been being*

Keeping It Simple

Present, past, and future are the so-called *simple tenses,* which aren't always as simple as people like to think, as explained in the following sections.

> **DEFINITION**
>
> **Simple tenses** indicate only the time of the action, not whether the action has been completed or is ongoing.

Present

Use the present tense to describe action that happens right now:

> I <u>understand</u> your concern.
>
> The peaches <u>are</u> ripe.

The present tense is also commonly used to describe facts or habitual action, as in the following examples:

> I always <u>call</u> my mom on Mother's Day.
>
> Jennifer <u>swims</u> the 400-meter freestyle. Mark <u>swims</u> the 200-meter butterfly.

People rarely run into problems knowing when to use the present tense, except when they mix the present and past tense while referring to something that still exists in the present:

> Last week, I wrote a letter to our CEO. My letter <u>questioned</u> his judgment in laying off 25 percent of the company's employees.
>
> Last week, I watched a documentary that <u>claimed</u> global warming <u>was</u> a hoax.

In these examples, the letter, the documentary, and the topic of global warming are still in existence and always will be, so you need to describe them in the present tense:

> Last week, I wrote a letter to our CEO. My letter <u>questions</u> his judgment in laying off 25 percent of the company's employees.
>
> Last week, I watched a documentary that <u>claims</u> global warming <u>is</u> a hoax.

Past

Use the past tense to express past action that's over, done, finished:

> We <u>ate</u> catfish last night.
>
> Sally and Roger <u>traveled</u> to Denver for spring break.

Future

If you're like most people, you have little trouble figuring out when to use the future tense or how to form it, but you do need to be aware of the following subtleties:

In the old days, people used *shall* instead of *will* with *I* or *we*, as in "We <u>shall</u> overcome." This is no longer a rule, but when you're offering to help someone, you should use *shall* instead of *will*, as in "<u>Shall</u> I help you carry your groceries?" To avoid sounding stuffy, avoid *shall* altogether in such cases: for example, "<u>May</u> I help you carry your groceries?"

You can also express future action by using a form of the verb *go* with the infinitive of the action verb; for example, "I am going to discuss this with my supervisor."

You can also use the present or present progressive tense to express future action, as in "Cindy <u>leaves</u> for Las Vegas later today" or "Cindy <u>is leaving</u> for Las Vegas later today."

Recognizing the Perfect Tenses

English has three *perfect tenses* used to describe action that occurred just prior to the present, past, or future. The following sections explain the perfect tenses and explore their nuances.

> **DEFINITION**
>
> The **perfect tenses** express action completed before another action occurred, occurs, or will occur. For example, the future perfect tense expresses future action that has been completed prior to another future action.

Present Perfect

Use the present perfect to express action leading up to the present and possibly still occurring, as in the following examples:

> Patrick <u>has</u> often <u>dreamed</u> about owning his own farm. (Patrick dreamed in the past and presumably is not done dreaming about this.)

> My parents <u>have spent</u> every winter in Alabama since I can remember. (Action occurred in the past and continues to the present.)

A common mistake is to use present perfect to express action that happened sometime in the past and is over. For example:

> I already <u>have responded</u> to your email message!

> Congress <u>has voted</u> on the legislation and is now waiting for the president to sign it into law.

For action completed in the past, use the simple past tense:

> I already <u>responded</u> to your email message!

> Congress <u>voted</u> on the legislation and is now waiting for the president to sign it into law.

Past Perfect

Use the past perfect tense to express action completed prior to another past action, as in the following examples:

> James <u>had called</u> home before he <u>left</u> work. (Both actions occurred in the past, but <u>had called</u> came first.)

> The buyers <u>signed</u> the contract moments after the sellers <u>had lowered</u> their price. (Both actions occurred in the past, but <u>had lowered</u> came first.)

Often, people mistakenly use the past tense for all actions that occurred in the past, even when some past actions occurred before others:

> Natalie's eyes <u>expressed</u> her disappointment with the engagement ring her fiancé <u>gave</u> her. (The verb <u>gave</u> should be <u>had given</u>, because the fiancé gave the ring before Natalie's eyes expressed disappointment.)

Future Perfect

Use the future perfect tense to express action completed sometime in the future, as in the following examples:

> My father <u>will have turned</u> 65 years old on his next birthday. (The father's birthday will happen in the future, but he will have turned 65 years old by that time.)

> Ten days from now, most of the seeds you planted <u>will have sprouted</u>. (Some seeds may sprout before the ten days have passed.)

Recognizing the Progressive Tenses

The progressive tenses all use the *–ing* form of the action verb to indicate that the action is happening in the specified time frame—present, past, or future. The following sections provide guidance on when to use each of these progressive tenses.

Present Progressive

Use the present progressive tense to express action that's occurring right now, as in the following examples:

A frog <u>is hiding</u> underneath this lily pad.

Rays of sunlight <u>are sparkling</u> on the lake's surface.

You can also use the present progressive tense to express future action, as shown here:

I don't know about you, but I <u>am sleeping</u> in tomorrow morning. (You could also use the future progressive tense, as explained later.)

Past Progressive

Use the past progressive tense to express action that was happening in the past. This tense comes in handy particularly when a past action is interrupted by another past action, as in the following examples:

I <u>was minding</u> my own business when the lion attacked me.

Jenny <u>was crossing</u> the street when she bumped into her neighbor.

You can also use the past progressive tense to exaggerate a habitual action:

The professor <u>was</u> constantly <u>berating</u> his students.

Future Progressive

Use the future progressive tense to express action that will be happening sometime in the future. The future progressive tense is particularly helpful for expressing a future action leading up to or interrupted by a future event, as in the following examples:

I <u>will be driving</u> home from work when the game starts.

By the time I get there, everyone <u>will be leaving</u>.

The future progressive tense is also useful for expressing future action that's in progress. Note the subtle difference in meaning between the future and future progressive tenses:

Future: I <u>will install</u> your water heater tomorrow.

Future progressive: I'm sorry, tomorrow doesn't work for me. I <u>will be installing</u> four water heaters on the other side of town.

Noting the Perfect Progressive Tenses

Use the *perfect progressive tenses* to express ongoing action completed in the past, present, or future.

> **DEFINITION**
>
> The **perfect progressive tenses** express ongoing action completed in the past, present, or future.

Present Perfect Progressive

Use the present perfect progressive to express action that started in the past and continues in the present, as in the following example:

> The auditor <u>has been reviewing</u> the financial records for the past three days. (The action started three days ago and is still in progress.)

You can also use the present perfect progressive to express continuous action sometime in the recent past, as in the following examples:

> The elephants <u>have been eating</u> a little more than usual.

> <u>Have</u> you <u>been following</u> the news?

Past Perfect Progressive

Use the past perfect progressive tense to express continuous action completed sometime in the past, as in the following examples:

> How long <u>had</u> you <u>been waiting</u> before the airline let you board the plane?

> The candle <u>had been burning</u> all night before someone blew it out.

The past perfect progressive also comes in handy for showing cause and effect. Here are a couple examples:

> We achieved our goal because we <u>had been working</u> as a team.

> Because he <u>had not been showing up</u> for work, he lost his job.

Be careful not to confuse the past progressive and the past perfect progressive. The past progressive is more about interrupting an action in the past. With the past perfect progressive, the emphasis is on duration of time. Note the subtle difference in meaning of the following sentences:

Past progressive: We <u>were standing</u> on the corner when the motorcade passed. (The emphasis here is on what we were doing at the very moment when the motorcade passed.)

Past perfect progressive: We <u>had been standing</u> on the corner for at least 45 minutes when the motorcade passed. (The emphasis here is on how long we were standing on that corner.)

Future Perfect Progressive

Use the future perfect progressive to express ongoing action in the future that's interrupted by a future action or event, as in the following examples:

The Sherpa <u>will have been climbing</u> for 48 hours by the time he reaches the summit.

How long <u>will</u> you <u>have been working</u> at Xenon Enterprises when you reach retirement age?

You may also use the future perfect progressive along with the simple future to show cause and effect, as shown here:

The workers will be exhausted at the end of the day because they <u>will have been working</u> nonstop for over 8 hours.

Again, be careful to distinguish the future progressive from the future perfect progressive. Use the future progressive to express an action that gets interrupted by another future action. Use the future perfect progressive to suggest a period of time. These examples shed light on the difference:

Future progressive: The fans <u>will be standing</u> at the start of the National Anthem.

Future perfect progressive: The fans <u>will have been standing</u> for 15 minutes prior to the playing of the National Anthem.

Sticking to Your Timeline

One of the most important rules to follow when describing action is to adhere to a consistent timeline. Choose a tense—usually present or past—and change tense only when necessary to reference time periods relative to your baseline tense. Any unnecessary or illogical shifts in tense are likely to confuse readers. Here's an example of a paragraph with awkward shifts in verb tense followed by a corrected version:

Awkward tense shifts: We <u>received</u> your cover letter and résumé. Although we <u>had</u> no openings at this time, your information <u>is entered</u> into our database, and you <u>will be considered</u> for any future openings that <u>required</u> your skills and expertise.

Smooth tense shifts: We <u>received</u> your cover letter and résumé. Although we <u>have</u> no openings at this time, your information <u>has been entered</u> into our database, and you <u>will be considered</u> for any future openings that <u>require</u> your skills and expertise.

Sorting Out *Lie* and *Lay*

People often struggle with the verbs *lie* and *lay:*

- *Lie* is an intransitive verb that means *to recline*, as in "I lie down to take a nap." (An *intransitive* verb does not require an object.)

- *Lay* is a transitive verb that means *to set down*, as in "Lay down your weapon." (*Transitive verbs* require objects; in this example, *weapon* is the object.)

So if the police show up at your home and incorrectly order you to "lie down your weapon," you could argue that you were confused as to whether you should lie down on the ground or lay down your weapon.

After you master that subtle distinction in meaning, you're only halfway home, having recognized the difference in the present tense. To master the other 11 tenses, you need to recognize how the verbs' principle forms differ:

Root	Past	Past Participle
lay	laid	laid
lie	lay	lain

As you can see, the past tense of *lie* is *lay*, which also happens to be the present tense of *lay*. Confusing, huh? So if your roommate is taking a nap, you might say something like "Tanya *lay* down to take a nap an hour ago." If you took a nap before she did, you might say, "And three hours before Tanya hit the sack, I *had lain* down to take my nap."

Practice

Write the correct verb form (tense) in each blank. Use the verb that appears in parentheses.

1. The zookeeper did not discover that the elephant _____ (escape) until she returned to work the next day.

2. By this time next year, the road crew _____ (complete) its work on the bridge.

3. The plane _____ (fly) for only 15 minutes when the pilot turned off the Fasten Seatbelts sign.

4. After his third Bahama Mama milkshake, Tom could not recall how much he _____ (drink).

5. At the same time police officers _____ (plan) their raid, the thieves were robbing another bank.

6. The locusts _____ (feast) on the crops all week [and still are].

7. Before the parents <u>lay</u> down to take a nap, they _____ (lie/lay) their baby in the crib. (Write the correct verb in its correct form in the blank.)

8. The critics raved about the film, many of them claiming it _____ (be) director Scorelli's most inspired work.

9. Upon hearing that his daughter _____ (incarcerate), John drove to the county jail to bail her out.

10. Since the beginning of the Industrial Revolution, hourly employees _____ (overwork) and _____ (underpay).

Answers:

1. The zookeeper did not discover that the elephant <u>had escaped</u> until she returned to work the next day.

2. By this time next year, the road crew <u>will have completed</u> its work on the bridge.

3. The plane <u>had been flying</u> for only 15 minutes when the pilot turned off the Fasten Seatbelts sign.

4. After his third Bahama Mama milkshake, Tom could not recall how much he <u>had drunk</u>.

5. At the same time police officers <u>were planning</u> their raid, the thieves were robbing another bank.

6. The locusts <u>have been feasting</u> on the crops all week.

7. Before the parents lay down to take a nap, they <u>had laid</u> their baby in the crib.

8. The critics raved about the film, many of them claiming it <u>is</u> director Scorelli's most inspired work.

9. Upon hearing that his daughter <u>had been incarcerated,</u> John drove to the county jail to bail her out.

10. Since the beginning of the Industrial Revolution, hourly employees <u>have been over-worked</u> and <u>underpaid</u>.

Making Sure Your Nouns and Verbs Agree

Every sentence has an actor and an action, a noun and a verb, and the noun and verb must agree in person and number. Singular subjects take singular verbs; plural subjects require plural verbs. Likewise, the verb must reflect the person performing the action: I, you (singular), he/she/it, we, you (plural), or they.

Every verb has six person/number forms—three singular persons and three plural persons. Here are the six present noun forms for the regular verb *love:*

	Singular	**Plural**
1st Person	I *love*	We *love*
2nd Person	You *love*	You *love*
3rd Person	He/she/it *loves*	They *love*

USAGE TIDBIT

The good news is that you don't have to think about person and number when dealing with any tense other than the present, because in the other tenses, the verb form is the same regardless of which subject(s) are performing the action. For example, *I, you* (singular), *he, she, it, we, you* (plural), and *they* all *loved, will love, have loved, had loved,* and so on.

Most people have little trouble choosing the right verb form when the noun performing the action is clear and near to the verb. When other words get between the subject and the verb—making the subject of the sentence fuzzy—choosing the right form gets complicated. In the following sections, I provide guidance on how to deal with the trickiest situations.

Dealing with Compound Subjects

When a plural subject or two or more subjects—called a *compound subject*—perform an action, choose the appropriate plural verb form—the form for *we, you* (plural), or *they.* Obvious, right? Well, in some cases, the choice isn't so clear. Here are some guidelines to help you in a pinch:

- Two or more subjects connected by *and* are *they,* so use the third-person plural verb form:

  Sally and Dan dance together on Fridays.

- When two or more subjects are connected by *or* or *nor,* only one or none of the subjects is acting, so use the third-person singular verb form:

  Neither Sally nor Dan likes ballroom dancing.

- Likewise, if *either* or *neither* is the subject of the sentence, use a singular verb:

  Either of us makes a fine candidate for mayor.

- When *I* is one of two or more subjects separated by *or* or *nor*, place it last and use the first-person singular verb form:

  Neither Ms. Drake nor I am taking the train into town.

- When the compound subject includes a singular and a plural noun connected by *or* or *nor*, place the plural noun last and use a plural verb form.

  Neither Bryce nor the other anglers go fishing at noon.

- When a singular subject performs an action along with, as well as, or besides another noun, use a singular verb form:

  Senator Brewer, as well as Senator Ditch, <u>supports</u> the amendment.

> **DEFINITION**
>
> A **compound subject** is made up of two or more nouns or pronouns joined by *and, but, or, for,* or *nor* sharing the same verb(s).

Accounting for Collective Nouns

A *collective noun,* such as crowd, denotes a group of individuals. Often, a collective noun takes a singular verb form:

> The crowd <u>roars</u>.

> The team <u>wins</u> its first tournament game.

> Sometimes, the collective noun is treated as plural:

> The faculty <u>were</u> outraged.

> The sheep <u>run</u> around the field.

To figure out whether a singular or plural verb form is appropriate, see if the collective noun is acting as one, coherent entity or a bunch of singular entities. Either could be correct, depending on the situation.

For example, if a group is experiencing some discord—or you want to distinguish the members of the group for some other reason—use the plural verb form:

> Team members <u>disagree</u> on the presentation format.

Recognizing Singular Indefinite Pronouns

Further complicating the selection of singular and plural noun forms are the singular indefinite pronouns *anybody, each, everybody, everyone, every one, nobody, no one, somebody,* and *someone* when followed by a plural noun, as in the following examples:

Every one of the lizards eats both plants and insects regularly.

Everybody, especially the fans, appreciates good sportsmanship.

> **PRACTICAL POINT**
>
> Interestingly, the pronoun *none* can be singular or plural depending on whether you intend it to mean "not one" (singular) or "not any" (plural). Both of the following are correct:
>
> None of the doctors agrees on the diagnosis. (Not one of the doctors agrees.)
>
> None of the doctors agree on the diagnosis. (Not any of the doctors agree.)

Maintaining Agreement with Amounts and Number of ...

When discussing portions using words such as *part of, majority of, some of, all of, none of, remainder of,* or a *percentage* or *fraction of,* look at the noun following *of* to determine whether to use a singular or plural noun form. If the noun is singular, use the singular verb form. If the noun is plural, use the plural verb form. Here are a couple examples:

Half of the island <u>is</u> underwater. (Use the singular verb *is* because *island* is singular.)

Half of the peaches <u>were</u> lost to frost. (Use the plural verb *were* because *peaches* is plural.)

When using *number of,* however, different rules apply:

- When using <u>*the*</u> *number of,* use a singular verb, as in "The number of guests we need to feed <u>is</u> 150."

- <u>When</u> using *a number of,* use a plural verb, as in "A number of guests <u>have requested</u> drinks."

Treat a dollar amount or a period of time as a singular noun and use a singular verb:

Twenty-five dollars <u>is</u> the price I'm asking.

Two months <u>seems</u> a long time to be away from home.

Practice

In the following sentences, underline the correct singular or plural verb form:

1. Neither Jerry nor his neighbors is/are happy about the new parking restrictions.

2. The finance committee have/has approved next year's budget.

3. Nobody, including the employees, was/were happy with the new benefit package.

4. Mrs. Bower's cat, along with her dog, cross/crosses the street at the intersection.

5. Over half of the islanders was/were left homeless.

Answers:

1. Neither Jerry nor his neighbors is/<u>are</u> happy about the new parking restrictions.

2. The finance committee have/<u>has</u> approved next year's budget.

3. Nobody, including the employees, <u>was</u>/were happy with the new benefit package.

4. Mrs. Bower's cat, along with her dog, cross/<u>crosses</u> the street at the intersection.

5. Over half of the islanders was/<u>were</u> left homeless.

Setting the Right Mood

A verb's *mood* conveys the attitude of the speaker. English verbs have three moods:

* **Indicative** states a fact:
  The king cobra is a menacing reptile.

* **Imperative** issues a command:
  Don't pet the king cobra!

* **Subjunctive** indicates the statement is not factual but likely or unlikely, hoped for, or feared:
  If I were a king cobra, I would be menacing.

> **DEFINITION**
>
> **Mood** is a feature of verbs that conveys the attitude of the speaker or writer toward what is being stated.

Most people don't have trouble with the indicative or the imperative, but they have no idea of when to use the subjunctive or how to form it.

Use the subjunctive mood to express a wish, suggestion, or demand or a condition that's contrary to fact, as in the following examples:

Wish: Sandy wishes she <u>were</u> more outgoing.

Suggestion: Paul suggests we <u>write</u> letters to our representatives.

Demand: The FDA has mandated that all over-the-counter sleep medications <u>be</u> pulled from the shelves.

Condition contrary to fact: If I <u>were</u> leading the country, everyone <u>would</u> work a 30-hour week. (The condition is contrary to fact, because I'm not leading the country.)

Forming the present and past subjunctive is fairly straightforward. For nearly every verb, you simply use the verb's root: *ask, walk, talk,* whatever. In the case of the verb *to be,* you still use the root (be) to form the present subjunctive, but to form the past subjunctive, use *were* instead of *was.*

If the action that's contrary to fact occurs before another action that occurred in the past, use *had + past participle* of the verb, as in the following examples:

<u>Had</u> I <u>known</u> of the risks, I never would <u>have invested</u> all that money.

I would <u>have filled</u> the tank if the gas <u>had been</u> on sale.

Practice

In the following sentences, underline the verb that's in the subjunctive mood.

1. Our policy manual demands that all employees be/are on time.

2. If the pizza were/was here, we would break for lunch.

3. Christine requested that her boyfriend not call/calls her during work hours.

4. The tour guide recommended that everyone packs/pack bottled water and a few snacks for the day.

5. Have/Had the parents been informed of the details, they would never have given their permission.

Answers:

1. Our policy manual demands that all employees <u>be</u>/are on time.

2. If the pizza <u>were</u>/was here, we would break for lunch.

3. Christine requested that her boyfriend not <u>call</u>/calls her during work hours.

4. The tour guide recommended that everyone packs/<u>pack</u> bottled water and a few snacks for the day.

5. Have/<u>Had</u> the parents been informed of the details, they would never have given their permission.

Choosing a Voice

A verb's *voice* reveals or conceals the subject of the sentence:

• With the *active voice*, you know from the get-go who's performing the action:

The gecko sold far more auto insurance policies than did the walrus.

We released the information prematurely.

• With the *passive voice*, you don't find out who's performing the action until later, if at all:

Far more auto insurance policies were sold by the gecko than by the walrus.

The information was released prematurely.

In most cases, use the active voice, because it's clear and direct. Use the passive voice when you want to avoid taking or placing blame. In other cases, the passive voice is appropriate because you want to emphasize the action or whoever is performing the action is irrelevant, as in scientific studies.

DEFINITION

Voice conveys the relationship between the action or state of being and the doer or recipient of the action. In the active voice, someone or something performs the action. In the passive voice, the action is performed on someone or something.

Practice

Change each of the following sentences from passive to active voice:

1. Numerous complaints had been filed by irate customers.

_____

2. New medications are developed each year by the pharmaceutical companies.

_____

3. All of the cracks in the bathtub were sealed with epoxy.

_____

4. The people who were affected by the floods were not allowed to return to their homes by the authorities.

_____

5. A standing ovation was given to the cast and crew.

_____

Answers:

1. Irate customers <u>had filed</u> numerous complaints.

2. Pharmaceutical companies <u>develop</u> new medications each year.

3. Epoxy <u>sealed</u> all of the cracks in the bath tub.

4. The authorities <u>did not allow</u> the people who were affected by the floods to return to their homes.

5. The cast and crew <u>received</u> a standing ovation.

The Least You Need to Know

- Use the four verb forms—root, present participle, past, and past participle—to form the 12 tenses.
- Use the simple tenses to express action in the past, present, or future; the perfect tenses to express completed action; and the conditional (progressive) tenses to express ongoing action.
- Keep your eye on the timeline when shifting tense.
- The subject of a sentence must agree with the verb in person and number.
- Use the subjunctive mood to express a wish, suggestion, or demand—or a condition that's contrary to fact.
- The active voice generally is clearer and more direct than the passive voice.

Describing Words: Adjectives and Adverbs

Nouns and verbs do the heavy lifting of language, but there's more to language than heavy lifting. If there were nothing but nouns and verbs, we'd all sound a little like a toddler or the Hulk. You can only say so much with sentences such as "Want toy!" and "Hulk smash!"

That's where adjectives and adverbs come in. These words modify other words, adding color, detail, and vibrancy to people, places, things, actions, and conditions.

Without adjectives and adverbs, writing would be short, simplistic, and boring. You'd never be able to talk about a stirring speech, a danceable song, a loud noise, or a diabolical villain. You couldn't say that you barely passed a test, happily married your best friend, or truthfully answered a question.

Adjectives and adverbs help us paint a picture of the world. Without them, the canvas of language would be mostly blank.

In This Chapter

- Describing nouns and pronouns with adjectives
- Looking at different types of adjectives
- Using definite and indefinite articles
- Describing verbs, adjectives, and other adverbs with adverbs

Adjectives: Describing Words

There's more to life than people, places, and things. There are tall people, exciting places, and annoying things. Without adjectives, we'd be at a loss to describe just about everything. Adjectives paint a more detailed picture of the world.

Adjectives describe everything that can be described. Some describe color:

> black
>
> blue
>
> brown
>
> green
>
> lavender
>
> orange
>
> pink
>
> purple
>
> red
>
> teal

Others describe size:

> big
>
> cumbersome
>
> enormous
>
> gigantic
>
> itty-bitty
>
> large
>
> little
>
> medium
>
> sizable
>
> teeny-weeny

These adjectives describe the texture of an object:

damp

fuzzy

grainy

gritty

hard

jagged

porous

rough

smooth

Someone's personality can be described in the following ways—and many others:

buoyant

courageous

depressed

fearful

happy

hilarious

jovial

passive-aggressive

quiet

weird

When the weather's hot, there are many adjectives besides *hot* you can use:

blazing

hellish

scorching

tropical

warm

There are even adjectives to describe things that can't be described or understood:

incomprehensible

indescribable

ineffable

mysterious

unfathomable

unknowable

unspeakable

unthinkable

Such lists could continue for hundreds of pages (and you can find such lists in a thesaurus). For now, you should know that there are many adjectives out there and that it's important to find the right one for your writing situation.

Types of Adjectives

There are four main types of adjectives: common, proper, compound, and indefinite. Knowing the types of adjectives will help you find the appropriate terms to describe your nouns and pronouns.

Common

A common adjective is a plain old adjective that consists of one word and is not capitalized. Common adjectives include *red*, *historical*, *fuzzy*, and *huge*.

Proper

A proper adjective, like a proper noun, is capitalized. Most proper adjectives are variations of names, as in the following example.

The Shield is a <u>Shakespearian</u> tragedy.

Are you familiar with <u>Aristotelian</u> logic?

That story is <u>Kafkaesque</u>!

The suspicious behavior of the president seems a little <u>Nixon-y</u>.

Do you like <u>Chicago-style</u> hot dogs?

> **PRACTICAL POINT**
>
> As you can see, many proper adjectives are also eponyms: words derived from people's names. Adjectives such as *Shakespearian* and *Draconian* are taken from names, but eponyms can be other parts of speech as well. Nouns such as *shrapnel* and verbs such as *boycott* are also eponyms.

Compound

In the previous section, the word *Chicago-style* was used as an example of a proper adjective: *Chicago-style* is also a compound adjective.

Compound adjectives consist of two words, and they are usually joined by a hyphen:

> Is this gizmo <u>battery-operated</u>?
>
> My son is <u>left-handed</u>.
>
> The <u>ring-tailed</u> lemur is cute.
>
> I have a <u>part-time</u> job.
>
> I like <u>foot-long</u> hot dogs.

For more on hyphens, see Chapter 19.

Just as other compound words can exist without a hyphen, sometimes a compound adjective has no hyphen, as in this example:

> She is my <u>longtime</u> friend.

Also, a compound adjective is sometimes two separate words:

> Did you go to the <u>Pink Floyd</u> concert?

Though many compound adjectives are hyphenated, don't get confused if you see an adverb followed by an adjective, as in these examples:

> Let's go to the highly anticipated lecture.
>
> I made freshly grilled hamburgers
>
> Let's watch the newly chosen winners.

In those sentences, the adverb modifies the adjective, so these are not compound adjectives; therefore, you don't use a hyphen. Remember, hyphens should be used to add clarity and create compound adjectives, but an adverb plus an adjective cannot be a compound adjective.

Practice

In the following sentences, indicate whether or not there is a compound adjective that should be hyphenated:

1. I like this brightly lit room.

2. My client is unjustly accused.

3. Do you like my flat top haircut?

4. That is flatly untrue.

5. Follow that backpack wearing man!

6. The book has dog eared pages.

7. I love the smell of newly mown grass.

8. The artist specializes in ready made pieces.

9. I have a do it yourself attitude.

10. This shirt was badly made.

Answers:

1. I like this brightly lit room. (No hyphen.)

2. My client is unjustly accused. (No hyphen.)

3. Do you like my <u>flat-top</u> haircut?

4. That is flatly untrue. (No hyphen.)

5. Follow that <u>backpack-wearing</u> man!

6. The book has <u>dog-eared</u> pages.

7. I love the smell of newly mown grass. (No hyphen.)

8. The artist specializes in <u>ready-made</u> pieces.

9. I have a <u>do-it-yourself</u> attitude.

10. This shirt was badly made. (No hyphen.)

Indefinite

As you might guess, indefinite adjectives are not as specific as adjectives such as *green* and *Orwellian*. Indefinite adjectives refer to vaguer concepts, mainly numbers—but not exact numbers. These are the most common:

> all
>
> any
>
> each
>
> few
>
> many
>
> most
>
> several
>
> some

Here are some indefinite pronouns used in sentences:

> Do you have <u>any</u> comic books?
>
> I like <u>most</u> Christopher Nolan films.
>
> I only have a <u>few</u> good friends.
>
> There are <u>several</u> dogs playing in the park.
>
> I don't have a lot of money, but I have <u>some</u> money.

Notice how those adjectives don't refer to exact amounts? That's how you know they're indefinite.

Practice

For the following sentences, mark whether the adjective is common, proper, compound, or indefinite:

1. My sweater is <u>yellow</u>.

2. I need to make a <u>left-hand</u> turn.

3. What is the <u>Christian</u> thing to do?

4. This is a <u>hardwood</u> floor.

5. I don't have <u>many</u> DVDs.

6. You should give a <u>clean</u> napkin to each customer.

7. Which <u>red-bellied</u> bird is that?

8. Your music is very <u>Wagnerian</u>.

9. I smell something <u>gross</u>.

10. I got hit by the <u>spring-loaded</u> boxing glove.

Answers:

1. My sweater is <u>yellow</u>. (Common.)

2. I need to make a <u>left-hand</u> turn. (Compound.)

3. What is the <u>Christian</u> thing to do? (Proper.)

4. This is a <u>hardwood</u> floor. (Compound.)

5. I don't have <u>many</u> DVDs. (Indefinite.)

6. You should give a <u>clean</u> napkin to each customer. (Common.)

7. Which <u>red-bellied</u> bird is that? (Compound.)

8. Your music is very <u>Wagnerian</u>. (Proper.)

9. I smell something <u>gross</u>. (Common.)

10. I got hit by the <u>spring-loaded</u> boxing glove. (Compound.)

How to Use Adjectives

In English, the adjective often goes before the noun it modifies:

a tasty chicken

a breathtaking view

an enormous horse

some lazy children

our adorable dog

Now let's put similar terms in sentences:

I have a <u>splitting</u> headache.

My dog has <u>white</u> fur.

Canada is a <u>cold</u> country.

Staples are <u>tiny</u> devices.

I have a <u>runny</u> nose.

All those examples involve one adjective modifying one noun, but you can add more than one adjective to these sentences.

I have a <u>horrible, splitting</u> headache.

My dog has <u>white, wiry, thick</u> fur.

Canada is a <u>cold, wintry, peaceful, northern</u> country.

Staples are <u>metal, bendy, tiny</u> devices.

I have a <u>runny, sore, swelling</u> nose.

Use commas to separate the adjectives, but don't put a comma between the final adjective and the noun.

Adjectives and *To Be*

You can also use a form of *to be* with adjectives.

My pet rabbit is stinky.

Coffee is addictive.

Cupcakes are sweet.

Pizza is amazing.

September is refreshing.

Both these methods can be used in one sentence:

My mangy pet rabbit is stinky.

Strong coffee is addictive.

Chocolate cupcakes are sweet.

Spicy pizza is amazing.

Cool September is refreshing.

The longer the sentence, the more opportunities to use adjectives. Anytime you see a noun or a pronoun, you can modify it with adjectives.

Finding the Right Adjective

Think of adjectives as a box of crayons—a box of crayons that has thousands of colors. Every time you use an adjective, you should use the one that is just right for your situation.

Let's say you're trying to describe a TV show you like, such as *Arrested Development*. Here's a sentence that includes some poorly chosen adjectives:

> *Arrested Development* is a good, funny comedy.

The problems start with *good*. Ironically, *good* is one of the least good words in English. It's too vague. I wouldn't say you should never use it, but if you do, you'd better follow it up with more specific words that show *why* what you're describing is good.

The second problem with this sentence is *funny*. That's more specific than *good,* but it's a little redundant next to the word *comedy*. If *Arrested Development* is a good comedy, of course it's funny.

Off the top of my head—and without revision, I promise—here are 20 adjectives that could apply to *Arrested Development:*

American

bizarre

catchphrase-oriented

character-driven

cult

documentary-style

family

fast-paced

ground-breaking

goofy

innovative

intricate

political

quirky

quick

quotable

satirical

unusual

unpopular

witty

All of these words—which include compound adjectives like *character-driven* and proper adjectives like *American*—are better than *good* and *funny*, and many could be used to write something specific and interesting about *Arrested Development*. However, a well-chosen adjective isn't enough. The word *witty*, like *good*, makes a reader ask "Why?" You have to back up your adjectives with details and examples.

For example, if I said *Arrested Development* is a goofy show, I would have to give an example such as the silly chicken dance of Gob Bluth. If I said it was a quotable show, I would have to mention some of the catchphrases fans often repeat, such as "I've made a huge mistake" and "No touching!" If I said it was a family show, I'd have to talk about the show's focus on the Bluth family. If I said that family is bizarre—which they are—I'd have to give examples of that, such as the fact that one Bluth brother drives an airport staircar down the street and another has a hook for a hand.

Your writing will be vivid and clear if you back up your adjectives with examples that will make your readers see, hear, feel, smell, touch, and experience what you're writing about.

Here's another bad example:

> I hear something weird.

If you said this, someone would say, "What do you hear? Why is it weird?" If you wrote this, the reader would ask similar questions—or just stop reading out of confusion. When using a vague word like *weird*, follow it up with specifics to make the reader understand your meaning:

> I hear something weird. It sounds like a dog's bark mixed with a cat's meow.

See how much clearer that is? Now you understand why the writer thinks the sound is weird, and you can probably imagine the weird sound yourself.

Specifics make for better writing. Adjectives can help you be specific, but don't rely on them to do all the work.

Forming Comparisons: Fast, Faster, Fastest

One of the most important jobs of adjectives is in making comparisons. The suffixes *–er* and *–est* are helpful in transforming words.

> Joe was quick, but Jan was quicker.
>
> My dog is dumb, but he's not the dumbest dog I know.
>
> My sister is pretty. She's much prettier than my cousin.
>
> Football players are strong. Most are much stronger than basketball players. However, weightlifters are probably the strongest athletes.

Words of this type have three forms: the positive, the comparative, and the superlative.

positive	comparative	superlative
deep	deeper	deepest
odd	odder	oddest
red	redder	reddest
silly	sillier	silliest
smart	smarter	smartest
tall	taller	tallest
thin	thinner	thinnest
weak	weaker	weakest

The positive is used when there's only one item.

> The bear is <u>angry</u>.

The comparative is used when you're discussing two items.

> The bear is <u>angrier</u> than the camper.

The superlative is used when you're discussing at least three items.

> Out of the bear, the camper, and the lion, the bear is <u>angriest</u>.

Some words have no comparative and superlative. For example, you have to write *more intelligent* and *most intelligent*.

Practice

For the following sentences, note whether the adjective is the positive, the comparative, or the superlative.

1. Birds are intelligent.

2. Pigs are the smartest animal in the world.

3. Canada is a colder country than the United States.

4. I love cupcakes because they're sweet.

5. I love cake because it's the sweetest dessert in the world.

Answers:

1. Birds are intelligent. (Positive.)

2. Pigs are the smartest animal in the world. (Superlative.)

3. Canada is a colder country than the United States. (Comparative.)

4. I love cupcakes because they're sweet. (Positive.)

5. I love cake because it's the sweetest dessert in the world. (Superlative.)

When *Not* to Use Adjectives

Adjectives have a little bit of a bad reputation. Many writers have claimed that they're soft words that don't carry the force of nouns and verbs. This advice is, like so much writing advice, a little bit true and a little bit false.

There's no question that an overload of adjectives can lead to fluffy, sloppy writing that doesn't say much. However, vague or inappropriate word choices will hurt your writing across the board, for every part of speech, not just adjectives.

Advice on adjectives is often contradictory. For example, professional linguists—such as Geoffrey Pullum—have noted that William Strunk and E. B. White's advice in *The Elements of Style* is inconsistent and not even followed by the authors. Strunk and White write, "The adjective hasn't been built that can pull a weak or inaccurate noun out of a tight place." As Pullum (chronicle. com/article/50-Years-of-Stupid-Grammar/25497) notes, this is an odd way to slam the adjective, since this sentence includes three of them.

In fact, it's hard to write without adjectives, and there's no reason not to use them. Just use adjectives that are specific and suited to your purpose, as all words you choose should be. If your adjectives are clear and appropriate, your writing will be, too.

Articles: Little Words with Big Jobs

Articles are a type of adjective with a specific purpose: they introduce nouns, but they also modify them, like all adjectives.

Definite Articles

In English, the definite article is *the*. Use *the* when you're referring to a specific thing, not one of several things.

> Please hand me the large fork.
>
> Did you see the World Series?
>
> I love the show *Seinfeld*.
>
> Are you watching the TV?
>
> What's the big deal?

All those uses of *the* refer to a singular, specific thing. For situations that are more general, use one of the indefinite articles.

Indefinite Articles

In English, the indefinite articles are *a* and *an*. *A* comes before words that start with a consonant sound, and *an* comes before words that start with a vowel sound. So you would never refer to *a elephant* or *an table:* it's *an elephant* and *a table*. Here are some more examples of indefinite articles at work:

> Please hand me a doughnut.
>
> Do you have a dog?
>
> Can you give me an example?
>
> Is your dad a politician?
>
> Is that animal an emu?

Articles can be tricky for people who are new to English, especially if their first language doesn't use articles. Remember that indefinite articles refer to a general or nonspecific entity, while the definite article is more specific.

> "Do you have a dog?" doesn't refer to a specific dog. There might not even be a dog.
>
> "Look at the dog begging!" refers to a specific dog.

Be sure to pay attention to articles as you read, as seeing articles in use will help you learn how to use them correctly yourself.

> **USAGE TIDBIT**
>
> Since *an* comes before words that start with a vowel sound, sometimes this includes words that start with a consonant. For example, it's *an NBA coach*, not *a NBA coach*, because *NBA* starts with an *en* sound.

Adverbs: Describing Verbs, Adjectives, and Other Adverbs

Adjectives have some close relatives: adverbs. Adverbs also describe, but they have the power to describe verbs, adjectives, and even other adverbs.

Transforming Adjectives into Adverbs

One of the defining traits of words is that they can be changed. Nouns become verbs. Verbs become nouns. Adjectives become adverbs, too. In fact, going from adjective to adverb is one of the easiest transitions in grammar. Let's start with some sentences with adjectives:

> After the tragedy, the president was <u>solemn</u>.
>
> The crying baby was <u>loud</u>.
>
> In the afternoon, the sun is <u>bright</u>.

These adjectives can become adverbs with the addition of *−ly*. Here's how they might work in new sentences:

> The president spoke <u>solemnly</u> about the tragedy.
>
> The baby cried <u>loudly</u>.
>
> In the afternoon, the sun shines <u>brightly</u>.

These sentences have similar meanings to the previous sentences, but the grammar is different. In the first group, *solemn* modifies *president, loud* modifies *baby,* and *bright* modifies *sun:* three cases of adjectives modifying nouns. In the second group of examples, *solemnly* modifies *spoke, loudly* modifies *cried,* and *brightly* modifies *shines:* three cases of adverbs modifying verbs.

How do you decide what's the best structure for your sentence? It depends on the situation. If it's important to describe how an action is happening, especially the exact way someone is doing something, then adverbs are the way to go.

> **PRACTICAL POINT**
>
> Most adverbs end in -ly, but not all. For example, *very* is an adverb, and some adjectives such as *hard* can act as adverbs, as in "I'm working hard." Also, -ly words can sometimes act as adjectives, such as *cowardly* and *bubbly*. The only way to know for sure if a word is an adjective or adverb is to see what kind of word it's modifying.

Using Adverbs to Describe Action

When it's important to describe an action, there are a few ways to use adverbs. Here are some examples.

Often, an adverb follows the verb it modifies, as in the following examples:

> The quarterback scrambled <u>desperately</u> to avoid defenders.
>
> Bees swarmed <u>wildly</u> over the picnic.
>
> Rain fell <u>steadily</u>.

Other times, an adverb comes before the verb it modifies.

> The kids <u>quickly</u> ran to the ice cream truck.
>
> The nurse <u>carefully</u> removed the cast.
>
> Snow <u>slowly</u> covered the lawn.

The adverb doesn't have to be right next to the verb it modifies. Sometimes they're separated by other words.

> The blind man crossed the street <u>slowly</u>.
>
> The writer composed a first draft <u>quickly</u>.
>
> Good comedians phrase their jokes <u>expertly</u>.

Using Adverbs to Describe Adjectives and Other Adverbs

Adjectives and adverbs are the two types of describing words, but sometimes adverbs describe adjectives, too.

> My dog is extremely annoying when he sees me eating.

(The adverb *extremely* describes the adjective *annoying*.)

> The president was extremely soft-spoken during the speech.

(The adverb *extremely* describes the adjective *soft-spoken*.)

> The actor's hideously contorted face grossed out the audience.

(The adverb *hideously* describes the adjective *contorted*.)

> The circumstances of some people's lives are depressingly unfortunate.

(The adverb *depressingly* describes the adjective *unfortunate*.)

Adverbs even have the power to describe other adverbs, often in a way that heightens them. For example:

> The spy very stealthily avoided detection.

(The adverb *very* describes the adverb *stealthily*.)

> I quite angrily shouted at the guy who didn't pick up after his dog.

(The adverb *quite* describes the adverb *angrily*.)

> I never really learned Spanish, even though I took three classes.

(The adverb *never* describes the adverb *really*.)

> I always thoroughly clean the stove.

(The adverb *always* describes the adverb *thoroughly*.)

Recognizing Adverbs That Moonlight as Conjunctions

Conjunctions connect. There are a group of conjunctive adverbs that connect, too. These are some of the most common conjunctive adverbs:

accordingly
also

anyway
besides
consequently
conversely
finally

further
furthermore
hence

however

indeed
instead
likewise
meanwhile
moreover
nevertheless
next

nonetheless
otherwise
similarly
still
subsequently
then

thereafter
therefore
thus

Conjunctive adverbs join two clauses, much like conjunctions. Here they are at work in the following sentences:

I hate speeches; <u>nonetheless</u>, I'll join you for this speech.

My dog threw up on the rug. <u>Subsequently</u>, I washed it.

I like cheese. <u>Consequently</u>, I bought a dairy farm.

I'm tired; <u>still</u>, I could come to the party.

I went to the bank. <u>Next</u>, I went to the gym.

Whether the clauses take the form of one sentence or two, the conjunctive adjective comes between the clauses: it's the glue holding them together.

The Least You Need to Know

- Adjectives are used to describe nouns and pronouns.
- The main types of adjective are common, proper, compound, and indefinite.
- Definite (*the*) and indefinite articles (*a, an*) are adjectives that introduce nouns.
- Adverbs are mainly used to describe verbs, but they can also describe adjectives and other adverbs.
- Conjunctive adverbs join independent clauses.

Wrapping Up Action with Complements

A compliment is a nice thing to say, like "That's a cool hat" or "You did a good job on the Penske file." People love to receive compliments, especially when they've had a haircut or bought some new clothes. Many romantic relationships suffer when one person doesn't compliment the other enough, and no one wants to work for a boss who never offers any compliments.

A complement is something different: to complement something is to enhance or support it in some way. A hat could complement the rest of your outfit, which could result in your getting a compliment. Vegetables complement many meals, just as a painting can complement a room.

In grammar, complements also enhance something: the subject, verb, or object of the sentence. In this chapter, you'll learn how complements work and how to use them to make your writing clearer and more interesting to read.

In This Chapter

- How subject complements work
- How object complements work
- How verb complements work
- Infinitives, gerunds, and noun phrases as verb complements

Linking to a Subject Complement

The following sentences all have subject complements:

> My dog is a <u>rat terrier</u>.
>
> Children can be <u>noisy</u>.
>
> My cousin is <u>creepy</u>.
>
> This iced coffee is <u>creamy and delicious</u>.
>
> September is <u>the best month of the year</u>.

You can tell these are complements because the information after the verb tells you more about the subject, rather than telling you what the subject is acting upon.

Some complements are noun phrases, like the following:

> Beards are <u>facial hair</u>.
>
> The Emmys are <u>a major event</u>.
>
> My friend is <u>a lawyer</u>.
>
> That baby is <u>a pain in the neck</u>.
>
> Rabbits are <u>adorable pets</u>.

A complement follows a linking verb, which is often a form of *be*. When the complement is a noun phrase, it tells you new information about the subject or puts the subject in different words. In the previous examples, *beard* and *facial hair*, as well as *rabbits* and *adorable pets*, are the same things.

Don't confuse complements with objects, which are separate entities from the subject. Here are similar sentences with objects instead of complements:

> Beards disgust <u>my sister</u>.
>
> The Emmys ruined <u>my career</u>.
>
> My friend sued <u>me</u>.
>
> That baby peed on <u>my couch</u>.
>
> Rabbits eat <u>grass</u>.

When the complement is the same entity as the subject, you have a complement. When the object is a separate entity, you have an object.

> Complement: Rabbits are <u>adorable pets</u>.

> Object: Rabbits eat <u>grass</u>.

Complements can also be adjective phrases, like the following:

> Puppies are <u>cute</u>.

> My legs are <u>tired and sore</u>.

> Michael Jordan's performance in the NBA finals was <u>superlative and historic</u>.

> My dog runs <u>so fast</u>.

> This cake is <u>disgusting</u>.

USAGE TIDBIT

As you can see, subject complements are useful when explaining or describing something. They're also helpful when evaluating. Next time you read a review of a movie, TV show, or album, look out for the subject complements.

Complementing a Direct Object: The Object Complement

Objects can have complements, too. Just as subject complements rename or add additional information about the subject, object complements rename or add additional information about the object. The object complements are underlined in the following examples:

> My dog scared the mailman <u>to death</u>.

> I called my brother Jimmy <u>a jerk</u>.

> Some people call jean shorts <u>jorts</u>.

> The comedian made the people <u>happy</u>.

> I often call my dog <u>a good boy</u>.

As with subject complements, object complements can take several forms. Some are nouns or noun phrases:

> I refer to my cat as <u>a little gentleman</u>.
>
> I think of your mom as <u>my mom</u>.
>
> We all know your brother <u>the supervillain</u>.
>
> The company named me <u>acting president</u>.
>
> Jerry called his girlfriend <u>schmoopie</u>.

Others consist of adjectives:

> Powerful movies make people <u>sad</u>.
>
> An accident makes traffic <u>worse</u>.
>
> I considered your mom <u>friendly</u>.
>
> Depression makes sufferers <u>tired</u>.
>
> I want this room <u>clean</u>!

Sometimes the object complement can be a prepositional phrase, as in these examples:

> The dog chased the squirrel <u>up the tree</u>.
>
> My mom's voicemails drive me <u>up the wall</u>.
>
> I learned to read novels <u>in the dark</u>.
>
> I hid the stolen artifact <u>under my bed</u>.
>
> The wind blew the garbage <u>into the river</u>.

Practice

In the following sentences, identify the subject or object complement. Hint: some sentences may have no complements at all.

1. Joe drove Jillian to the store.

2. Where I come from, we call soda pop.

3. My hair is shiny and silky.

4. The scandal ruined the president's life.

5. The singer is a great man.

6. Cats are independent and quirky.

7. Poodles are hypoallergenic dogs.

8. I throw a football like a loser.

9. The coffee shop is pretentious and annoying.

10. The snowboarder is a drug addict.

11. I learned to juggle knives.

12. My brother's singing drives me out of my mind.

13. Drinking beer is a good time.

14. Drinking wine is a bad idea.

15. That man's beard scared my children silly.

16. The manicure was shiny.

17. The weather will make everyone wet.

18. I like writing on the chalkboard.

19. I gave up on my dreams.

20. The criminals left the bank a disaster area.

Answers:

1. Joe drove Jillian <u>to the store</u>. (Object complement.)

2. Where I come from, we call soda <u>pop</u>. (Object complement.)

3. My hair is <u>shiny and silky</u>. (Subject complement.)

4. The scandal ruined the president's life. (No complement.)

5. The singer is <u>a great man</u>. (Subject complement.)

6. Cats are <u>independent and quirky</u>. (Subject complement.)

7. Poodles are <u>hypoallergenic dogs</u>. (Subject complement.)

8. I throw a football like a loser. (No complement.)

9. The coffee shop is <u>pretentious and annoying</u>. (Subject complement.)

10. The snowboarder is <u>a drug addict</u>. (Subject complement.)

11. I learned to juggle knives. (No complement.)

12. My brother's singing drives me <u>out of my mind</u>. (Object complement.)

13. Drinking beer is <u>a good time</u>. (Subject complement.)

14. Drinking wine is <u>a bad idea</u>. (Subject complement.)

15. That man's beard scared my children <u>silly</u>. (Object complement.)

16. The manicure was <u>shiny</u>. (Subject complement.)

17. The weather will make everyone <u>wet</u>. (Object complement.)

18. I like writing on the chalkboard. (No complement.)

19. I gave up on my dreams. (No complement.)

20. The criminals left the bank <u>a disaster area</u>. (Object complement.)

> **USAGE TIDBIT**
>
> Remember, a direct object receives some action from the subject. Direct object complements expand on this relationship when appropriate. Sometimes you might want to write, "The dog ate the cake" and leave it at that. Other times you need more information, like "The dog ate the cake at the wedding."

Taking Action on Nouns with Verb Complements

Just as subjects and objects have complements, so do verbs. Verb complements add a little extra information, expanding on the verb, to explain exactly what the verb is doing.

Infinitives as Verb Complements

Remember how infinitives can operate as nouns and adverbs? Some of these uses are identical to an infinitive being used as a verb complement:

Jill wanted <u>to leave</u>.

Superman loves <u>to help</u>.

I'm working <u>to save money</u>.

My son is learning <u>to juggle</u>.

I like running <u>to lose weight</u>.

Gerunds as Verb Complements

A gerund can also be a verb complement, as in the following examples.

The girl likes <u>hunting</u>.

My dad is practicing <u>shooting a basketball</u>.

Today I will watch <u>bowling</u>.

I hate <u>jogging</u>.

You should do more <u>proofreading</u>.

This type of verb complement can also be classified as a direct object.

USAGE TIDBIT

Don't let the fact that some verb complements are also direct objects drive you crazy. Grammar is terribly complex. Why do you think so many people struggle with it, including the grammar checkers in your computer? If grammar were simple, everyone would be a master of it.

Noun Phrases as Verb Complements

Other times, the verb complement is a noun phrase or clause.

I wonder <u>what's on TV</u>.

Did you eat <u>what was in the refrigerator</u>?

I like <u>that you don't have a computer</u>.

I never know <u>when to go to sleep</u>.

My dad says <u>that I should get a job</u>.

For more on phrases and clauses, see Chapters 9 and 10, respectively.

Practice

For the following sentences, note what type of verb complement is used: infinitive, gerund, or noun phrase. Hint: some may have no verb complement.

1. John likes to grill.

2. I dropped my phone in the lake.

3. Sometimes I teach swimming.

4. My dog loves chewing things.

5. I hate that my mom is usually right.

6. My mom learned to shoot a gun.

7. I can never remember to tip.

8. Leanne's dog loves to chase.

9. Most cats like to scratch.

10. Some people think that the moon landing was faked.

11. I love hiking.

12. The thieves are planning to rob a bank.

13. I want to scream!

14. Let's dance.

15. I hate that I worry too much.

16. Where's the dog?

17. Batman loves to beat up criminals.

18. My friend Sara detests skateboarding.

19. I hate when it starts raining suddenly.

20. My dog chewed that shoe that I left out.

Answers:

1. John likes <u>to grill</u>. (Verb complement: infinitive.)

2. I dropped my phone in the lake. (No verb complement.)

3. Sometimes I teach <u>swimming</u>. (Verb complement: gerund.)

4. My dog loves <u>chewing things</u>. (Verb complement: gerund.)

5. I hate <u>that my mom is usually right</u>. (Verb complement: noun phrase.)

6. My mom learned <u>to shoot a gun</u>. (Verb complement: infinitive.)

7. I can never remember <u>to tip</u>. (Verb complement: infinitive.)

8. Leanne's dog loves <u>to chase</u>. (Verb complement: infinitive.)

9. Most cats like <u>to scratch</u>. (Verb complement: infinitive.)

10. Some people think <u>that the moon landing was faked</u>. (Verb complement: noun phrase.)

11. I love hiking. (No verb complement.)

12. The thieves are planning <u>to rob a bank</u>. (Verb complement: infinitive.)

13. I want <u>to scream</u>! (Verb complement: infinitive.)

14. Let's dance. (No verb complement.)

15. I hate <u>that I worry too much</u>. (Verb complement: noun phrase.)

16. Where's the dog? (No verb complement.)

17. Batman loves <u>to beat up criminals</u>. (Verb complement: infinitive.)

18. My friend Sara detests <u>skateboarding</u>. (Verb complement: gerund.)

19. I hate <u>when it starts raining suddenly</u>. (Verb complement: noun phrase.)

20. My dog chewed <u>that shoe that I left out</u>. (Verb complement: noun phrase.)

The Least You Need to Know

- Complements add information to a subject, verb, or object.
- Subject complements rephrase or supplement the subject, as in the sentences "My sister is a teacher" and "My brother is weird."
- Verb complements add information to a verb and can be infinitives, gerunds, or noun phrases.
- Object complements work exactly like subject complements, rephrasing or describing the object, as *secure* does in the sentence "The president made the country secure."

Using Phrases

"That's a nice turn of phrase." "I don't like that phrase." "What's the phrase I'm trying to think of?" "Could you rephrase that?"

People talk about phrases and phrasing all the time, but they likely don't have a clear understanding of what a phrase is in the grammatical sense.

This chapter will define phrases and introduce you to the different types of phrases. It will also distinguish phrases from clauses, which may have a similar length but aren't the same. To become a better writer, you need to be comfortable using phrases and moving them around as you revise.

The good news is that phrases give you vast choices. That's also the bad news: the flexibility of phrases gives you so many options that you might be overwhelmed. Don't be. With a little attention to the technical aspects of phrases, you'll be phrasing like a champ.

What a Phrase Is (and Isn't)

A phrase is a group of words that serves a function in a sentence but isn't a clause. Take the following sentence:

> My best friend in Maine is Joel.

This can be broken into three phrases:

> My best friend / in Maine / is Joel.

Each of those chunks of language has a distinctive meaning and purpose. Each is also a different type of phrase: a noun phrase, a prepositional phrase, and a verb phrase, respectively.

The Difference Between a Phrase and a Clause

The word *phrase* is often used very loosely to refer to almost any grouping of words, from a single term to a longer saying. However, in grammar, the word *phrase* means something specific—something that is different from a clause.

As you'll learn in Chapter 10, a clause is a group of words that has a subject and a verb. An independent clause can be a grammatical sentence, but a dependent clause cannot. The following are dependent clauses:

> when I eat cake
>
> that I got lost
>
> who offended my family
>
> which infuriates me to this day
>
> because it hurt my foot

All those examples have a subject and verb: for example, in "because it hurt my foot" the subject is *it* and the verb is *hurt*. There's even an object: *foot*. However, the word *because* prevents this group of words from being an independent clause. *Because* makes the clause dependent.

On the other hand, a phrase—though it might look a lot like a clause—has a key difference: it doesn't have a subject and verb. The following are examples of phrases:

> in summer
>
> running down the street
>
> the boy in the hat
>
> during May

out of my mind

drinking a milkshake

outside the gazebo

at the tip of my tongue

avenging my father

a giant poodle

Like dependent clauses, phrases are also not complete sentences. A great way to think about phrases is that they are building blocks for sentences.

USAGE TIDBIT

One good way to think about phrases is that they are somewhere between words and clauses: a phrase is more than one word, but not quite a clause.

Practice

For the following, indicate whether each is a phrase or clause:

1. riding the Green Line

2. a pointy hat

3. who wears a cashmere sweater

4. that I will never forget

5. a gentleman named Jeff

6. a Chicago-style hot dog

7. how I learned to juggle

8. that I forgot his birthday

9. in the middle of the night

10. who is my enemy

11. when the dog barks

12. until my friends get here

13. during the hottest part of the year

14. sawing the tree in half

15. when the war started

16. where I met Barbara

17. ate an entire pizza

18. for the love of country

19. on top of the mountain

20. which annoys me very much

Answers:

1. riding the Green Line (Phrase.)

2. a pointy hat (Phrase.)

3. who wears a cashmere sweater (Clause.)

4. that I will never forget (Clause.)

5. a gentleman named Jeff (Phrase.)

6. a Chicago-style hot dog (Phrase.)

7. how I learned to juggle (Clause.)

8. that I forgot his birthday (Clause.)

9. in the middle of the night (Phrase.)

10. who is my enemy (Clause.)

11. when the dog barks (Clause.)

12. until my friends get here (Clause.)

13. during the hottest part of the year (Phrase.)

14. sawing the tree in half (Phrase.)

15. when the war started (Clause.)

16. where I met Barbara (Clause.)

17. ate an entire pizza (Phrase.)

18. for the love of country (Phrase.)

19. on top of the mountain (Phrase.)

20. which annoys me very much (Clause.)

Forming Prepositional Phrases

Prepositions, as you learned in Chapter 3, are connecting words that help establish relationships. You can also use prepositions to form prepositional phrases.

Can you spot the prepositional phrases in the following?

> My dad put his keys on the dresser.
>
> In the other room, I keep my comic books.
>
> Who is in charge of this office?
>
> I've been in AA for about a year.
>
> I won't leave until you answer my questions.

Prepositional phrases begin with a preposition and then add a little more information. Here are the same sentences with the prepositional phrases underlined:

> My dad put his keys <u>on the dresser</u>.
>
> <u>In the other room</u>, I keep my comic books.
>
> Who is in charge <u>of this office</u>?
>
> I've been <u>in AA</u> for <u>about a year</u>.
>
> I won't leave <u>until you answer my questions</u>.

PRACTICAL POINT

Prepositional phrases answer questions such as where, when, why, what, and how.

Prepositional Phrases as Adjectives

Some prepositional phrases act as adjectives; they modify a noun.

> I am a friend <u>of the president</u>.
>
> I wrote a paper <u>on racism</u>.
>
> Those guys <u>in the store</u> look creepy.

Here are the nouns and the propositional phrases that modify them:

friend   of the president

paper   on racism

guys   in the store

Prepositional Phrases as Adverbs

Other prepositional phrases act as adverbs, which modify verbs, adjectives, and other adverbs. For example:

My dog sometimes hides under the bed during a storm.

Do you play tennis on the weekends?

Until further notice, I won't help you with your homework.

Sometimes it's hard to tell if the prepositional phrase is modifying a noun or verb. Let's look at this sentence again:

Do you play tennis <u>on the weekends</u>?

Though *on the weekends* seems like it could be modifying *tennis,* it is actually modifying play. Here's how you can tell: pull the word *tennis* out:

Do you play on the weekends?

That sentence makes sense, so the prepositional phrase must be modifying *play*. Now let's look at the opposite:

Do you tennis on the weekends?

Since that version doesn't make sense, *on the weekends* must not modify *tennis.*

In the above example sentences, there's also a case of a prepositional phrase modifying another prepositional phrase, which is like an adverb modifying an adverb. Read this sentence again:

My dog sometimes hides under the bed during a storm.

While *under the bed* acts as an adverb modifying *hides, during a storm* acts as an adverb modifying *under the bed.*

Using Verbs as Adjectives, Adverbs, and Nouns

Verbs and verb phrases are all about action, but sometimes they can function as adjectives, adverbs, and nouns. Read on to learn more about the versatility of verbs and verb phrases.

Using Participles to Describe

Participles are verbs—which usually end in *–ing* or *–ed*—that are used as adjectives. In other words, an action is turned into a description. The participles are underlined in the following examples:

Look at the <u>frolicking</u> dog.

My uncle is a <u>defeated</u> man.

The classroom is full of <u>studying</u> children.

The <u>purring</u> cat is adorable.

The <u>fallen</u> vase is in pieces.

The <u>crashed</u> plane killed two people.

Were you on the <u>winning</u> team?

The <u>laughing</u> kids would not shut up.

The <u>quivering</u> dog was afraid of fireworks.

The <u>screaming</u> parents and <u>crying</u> child were quite a combination.

Transforming a Verb into a Noun: Gerunds

The suffix *–ing* is added to a verb to form the present participle, as seen in these examples:

I love <u>swimming</u> in the lake.

What are you <u>drawing</u>?

I enjoy <u>parenting</u> with my wife.

Stop <u>lying</u> to me!

Who's that <u>lurking</u> around?

This form of verb can also be used as the subject of a sentence when an activity is treated as a thing. This creates a gerund. The following examples all use present participles as gerunds that function as the subject of sentences:

> Swimming in the lake is fun.
>
> Drawing is difficult.
>
> Parenting takes love and patience.
>
> Lying is a bad habit.
>
> Lurking is creepy.

In other sentences, these gerunds could be objects:

> I enjoy swimming.
>
> My sister studied drawing.
>
> I don't think I'd be good at parenting.
>
> I hate lying.
>
> I'm practicing my lurking.

A gerund can do anything another noun can do: it can be a subject, a direct object, an indirect object, or even a complement. Gerunds are versatile.

Getting More Mileage Out of Infinitives

Infinitives are also versatile. They can function as a noun, verb, or adjective. Here are infinitives that are working as nouns:

> To nap is wonderful.
>
> To eat pizza is fun.
>
> I hate to wake up in the morning.
>
> My dog loves to fetch.
>
> I need to write.

Note that sometimes the infinitive becomes an infinitive phrase, as in *to wake up*.

In other cases, an infinitive or infinitive phrase can be an adjective, as in these examples:

> Superman has the power to fly.
>
> Michael Jordan had the will to win.

Right now, I don't have the desire <u>to eat</u>.

Do you even have the ability <u>to love</u>?

I lack the resources <u>to buy a house</u>.

Sometimes, the infinitive acts as an adverb. In the following cases, infinitives or infinitive phrases modify verbs:

You must interview <u>to get the job</u>.

I worked hard <u>to succeed</u>.

I drink <u>to forget</u>.

Are you arguing <u>to distract me</u>?

I fight <u>to win</u>.

Elaborating on Nouns with Appositives

Your most important goal as a writer is to communicate, and to communicate you must be clear. While trying to be clear, sometimes you have to repeat or rephrase some information. An appositive is a phrase that puts your subject in different language: it rephrases a noun, usually adding some details to the sentence. The appositives are underlined in the following examples:

I have two brothers, <u>Bill and Joe</u>.

The president and vice-president, <u>Mr. Obama and Mr. Biden</u>, attended the funeral.

The hospital, <u>a major medical center</u>, was located just off the highway.

The sandwich, <u>a beef on wick</u>, was delicious.

The comic book, <u>a new graphic novel</u>, was amazing.

Facebook, <u>a social network</u>, can be very annoying.

If you have a concussion, <u>a trauma to the brain</u>, you should go to the doctor.

The new tax, <u>an increase in government revenue</u>, goes into effect soon.

I love Jane, <u>my wife</u>.

My favorite pet is my dog, <u>a rat terrier</u>.

Appositives always put the noun in different words, but there's a lot of freedom as to what kind of words. In some cases, an appositive is simply a synonym, such as *graphic novel* for *comic book*. Sometimes an appositive explains who someone is, like *my wife*. Sometimes an appositive gives extra information, like the breed of a dog (*a rat terrier*). You have a lot of freedom and possibilities when using appositives.

> **USAGE TIDBIT**
>
> With all these types of phrases—not to mention clauses—available, how do you decide what kind to use? First, go with what's clearest. Second, remember the importance of sentence variety. If the form of many of your sentences in a paragraph is the same, the paragraph will feel repetitive and annoying. Adding an appositive—or taking one out—can help keep your writing fresh.

Rearranging Phrases to Clarify and Emphasize

Moving around phrases is one of the handiest ways to make clearer, stronger sentences. This is particularly easy with prepositional phrases. For example, take the following sentences:

> In the morning, I like to eat bacon.

The prepositional phrase can easily be moved if you want to emphasize the subject and downplay the time:

> I like to eat bacon in the morning.

As you revise, always leave enough time to deconstruct and reconstruct your sentences as needed. Take full advantage of the mobility of phrases.

Don't go overboard with prepositional phrases. Sentences can get a little odd-sounding if you have one prepositional phrase after another. Here's an extreme example:

> I like eating breakfast with my friends at the diner near the airport on weekends.

That's not a very long sentence, but it has four prepositional phrases. Here they are:

> with my friends
>
> at the diner
>
> near the airport
>
> on weekends

That's too many propositional phrases for one sentence. It's almost as bad as if you had that many one-word adverbs in a sentence:

> I like eating breakfast sloppily, hungrily, quickly, and thoughtlessly.

That's just too many adverbs. Too much of anything can annoy your readers, so remember to edit and refine your work to keep it fresh and interesting to readers.

Your prose should appear effortless to readers. Unfortunately, that takes a lot of effort on your part.

The Least You Need to Know

- A phrase is a group of words that serves a function in a sentence and may have a noun or verb, but not both.
- Propositional phrases act as adjectives and adverbs.
- Verbs can be used as nouns, adjectives, and adverbs in the infinitive form.
- Verbs can become participles with the addition of *-ing* or *-ed*, which creates adjectives.
- A gerund is a verb plus *-ing* that is used as a noun.
- An appositive is a phrase that adds extra information to describe a noun.

CHAPTER 10

Adding Clauses

There are a lot of ways to say similar things in grammar. A complete sentence is also a complete thought. You can also call it an independent clause, which is one of the main types of clauses you'll learn about in this chapter.

The clause is one of the most important parts of grammar. Clauses are a lot like sentences, and some clauses (the independent kind) can be sentences. Learning to identify independent clauses and dependent clauses is a crucial part of becoming a skilled writer in English.

In the previous chapter, you learned about phrases, which are easy to confuse with clauses. They are quite different, with different forms and purposes, and we'll explain what distinguishes them.

If you know your clauses, you're more than halfway to knowing your grammar. Knowing clauses well separates people who know just a little about grammar from those who truly understand it.

In This Chapter

- What makes a clause a clause?
- Two types: the difference between independent and dependent clauses
- The three types of dependent clauses: noun, adjective, and adverb
- How to arrange and rearrange clauses for clarity and emphasis

Recognizing the Two Main Clause Types

A clause is a group of words that has a subject and a verb. Sounds like a sentence, right? Not necessarily. One kind of clause can be a sentence, but the other kind cannot.

Using clauses is one of the most basic aspects of writing. If you can't write and recognize a clause, you won't get far as a writer. Clauses are important building blocks of writing, and yes, "Clauses are important building blocks of writing" is a clause.

Read on to learn more about the two kinds of clauses: independent and dependent.

Independent Clauses

An independent clause consists of a subject and a verb. It's also a complete thought. Independent clauses can be short, as in these examples:

> Men shouted.
>
> The dog howled.
>
> I'm sad.
>
> It's raining.
>
> Today is Sunday.

The key part is that they have a subject and a verb. Some sentences have more than one independent clause, as in the following examples, which each have two:

> Canada is near Buffalo; Lake Erie is nearby, too.
>
> I just took a nap, and now I feel refreshed.
>
> My dog smells weird: I think he rolled in something disgusting.
>
> *Anchorman* is my favorite comedy; I love Will Ferrell.
>
> I think I'm going through a midlife crisis: I just bought a Corvette.

Practice

In the following sentences, mark the number of independent clauses: 0, 1, 2, or more:

1. I feel tired.

2. There's a cat in a tree; someone should call a fireman.

3. Which is a real problem for me.

4. I forgot to pay my taxes: I think I'm in trouble, and I might go to jail.

5. Why is the sky purple?

6. I look like a police officer, but I'm actually an actor.

7. In the event of my death or serious injury.

8. Let's go to the beach; it's a nice day.

9. I burned my tongue on the soup.

10. My mom's corn muffins are awesome; you have to try them, and you should also try her waffles.

11. Swedish pancakes are my favorite food.

12. My uncle is a waiter and a creep.

13. Superman is the oldest superhero but not the best.

14. Try this shirt on—I think it'll fit you.

15. My shoes got soaked in the rain; man, I hate spring.

Answers:

1. I feel tired. (1 independent clause.)

2. There's a cat in a tree; someone should call a fireman. (2 independent clauses.)

3. Which is a real problem for me. (0 independent clauses.)

4. I forgot to pay my taxes: I think I'm in trouble, and I might go to jail. (3 independent clauses.)

5. Why is the sky purple? (1 independent clause.)

6. I look like a police officer, but I'm actually an actor. (2 independent clauses.)

7. In the event of my death or serious injury. (0 independent clauses.)

8. Let's go to the beach; it's a nice day. (2 independent clauses.)

9. I burned my tongue on the soup. (1 independent clause.)

10. My mom's corn muffins are awesome; you have to try them, and you should also try her waffles. (3 independent clauses.)

11. Swedish pancakes are my favorite food. (1 independent clause.)

12. My uncle is a waiter and a creep. (1 independent clause.)

13. Superman is the oldest superhero but not the best. (1 independent clause.)

14. Try this shirt on—I think it'll fit you. (2 independent clauses.)

15. My shoes got soaked in the rain; man, I hate spring. (2 independent clauses.)

Dependent Clauses

An independent clause can stand alone, but a dependent clause cannot. Like an independent clause, a dependent clause has a subject and a verb. Here's the big difference: a dependent clause is not a complete thought. The following are examples of dependent clauses:

> when I get a headache
>
> who I later learned was a barber
>
> that I'll never forget
>
> after walking the dog
>
> if I went to Australia

Words such as *when, if,* and *that* are a clue that you're dealing with dependent clauses. For example:

> Independent clause: I went to Australia.
>
> Dependent clause: If I went to Australia.

That *If* demands further information to make a complete sentence. It makes the reader wonder, "Well, if you went to Australia, then what?" Dependent clauses must be joined with independent clauses to form complete, grammatical sentences. Here's another example:

> Independent clause: My back hurts.
>
> Dependent clause: When my back hurts.

"My back hurts" is a complete thought, but "When my back hurts" is not. Adding *When* to "My back hurts" turns an independent clause into a dependent clause.

> **DANGER ZONE**
>
> Since a dependent clause has a subject and a verb, it can feel like a complete thought—even though it is actually a sentence fragment. Writing a dependent clause as a complete sentence is one of the most common writing errors. For more on how to identify and fix this problem, jump to Chapter 15.

There are three kinds of dependent clauses, which mirror three of the main types of words: noun, adjective, and adverb. Knowing the difference among these types of dependent clauses will help you craft sentences, avoid errors, and introduce variety into your prose.

Noun Clauses

A noun clause can be the subject of a sentence: it can also be the object or a complement. Typically, noun clauses begin with one of the following words:

how

if

that

what

whatever

when

whenever

where

whether

which

who

whoever

whose

why

The following are examples of noun clauses:

where I learned to juggle

where I grew up

why I won't bike on the sidewalk

whatever my dad says

why I hate heights

whoever took the last muffin

who my grandmother married

how experts do it

that town bordering the lake

when my sister got married

To figure out if a clause is a noun clause, you have to see if it sounds like a noun. Ask yourself: is it a person, place, or thing? By putting the above noun clauses into sentences, we can see that they do function as nouns:

That school is <u>where I learned to juggle</u>.

Buffalo is <u>where I grew up</u>.

Traffic laws and common sense are <u>why I won't bike on the sidewalk</u>.

I do <u>whatever my dad says</u>.

A childhood trauma is <u>why I hate heights</u>.

I'm going to murder <u>whoever took the last muffin</u>.

Joe is the guy <u>who my grandmother married</u>.

I'm new to cooking; I want to learn <u>how experts do it</u>.

I'd like to visit <u>that town bordering the lake</u>.

I remember <u>when my sister got married</u>.

> **PRACTICAL POINT**
>
> You may sometimes see dependent clauses referred to as subordinate clauses. Don't be confused. A dependent clause is the same thing as a subordinate clause. If you forget, remember that the words dependent and subordinate both indicate a lack of independence. Dependent people and subordinate people don't have the power to act alone: the same is true of dependent/subordinate clauses.

Adjective Clauses

Adjective clauses—also known as relative clauses—typically begin with one of the following relative pronouns:

of which

that

which

who

whoever

whom

whomever

whose

Like adjectives themselves, adjective clauses describe nouns and pronouns. Adjective clauses are descriptive, giving extra information that adds color and vividness to your writing. The following are all adjective clauses:

that I grew up in

that I ate for breakfast

which is kind of lumpy

whose brother I know

who loves hamburgers

who works as a security guard

that I need for this job

whose wallet I found

that upset my stomach

Here's how those clauses might fit into sentences to describe some nouns:

Did you buy the house <u>that I grew up in</u>?

Cereal is the food <u>that I ate for breakfast</u>.

I like oatmeal, <u>which is kind of lumpy</u>.

I just met James, <u>whose brother I know</u>.

Jill is a friend <u>who loves hamburgers</u>.

Greg is a guy <u>who works as a security guard</u>.

A working knowledge of spreadsheets is something <u>that I need for this job</u>.

Bernie Baldwin is the man <u>whose wallet I found</u>.

Chili is the food <u>that upset my stomach</u>.

See how those clauses describe nouns? Let's look at one example:

> I like oatmeal, <u>which is kind of lumpy</u>.

The clause describes *oatmeal*. Of course, you could say "I like lumpy oatmeal," but that would have a different meaning. Both sentences are grammatical, so you should choose the one that best conveys your meaning.

The important thing to remember is that adjective clauses describe. Look at how they answer a reader's potential questions in these examples:

> Greg is a guy <u>who works as a security guard</u>.
>
> What kind of guy is Greg? One who works as a security guard.

> Chili is the food <u>that upset my stomach</u>.
>
> What kind of food is chili? The food that upset my stomach.

> Did you buy the house <u>that I grew up in</u>?
>
> Did you buy the house? Which house? The one I grew up in.

If the dependent clause doesn't describe, it must not be an adjective clause.

Adverb Clauses

Like an adverb, an adverb clause modifies verbs, as well as adjectives and other adverbs. Typically, an adverb clause begins with one of the following words:

> after
>
> although
>
> as
>
> as if
>
> because
>
> before
>
> even though
>
> if
>
> since
>
> so that

than

that

though

unless

until

when

whether

while

The following are examples of adverb clauses:

when the days get shorter

while Bill Clinton was president

since I have a headache

although cats are more independent

until the sun blows up

whether you like it or not

before the end of the month

if that's your sort of thing

after watching me do it first

though I have my reservations

Adverb clauses usually say how, why, where, or when something is happening. They often state a condition. For example, the adverb clause, "though I have my reservations" could be used in several sentences, such as:

Though I have my reservations, I will sign the contract.

I married her, though I have my reservations.

Though I have my reservations, I moved to Buffalo, New York.

Though I have my reservations, I bought a fedora.

I decided to have children, though I have my reservations.

Here's how another adverb clause might fit in several sentences:

>You must pay the rent before the end of the month.

>Want to get a drink before the end of the month?

>Please write 20 pages before the end of the month.

>Before the end of the month, my wife will give birth.

>I think the world will end before the end of the month.

In all those cases, "before the end of the month" answers the question "When?"

Practice

For the following examples, note whether the dependent clause is an adjective, adverb, or noun clause.

1. I grew up in the house where Abraham Lincoln was born.

2. Whoever owns that car is my hero.

3. Whatever is wrong with my cousin is also wrong with me.

4. I won't marry you even though we've dated three years.

5. This is the shirt that my uncle died in.

6. Whenever I eat beets, my stomach grumbles.

7. I feel happy wherever I am.

8. This is the money that I wanted to spend on travel.

9. When it rains, my knee hurts.

10. That's the girl who broke my heart.

Answers:

1. I grew up in the house <u>where Abraham Lincoln was born</u>. (Adjective.)

2. <u>Whoever owns that car</u> is my hero. (Noun.)

3. <u>Whatever is wrong with my cousin</u> is also wrong with me. (Noun.)

4. I won't marry you <u>even though we've dated three years</u>. (Adverb.)

5. This is the shirt <u>that my uncle died in</u>. (Adjective.)

6. <u>Whenever I eat beets</u>, my stomach grumbles. (Adverb.)

7. I feel happy <u>wherever I am</u>. (Adverb.)

8. This is the money <u>that I wanted to spend on travel</u>. (Adjective.)

9. <u>When it rains</u>, my knee hurts. (Adverb.)

10. That's the girl <u>who broke my heart</u>. (Adverb.)

Rearranging Clauses to Clarify and Emphasize

As you can probably already tell, clauses are easy to move around in a sentence. Depending on what you want to emphasize, you can flip clauses around as needed. For example, let's go back to the noun clause "where I grew up."

There are many sentences that could be written with this clause. It can start sentences:

Where I grew up was chilly.

Where I grew up is now a parking lot.

Where I grew up is where my children will grow up.

The same clause can also end sentences:

I love where I grew up.

My parents still live where I grew up.

Don't visit where I grew up.

In different sentences, "where I grew up" can function as an adjective or adverb phrase instead of a noun phrase:

That's the house where I grew up.

Where I grew up, people had manners.

I've never loved anything as much as the town where I grew up.

Depending on the purpose of your sentence and the other sentences, you can and should move your clauses around. Don't leave them as they were in your first draft. Take advantage of the combinatory possibilities of clauses. They are a writer's friends.

The Least You Need to Know

- A dependent clause has a subject and a verb, but it's not a complete thought and it can't be a grammatical sentence on its own.
- Independent clauses are complete thoughts and can function as sentences on their own.
- Dependent clauses can be one of three types: noun, adjective, or adverb.
- Clauses can be rearranged in many ways, depending on what you want to emphasize in your sentence.

Writing with Style

Grammar is only half the story when it comes to writing. You could have perfect grammar and still write a paper, article, or story that is terrible. These chapters will show how the rules and elements of grammar can be used to craft writing that packs a punch and tells a story. The grammar chapters are about the raw material of language. The style chapters tell you how to mold that raw material into compelling prose.

That's where the seven Cs of good writing come in. If you're feeling overwhelmed by the terminology and rules of other chapters, the seven Cs are another way to look at writing that can help you focus on the big picture.

In these chapters, you'll also learn some rules of thumb and tricks of the trade for writing with style. One of the most important aspects of style is sentence variety. You'll learn how to vary your sentences in terms of length and type—and why this is so important. I'll also discuss diction: word choice. I'll show you how to make strong word choices while (usually) avoiding clichés, euphemisms, slang, and jargon. Parallelism is another tool that helps you craft smooth, clear sentences. In another chapter, I'll review some of the most common writing errors and how to avoid them.

I'll also discuss how to keep your writing free of bias. This can be tricky when discussing gender, race, sexual orientation, and other identity issues, but there are some general guidelines that will keep you from accidentally being offensive or unfair.

The Seven Cs of Good Writing

As discussed in Chapter 2, alliteration can be a very useful literary device. It's particularly helpful for making something memorable, and this is true of the seven Cs of good writing.

These are seven words, all starting with the letter *C*, that should describe your writing. When your head is spinning from thinking about phrases, semicolons, participles, and gerunds, it can help to look at the big picture. That's where the seven Cs come in.

If you go googling, you'll see many versions of the seven Cs (or even another number), but the following are the most important ones for writing well:

- Clear
- Compelling
- Consistent
- Concise
- Convincing
- Concrete
- Correct

If you find yourself getting lost in the details and rules and guidelines of other chapters, the seven Cs can help you remember why all this is important. Think of them as rules of thumb that should guide everything you write.

In This Chapter:

- Another way to look at style and grammar
- Applying the seven Cs to your writing
- The importance of following style guides
- Quoting, paraphrasing, and summarizing
- How and why to avoid plagiarism

Clear

Good writing is clear. In clear writing, the paper or article has an explicit overall purpose. Readers can understand the meaning of sentences without reading them several times or looking up many words in the dictionary. The organization helps the reader move smoothly from paragraph to paragraph. In short, clear writing is easy and enjoyable to read.

Making your writing clear isn't as simple as it sounds. What sounds clear in your head may be a muddle on paper. Here are a few tricks to help make your writing clear:

Replace vague language with specific language. Replace *bad* with *dangerous*. Replace *huge* with *500 pounds*. Replace *some people* with *women from Indiana*. The more specific you are, the clearer your writing will be.

Use an outline. If your work has a logical flow of ideas and paragraphs, the overall point will be clear. Remember, it's okay to start writing and then outline your work to check and improve the organization. All that matters is that the final result is organized.

Show it to someone else, especially someone who's not an expert on the subject. If someone who is unfamiliar with the subject understands what you're saying, your work must be clear. A fresh set of eyes can be a huge help in this regard.

Compelling

You know how a really good book is hard to put down? Even if you're not writing a mystery or thriller, you want your writing to have that hard-to-put-down feeling.

Good writing is compelling. This is another way of saying you need to write in a way that makes people want to read it. Following are a few qualities that can make writing compelling.

Humor

Do you enjoy people who are always completely serious, who never crack a joke or smile? Even if you do, most people don't. Just as a teacher can liven up a dull lecture with a little humor, you can use some humor to make your writing more fun to read.

Instead of thinking you have to include a lot of jokes, think of humor as an attitude. If you don't take yourself too seriously, that can add a positive element to your writing.

 DANGER ZONE

Be careful when using humor. Often, the risks outweigh the rewards. Sexual or racial humor will rarely, if ever, be appropriate. A joke that might seem innocent to you could offend someone else. Use humor sparingly and cautiously.

Fresh Language

You're a unique person who sees the world in your own way. Let that uniqueness be part of your writing. Don't settle for the same tired phrases and terms everyone else is using. I discuss language to avoid, such as euphemisms, clichés, and jargon, in Chapter 12.

It's easier to turn stale language into fresh language if you're not writing in a rush. If you give yourself enough time to thoroughly revise and edit your work, you'll have more chances to edit out phrases that are dull and worn out.

Headings and Transitions

Transitions help readers get a feel for where an essay is headed, and they're a huge help in making your writing compelling. Think of transitions—and headings in longer papers—as little signs along the way that keep your readers headed in the right direction. Headings and directions keep readers from getting lost, and readers who know where they're going will be compelled to continue.

Consistent

Good writing is consistent. Unfortunately, there are many aspects of writing where inconsistency can creep in. Following are some of the most common types of consistency errors that you should work to avoid.

Grammar

Grammar is one area where consistency is important. Look at the following sentences:

> The boys are playing outside. They were having fun.

Do you see the problem? First, the boys are playing outside now. Then, the boys were having fun in the past. This is likely a mistake, and it's a common one. It's important to keep your verb tenses consistent to avoid confusion. If revised for consistency, the sentences will make more sense:

> The boys are playing outside. They are having fun.

Pronouns

In Chapter 16, you'll read a variety of ways to handle pronouns while avoiding sexism. Whatever method you choose, be consistent. If you use *he/she* in one part of a paper, don't start using singular *they* in another part.

Diction

Be consistent with terminology. Sloppiness with word choice can cause confusion.

For example, let's say a supervisor is telling a subordinate about a new assignment in an email. In part of the email, the supervisor writes, "I'll expect this to be finished by next Wednesday." In another part of the email, the supervisor writes, "Remember, this is an optional assignment." What is the employee supposed to think?

There's a language problem there. If the assignment is truly optional, then the employee doesn't have to do it. If the supervisor expects the assignment to be completed by a certain date, then the employee does have to do it. Inconsistent word choices cause problems.

While varying your vocabulary can help your writing stay lively, don't sacrifice consistency for the sake of variety. In most writing situations, consistency is more important than creativity.

Format

The main style guides are the Modern Language Association (MLA), the American Psychological Association (APA), and the Chicago Manual of Style (CMS).

You should be consistent in terms of the format you use. If a professor asks for a paper in APA format, don't use any elements of MLA format. This can be difficult if you're used to using MLA. Formatting takes patience and a willingness to fine-tune your work until you get it right.

Some books on writing—such as Diana Hacker's *A Writer's Reference*—provide basic information on all three major style guides. However, there's no substitute for going to the actual guidebook.

Be sure not to use an older version of APA format (or another style guide). Use the most current edition, which you can find by looking at the website for APA (apa.org), Chicago (chicagomanualofstyle.org), or MLA (mla.org).

Thesis Statement and Argument

If you're writing a paper, your thesis statement should be supported by the paper. A thesis statement is a sentence (sometimes two) that captures the argument of a paper. The following are examples of thesis statements:

> Until he wins at least six NBA titles, LeBron James cannot be considered a contender for the title of greatest basketball player ever.

> Comic book movies flourish while the comic book industry flounders because editors, writers, and artists are aiming for the wrong audience.

> Contrary to popular myths, texting and tweeting are actually making people better writers.

A thesis should be introduced in the beginning of a paper and supported throughout. If you contradict your own thesis, no one is going to believe your argument. Also, anything that doesn't fit within the thesis could prove distracting.

Assignment Directions or Guidelines

Being consistent with the directions or guidelines you are given is also important. When doing assignments for school, make sure you read the directions carefully. If you turn in a paper that doesn't answer the question or fit the assignment, you'll probably fail—even if your work is excellent. Don't be afraid to ask the teacher for clarification before you start writing. It's extremely important that what you write is consistent with what your audience—in this case, a teacher—expects.

> **PRACTICAL POINT**
>
> Some writers make the mistake of thinking they should memorize the rules of APA or MLA style, but this is not a good idea. Trying to remember all the guidelines is not a good use of your brain power. Looking up style rules is safer and easier. You should work to get faster at looking up material. Help yourself out by putting flags or notes in a physical copy of a manual or bookmarking internet pages. Odds are you'll use some pages over and over, so create shortcuts to those pages. With practice you will become more efficient at finding and understanding the rules.

Concise

Do you like it when someone has a "quick story" to tell that goes on for 20 minutes? Probably not. Writing is the same way: if you go on and on and on and on without saying much, your audience will be bored and stop reading.

Say what you have to say and finish.

Convincing

This point applies best to writing that makes an argument. If you're writing a movie review and you hated the movie, you probably want to argue that people shouldn't waste their money on that movie. If you accomplish that goal, your writing is convincing.

How do you convince your readers of something? Following are several ways to help do this.

Use Concrete Facts

The more specific details you give, the more you'll persuade your readers. For example, the following is not very credible:

> A lot of people have cancer from smoking.

How many people? Who says this is true? What kinds of cancer? A more specific statement will pass muster with readers:

> According to the American Cancer Society, 30 percent of all cancer deaths are the result of cigarette smoking.

Write Clean, Error-Free Prose

If your writing is error-free, it shows you've paid attention to details and taken your work seriously. This gives you credibility, and it makes your writing more convincing.

Of course, we all make writing mistakes. Writing is one of those things that will never be perfect, but it is also one of those things where you should strive for perfection, mainly for two reasons: communication and presentation.

Communication—which could easily be one of the Cs—is the goal of writing, and writing errors get in the way of communication. Think of them as static ruining a good song on the radio.

As for presentation, everything you write is a chance to present yourself as a certain kind of person. Do you want to present yourself as someone careful and considerate or thoughtless and incompetent? The fewer errors you make, the better impression you make on readers.

Don't Overstate Your Case

Avoid exaggerations and generalizations. Make a strong point, but don't go beyond it. It's easier to make a case that high school football should be banned than that all football should be banned. Keep your argument reasonable and don't overreach.

 DANGER ZONE

Some people, when asked to write an essay, feel that it's hard for them to write enough. These writers think they've said what they need to in 5 pages, but the teacher demands 10. They feel as if the teacher wants "fluff." No teachers—at least no good ones—want fluff. What they want is evidence. If you're trying to come up with more to write, think about adding more evidence. If that doesn't work, you might need to broaden your subject. Whatever you do, don't write fluff.

Complete

When you're writing an argument, completeness is important. For example, let's say your thesis statement is "Due to increasing knowledge of concussion-related brain injuries, high school football should be banned."

In that essay, you had better include thorough research on brain injuries—especially to high-school-age children. If you neglect the research on either brain damage or teens, your paper will be incomplete and your argument will be difficult to take seriously.

Correct

Most of this book is devoted to what's correct in writing. The following sections explain some of the specific types of correctness.

Grammar

Grammatical correctness is obviously very important or this book wouldn't exist. See Chapter 1 for a good start on getting your grammar under control.

Agreement is perhaps the most important grammatical concept. A noun must agree with its verb, so "Children play," not "Children plays." A large percentage of correctness is a form of agreement.

Facts

When writing, you should check and double-check your facts. If your writing spreads false information, it's not worth much. Take the time to research subjects thoroughly to provide the most correct and up-to-date information.

Your credibility is on the line with everything you write. Don't make yourself look foolish by ignoring, distorting, or mixing up the facts.

Format

If you're writing a paper for school, be sure you use the appropriate style guide. Don't use APA when your professor asked for MLA.

This may seem like a small point. After all, don't APA and MLA (and Chicago Manual of Style, for that matter) do the same thing? What's the difference between calling the list of sources "Works Cited" or "References"?

Though the differences are, in a sense, trivial and small, they make a big impression on readers—a negative impression. Just as misplacing a comma or calling someone by the wrong name can turn off the person you're writing to, using the wrong format or ignoring the rules of that format make you look like a sloppy, careless person. That's not an impression you ever want to make: not in school, not when applying for a job, and not even when writing a friend. Why make a bad impression when you could make a good one?

Also, formatting choices can have significant writing consequences. Since formats help you cite sources, bad citing could lead to accidental plagiarism.

Purpose

There are many reasons for writing: to inform, to entertain, to sell, to amuse, to argue, and to get a job are some common purposes. It's important that you understand your writing purpose and write accordingly.

For example, if your teacher or editor wants an objective research paper, don't turn in a personal essay. A research paper presents facts and makes an argument, while a personal essay tells a story and expresses emotions. If you start telling a story during a research paper, you've lost sight of your purpose.

Unfortunately, even if your writing is top-notch, if your writing fulfills the wrong purpose, it will probably be a failure (literally in school, figuratively elsewhere). Double-check your purpose before writing and remind yourself of it frequently while drafting and revising.

Consulting Style Guides for More Direction

Style guides are your friends. I've taught a lot of writing classes, and I wish my students would spend more time with these friends. Style guides are important: they answer many specific questions of what to do in your writing situation.

When in doubt, ask your teacher or editor what style guide they prefer.

USAGE TIDBIT

No style guide will be perfect for every situation, since they end up being used for more situations than they were designed. As an example, the APA manual is designed for formatting journal articles in psychology. However, APA format is used by many people for writing projects other than psychology papers. This can create gaps in style. For instance, students often wonder how to format a table of contents in APA. The answer is you can't. Since journal articles don't have a table of contents, that style is not included in APA. You have to figure out the format for a table of contents yourself using other sources. Sometimes a professor or editor will want your format to follow a rule that's not in APA or another manual. Should you ignore the professor and follow the manual? No! Give professors and editors what they want.

Steering Clear of Plagiarism

There are three ways to present other people's ideas in your work: quoting, paraphrasing, and summarizing. If you're familiar with these three methods, you won't have to worry about accidentally plagiarizing.

Quoting

When you quote, you use the exact words of a source, and you let the reader know with quotation marks. The following are examples of quoting:

> Christian Bale growled, "I'm Batman."

> My grandpa said, "Tarnation! The pig's loose again!"

> President Clinton said, "I feel your pain."

> I said, "I don't want to know!" when my sister started another embarrassing story.

> "Can you hear me now?" used to be Verizon's catchphrase.

For more on quotation marks, see Chapter 18.

When writing, it can be tempting to use a lot of quotations. If you have a 10-page paper, using 5 pages of quotations could cut your work in half. As long as you cite the quotations correctly, there's no problem with plagiarism. So what's the problem? Why not write a paper that's quote, quote, quote?

The problem is that by using an excessive number of quotations you've made more of a collage than a paper. Quoting is easy—too easy. It results in weak writing, and it avoids the task of writing itself. Don't give in to the temptation to overquote. It's a common symptom of weak writing that's easy for teachers, editors, and readers to spot.

Here's when you should include a quote: when something is extremely well said and emphasizes your point. Quote sparingly so what you do quote has an impact. Most of the time you should be paraphrasing your sources, which is a lot more work but results in much better writing.

Make Quotations Blend In

You should also integrate quotations into your writing. Introduce your quotations. The following is a bad way to start a paragraph:

> "Spain is lovely this time of year" (Brice 35).

This version is better:

> As Brice said, "Spain is lovely this time of year (35)."

Paraphrasing

Paraphrasing is when you take someone else's ideas and put them in your own words. The following are examples of paraphrasing:

> My dad always said how you treat others is important.

> Smith wrote about how families in America are like cesspools.

> The key to good basketball, according to Bill Simmons, is playing as a team.

Paraphrasing integrates other people's ideas into your own words. By paraphrasing, you make the ideas flow more smoothly, creating a coherent work.

Paraphrasing makes better writing, but it's not easy. In fact, it's hard work. If you don't paraphrase thoroughly, you could end up committing plagiarism. For example, let's say someone named Jennifer Walters wrote this sentence:

> Green is the color most associated with health and beauty.

Here's a bad paraphrase of that sentence:

> According to Walters, green is highly associated with health and beauty.

Though the author has cited Walter, the paraphrase is too close to the original. In fact, the words, "associated with health and beauty" are exactly the same. This is a type of plagiarism. One way to fix the problem is by using a partial quote:

> According to Walters, green is highly "associated with health and beauty."

Or you could keep working on the paraphrase until it is truly in your own words:

> According to Walters, there are healthy and beautiful connotations to the color green.

This is a better paraphrase because the structure of the sentence is different, but the ideas are about the same. Also, the paraphrase is the same length, which is important. A paraphrase should be about the same length as the original: don't paraphrase a sentence in a paragraph or vice versa.

If this sounds like a lot of work, it is. Paraphrasing takes a persistent willingness to write and rewrite sentences, shifting phrases and words around, all the while going back to the original to make sure the meaning has not been lost.

Practice

A good way to practice paraphrasing—and writing in general—is by doing exercises that involve writing different versions of a sentence. Take the following sentence and write 10 other sentences that say about the same thing:

> The FBI gives colorful nicknames to bank robbers.

There are no wrong answers. After you've finished, compare your sentences to the following 10 variations I came up with.

Answers:

1. Bank robbers receive colorful nicknames given by the FBI.

2. If you rob a bank, you could end up with a nickname given by the FBI.

3. One of the FBI's oddest functions is giving nicknames to bank robbers.

4. The distinctive nicknames for bank robbers help the FBI track down bank robbers.

5. Don't rob a bank unless you want an FBI nickname such as The Gilligan Bandit.

6. Robbing a bank is a good way to receive a vivid nickname from the FBI.

7. Bank robbers not only run the risk of going to jail: they often receive an unwanted nickname, courtesy of the FBI.

8. FBI agents don't just track down criminals; they nickname them, especially bank robbers.

9. The Beret Bandit and The Thong Bandit are a few of the colorful nicknames FBI agents have given bank robbers.

10. A bank robber with distinctive features could provide fodder for a colorful nickname: like the Super Sloth Bandit, who wore the word *Super* on a T-shirt and was extremely slow.

Some of these sentences move information around or add a little information. Deciding which sentence is best depends on what's happening in the rest of the paragraph and the paper. Only in grammar books will you ever deal with a sentence in isolation. However, by doing sentence-rearranging exercises, you can improve your ability to revise sentences. Just as physical exercises can improve your strength and agility, language exercises can make your writing stronger and smoother.

Summarizing

Summarizing is very similar to paraphrasing, except it does some shrinking: when you summarize, you take a longer batch of ideas and drill down to the overall or most essential idea. Summaries are shorter—sometimes much shorter—than the originals.

> Michael Adams' book claims slang is a form of poetry.

> Jennings explains the three types of Presidents in American history: the mavericks, the stewards, and the bridge salesmen.

> The teachings of Jesus were mostly about love.

You can summarize a paragraph, a page, an article, a chapter, a book, or even a series of books.

Often, you'll have to summarize your own work. For example, if you're writing a paper and someone asks what it's about, you can't recite the whole paper. You have to summarize. Being able to summarize your work is a sign that you know your purpose and project well.

Citing Your Work

"Avoid plagiarism" can be phrased in a more positive way: give credit to others for their words and ideas. The way to give credit is through citing.

In most style formats, there are two parts of citing. The first are in-text citations. Here are some sentences with in-text citations using MLA style:

> Families are increasingly awful (Miller 32).

> According to Jones (22), Magellan invented chairs.

> Walters said that "Coffee is great" (22).

In MLA, in-text citations include a page number. In APA format, these citations would look a little different. Since APA is often used for scientific writing, the year is prominent, letting readers know if the research is current.

> Families are increasingly awful (Miller 2011).

> According to Jones (2002), Magellan invented chairs.

> Walters (2009) said that "Coffee is great" (p. 22).

In APA, a page number is necessary only for a direct quotation.

Citing is only the half of it: you also need a works cited (in MLA) or reference (in APA) entry. Please consult the appropriate manuals for a lot more information on proper citing format.

Quotations, paraphrases, and summaries all need to be cited. If you don't cite, you've committed plagiarism—even if you've done so by accident.

This is one of the most important aspects of writing. A teacher or editor will almost always give you a chance to fix a comma error, but you could fail a paper (or class) if you commit plagiarism. Plagiarism is a serious issue.

Cite your quotations. Cite your paraphrases. Cite your summaries. When in doubt, cite it. Always give credit to others.

Take So-Called Plagiarism Checkers with a Grain of Salt

There are a lot of programs out there—such as Turnitin.com and SafeAssign.com—that are supposed to be plagiarism-checkers. They're not. All these programs do is match text in your paper with text in the program's database (plus the internet). The program highlights matched text—whether it's cited correctly or not.

Here's the brutal truth: there is no program that can check for plagiarism for you. You have to rely on your eyeballs and brain. You have to be careful and meticulous, double-checking your sources, quotations, paraphrases, summaries, and style guide.

Technology can do a lot of amazing things, but making your paper plagiarism-proof isn't one of them.

The Least You Need to Know

- Your writing should be clear, concise, and easy to understand.
- Make your writing compelling with humor, fresh language, and clear organization.
- Make your writing convincing by using credible facts, writing error-free prose, and being thorough and complete. Don't skip important information.
- Your writing should be correct in terms of grammar, facts, format, and purpose. Consult style guides for help.
- Always cite your work. Quotations, paraphrases, and summaries must be cited.

CHAPTER 12

Choosing the Right Words: Diction

People often feel choice fatigue when buying a cup of coffee. There are so many sizes, lattes, sugar substitutes, and flavors that it's hard to know what you want.

Choice fatigue is much worse with words. Words are your friends, but they are numerous friends who can be overwhelming. Writing can feel like being at a party with a million people.

When you flip through a thesaurus or dictionary, you might feel even worse. How do you use these tools without feeling used by them? How do you know the right word for the right situation? And what does the meaning of a word really mean anyway?

This chapter will help you feel more confident about these issues. You'll learn more about the tools and rules of thumb for choosing words. It's often difficult to choose between words, but you'll need to get comfortable making those choices. This chapter will help you make better decisions.

In This Chapter

- How to use a dictionary and thesaurus
- The difference between connotation and denotation
- Using slang and jargon in your writing
- The dangers (and uses) of clichés and euphemisms
- Eggcorns and other similar-sounding words

Word Books: The Dictionary and Thesaurus

Writing can be a daunting task, but you're not alone. In addition to grammar books like the one you're holding now, there are two main types of word books: dictionaries and thesauruses.

Different Types of Dictionaries

Though people speak about looking up a word in "the dictionary," there are actually many types of dictionaries. For example, some dictionaries are geared toward specific professions, like medical and legal dictionaries. There are slang dictionaries—like *Green's Dictionary of Slang*—that collect words that are irreverent and informal. If you're writing a song or poem, you should look at a rhyming dictionary, which groups words together by sound.

For the history of a word, try a historical dictionary; the biggest and best is the *Oxford English Dictionary.* Historical dictionaries not only define words, they offer example citations of the word being used over time, so you can see how it is used and has evolved. Another historical dictionary is the *Dictionary of American Regional English,* a huge project that collects terms that are used regionally in the United States, but not across the entire country.

For most purposes, you'll be well served by a general-use dictionary such as the *New Oxford American Dictionary* or the *Merriam-Webster Unabridged Dictionary.*

Online dictionaries can be helpful, too. One of the most innovative and helpful is *Wordnik,* which provides definitions from several print dictionaries, plus example sentences from around the internet.

Using a Thesaurus

A different type of word book is called a *thesaurus.* A thesaurus groups together words with similar meanings, which can help you find words you might not have considered otherwise. Words with the same meaning are called *synonyms.*

For example, let's say you're looking for another word that means nonsense. A thesaurus will turn up terms such as *rubbish, fiddle-faddle, balderdash, rot, twaddle, flapdoodle, tommyrot, hooey, malarkey, horsefeathers, hokum,* and *mumbo-jumbo* (plus a few words we can't print here).

The key to employing a thesaurus is to use it alongside a dictionary. Let's say you decided you liked the sound of *mumbo-jumbo.* By looking it up in a dictionary, you can see if *mumbo-jumbo* is the right type of nonsense for what you're writing.

Finding the Right Word

Flipping through a dictionary can feel overwhelming. There are so many words, and so many of them look or sound similar. It's a challenge for writers at all levels to find the right word for the right situation.

For example, let's say I'm in a romantic relationship with a woman. What's the right way to introduce her? There are many choices.

> This is my wife, Gwen.
>
> This is my girlfriend, Gwen.
>
> This is my main squeeze, Gwen.
>
> This is my significant other, Gwen.
>
> This is my partner, Gwen.

How do you choose? Whether or not to use *wife* (or *spouse*) is easy: it only applies to people who are married.

The word *partner* can also apply to a married couple, or at least a couple that is very stable and perhaps living together. *Partner* is often used by gay couples, especially when they haven't been legally allowed to get married.

Girlfriend and *boyfriend* are common words for people who are only dating but have made some level of commitment to each other. However, they sound a little odd when the couple in question is older. *Significant other* would sound right for many couples, but might be a little serious for couples that haven't been dating long. There are many other possible words for a sweetheart (like *sweetheart*).

There isn't always a 100 percent correct answer, but a dictionary can help you figure out your options. When writing, a dictionary should always be kept handy to help you make these decisions.

Checking a Word's Meaning as You Read

The best habit a writer can have is to read a lot. Read everything you can find: novels, newspapers, blogs, magazines, nonfiction books—everything. Absorbing the language and seeing how it's used will teach you how to use it yourself. Reading is the best writing teacher.

Another habit you should develop is to always look up unfamiliar words in a dictionary when reading. While you may be able to figure out part of the word's meaning from context, you'll likely miss out on something. If you read a lot and use the dictionary a lot, you'll be constantly improving your writing and vocabulary.

Denotation vs. Connotation

Denotation and connotation have to do with the meaning of a word. Denotation is the literal meaning of a word: the strict sense. Connotation is the flavor of a word. You can also think of it as the baggage a word carries from past associations.

For example, take the word *champagne*. The denotation is simple: champagne is a specific type of sparkling wine, one that is made from grapes in Champagne, France. Denotation—in other words, what a term denotes—is cut and dried.

However, *champagne* has connotations, too. Mostly, it is associated with success. If you've ever watched a sports team celebrating a championship in their locker room, you've probably seen the players pouring champagne on each other and spraying it into the air. After any success, it's appropriate to say "Let's break out some champagne!" Whether you're serious about actually drinking some champagne or not, the word *champagne* is shorthand for success.

Every word has denotation and connotation. The connotations may take time (and reading) to pick up, but they are important to consider. Using a word with a negative or inappropriate connotation can ruin a piece of writing and make a bad impression.

The Dangers of Careless Thesaurus Use

A thesaurus can be a useful tool, but it can also be dangerous. Careless thesaurus use can make your writing sound weird and inaccurate instead of smooth and clear.

Thesaurus problems often start when writers mistakenly think the goal of writing is to sound smart and clever, and the way to sound smart and clever is to dig into a thesaurus for big, fancy words. This rarely works out well.

For example, I once heard about a student in a creative writing class who described a glass as *fraught* with wine. That's a very emotional glass! Presumably, the student meant the glass was *full* of wine but thought *full* was too boring a word and went diving into the thesaurus headfirst. True, *fraught* does mean full—but only of emotion. By not investigating further, the student made an embarrassing mistake.

Should you throw out your thesaurus? Not necessarily. Use it, but use it cautiously. Specifically, you should use it for reminders of words you already know rather than as a source of brand-new words.

Avoiding the Double Negative

Good writing is consistent, and the double negative violates this principle. Here are some correctly worded negative statements:

> I have no wine.

> That isn't my car.

> We don't know each other.

A double negative would add confusion:

> I don't have no wine.

> No way that isn't my car.

> We don't not know each other.

Since two negatives equal a positive, these sentences are saying the opposite of what they should. You should avoid double negatives in almost all situations.

The exception—and there is almost always an exception when it comes to writing—is in fiction. If you're writing a character who is folksy, they might use a double negative because it's the way they talk. But writing should be different from talking.

Vague or Stale Language

When writing, you should strive for fresh, clear, strong, original language. That means you should avoid certain writing traps, and especially clichés and euphemisms.

Steering Clear of Clichés

Do you like taking it to another level, playing as hard as you work, and living life to the fullest? If so, good for you, but you should avoid those phrases when writing.

Why? Because they're clichés. Like a pair of jeans with holes in the knees, clichés are worn out. Language that has been repeated over and over and over again becomes a cliché. Clichés are a sign of unoriginal, stale writing. Writers resort to clichés when their creativity and imagination fail them.

A cliché can be a single term (like *the bottom line*) or a whole sentence (like "It is what it is.").

Not everyone agrees on which words and phrases are clichés, but if you've heard an expression a lot—and it makes you want to groan a little—it's probably a cliché.

Here are some very well-known clichés:

all in a day's work

at the end of my rope

at the end of the day

avoid like the plague

beacon of hope

better safe than sorry

better the devil you know than the devil you don't

bird in the hand

birds of a feather

bite the dust

bored to tears

by hook or by crook

can't cut the mustard

champing at the bit

close only counts in horseshoes and hand grenades

down and dirty

fool me once, shame on you

for the birds

good as gold

green with envy

hold your tongue

justice is blind

kiss and tell

light in the darkness

like trying to herd cats

lost his marbles

nip it in the bud

once bitten, twice shy

pain in the neck

pass the buck

raise one's game

silent but deadly

so close you can taste it

take it to the next level

the early bird catches the worm

thick as thieves

think outside the box

throw someone under the bus

till the fat lady sings

wild goose chase

work hard, play hard

worst nightmare

Some animals have a whole lexicon of clichés about them, such as dogs:

can't teach an old dog new tricks

dog days

every dog has its day

every dog is brave in his own yard

happy as a dog with two tails

let sleeping dogs lie

raining cats and dogs

sick as a dog

work like a dog

Besides the repetition factor, there's another reason to avoid clichés: they're often vague. Saying "You can't change horses in midstream" will probably not be as helpful to someone as specific advice.

> **USAGE TIDBIT**
>
> You can make a cliché sound fresh. One writing technique that's often successful is to vary the cliché. For example, "It's not what you know, it's who you know" is too old and tired to use as is, but you could write, "It's not what you know, it's who you marry" in an article on successful couples. This would allow you to take advantage of readers' knowledge of a cliché without repeating one mindlessly.

Avoiding Euphemisms—Most of the Time

Euphemisms have a bad reputation that is mostly deserved. Whenever a company talks about *downsizing* (firing employees), the government refers to *collateral damage* (civilian deaths), or a celebrity is hospitalized for *exhaustion* (drug problems), you can tell the truth is being smoothed over and obscured. Since clarity is one of the most important elements of writing, this alone is a great reason to avoid euphemisms. Also, many euphemisms tend to be clichés too—so they're both vague and worn out.

Here are some common euphemisms and their literal meanings:

assessment	test
challenges	disabilities
conflict	war
having financial issues	in debt
increase revenue	raise taxes
indulge	overeat
lady of the night	prostitute
laid off	fired
make love	have sex
misstatements	lies
passed away	died
with child	pregnant

Comedian George Carlin loved talking about euphemisms and how he thought they were harmful. In one routine, he talked about how the term *shellshock*—which once described the horrible toll of war on soldiers—was eventually renamed *battle fatigue,* then *post-traumatic stress disorder.* Each renaming added syllables while moving farther away from the grim reality of the condition.

I'm sure you can think of many more euphemisms yourself. Hint: there are many surrounding the topic of going to the bathroom, including "going to the bathroom" itself.

However, euphemisms aren't all bad. *Passed away* isn't as direct as *died,* but someone dealing with the death of a loved one deserves kinder and gentler words. Use euphemisms when you want to spare someone's feelings or just be tasteful.

For example, if someone suffered a horrible injury in a war (or anywhere for that matter) you might not want to draw attention to the specific nature of the injuries. Sometimes, being euphemistic is the right thing to do.

> **PRACTICAL POINT**
>
> Every year, the American Dialect Society picks a word of the year, along with other terms in categories such as Most Likely to Succeed and Most Unnecessary. One of the categories is Most Euphemistic, and over the years they've picked some doozies:
>
> hiking the Appalachian Trail: having an affair
>
> internal nutrition: a torture technique involving force-feeding
>
> daisy cutter: a bomb
>
> regime change: deposing or assassinating a foreign leader
>
> courtesy call: a telemarketer's unwanted call
>
> kinetic event: in Afghanistan, this is a term for a violent attack on U.S. troops
>
> badly sourced: untrue

Slang

Slang is difficult to define, but you can usually spot it when you see it, dude. In that sentence, *dude* is an example of slang.

Slang has a few qualities that distinguish it from other types of language. It tends to be humorous and informal. For example, calling someone's rolls of fat that stick out at the waist a *muffin top* is meant to be funny (and clever). One of the best books on slang—Michael Adams' *Slang: The People's Poetry*—focuses on the wild, creative, poetic aspects of slang.

Besides being creative, slang is social. It develops in specific groups. Teenagers—who are prolific generators of slang—don't use the same slang as adults or younger children. Different groups have their own slang, and slang is part of what makes them a group. If you speak the same way I do, it reinforces our connection.

For example, the difficult and deadly conditions of war have long made soldier slang a large language category. In the U.S. Civil War, to *skedaddle* was to retreat. Back in World War I, a *basket case* was a soldier who had lost all four limbs and needed to be carried in a basket. (Later, the term took on its current meaning, which refers to an extremely nervous person.)

Recent wars have also produced slang. In the Iraq War, *Mortaritaville* was any base that was constantly attacked; the name plays on the Jimmy Buffet song "Margaritaville," and the mortar is bombs. *Pope glass* referred to makeshift protection attached to a vehicle that looked like the windshield of the Popemobile. A *fobbit* was someone stationed at a forward operating base, also known as a FOB. *Fobbit* is a play on J. R. R. Tolkien's hobbits in more than just sound. The fobbits were thought to have it easier than soldiers who ventured away from the FOB, so fobbits were like hobbits, safe in the shire.

Jargon: Language Gets Professional

Jargon is slang's sibling who is all business.

The main meaning of *jargon* is the language of a profession. All professions have jargon, language that may be utterly meaningless to people outside the professional.

For example, the triangle offense—employed to such success by Coach Phil Jackson with the Chicago Bulls and Los Angeles Lakers—is part of the jargon of basketball. Another part of basketball jargon is calling player positions the 1, 2, 3, 4, and 5 (the point guard, shooting guard, small forward, power forward, and center, respectively). If you talked about how your 2 is making a play against the other team's 3 within the triangle, you'd better be talking to someone who knows their basketball. Otherwise, you'll mystify your audience.

There's a fine line between slang and jargon. Both create unity within groups, but since jargon is rooted to a profession, it has more practical uses. For example, some jargon consists of abbreviations that allow information to be relayed quickly. This can be helpful in professions that are dangerous (like being a police officer) or where speed is simply desirable (like being a waiter). The police term *APB* (all-points bulletin) is an example.

Be cautious when using slang and jargon in writing. Slang is most appropriate in speech, especially when talking to other members of the group that shares that slang. Some slang may also be okay in certain kinds of writing that are humorous or informal. However, if you use slang in a formal situation, it could make a terrible impression.

> **PRACTICAL POINT**
>
> There's another side to jargon. Often, the word *jargon* is used to mean language that is incomprehensible and also euphemistic. Business terms are notorious for this kind of odd, vague language. The TV show *30 Rock* made a brilliant spoof of business jargon when General Electric executive Jack Donaghy said he needed to *synergize backwards overflow*. That absurd, meaningless phrase has the same flavor of many real-life terms that are used to hide meaning rather than convey it.

Jargon poses different risks. While slang could be offensive to some people, jargon could just confuse them. Since the goal of writing is to communicate, you don't want to risk befuddling your readers (or listeners). Unless your audience is people who share the same jargon, you should put your ideas into words that are more likely to be understood. Assess your writing situation and use the most appropriate language.

Eggcorns: Mistakes That Make Sense

Do you feel bad about misspelling words? You really shouldn't. It happens to everyone sometimes, and making a mistake sometimes shows you're on the right track. Take the case of eggcorns.

An eggcorn is a linguistics term first discussed in 2003 on the popular linguistics blog *Language Log*. Simply put, an eggcorn is a spelling mistake that makes sense. For example, the word *eggcorn* itself came from a misspelling *of acorn*. If you didn't know how to spell *acorn*, but you knew what it was, *eggcorn* might seem right.

The following sentences all include eggcorns:

> For all intensive purposes, my brother is a bum.
>
> "Whoa is me!" said the depressed woman.
>
> You are star craving mad!
>
> I won't pay these exuberant prices.
>
> Without further adieu, I must leave.
>
> That's interesting, but it's a mute point.
>
> Be proactive and cease the opportunity.
>
> Why are you always so cautious and straight-laced?
>
> My vocal chords hurt.
>
> Some fashion trends are mind-bottling.

These sentences feature the correct spellings:

For <u>all intents and purposes</u>, my brother is a bum.

"<u>Woe is me</u>!" said the depressed woman.

You are <u>stark raving mad</u>!

I won't pay these <u>exorbitant prices</u>.

<u>Without further ado</u>, I must leave.

That's interesting, but it's a <u>moot point</u>.

Be proactive and <u>seize the opportunity</u>.

Why are you always so cautious and <u>strait-laced</u>?

My <u>vocal cords</u> hurt.

Some fashion trends are <u>mind-boggling</u>.

Do any of the eggcorns make more sense to you than the correct terms? It's logical to think a mind-boggling event could be mind-bottling, because when your mind is boggled, it can feel like it's been thrown in a bottle and swished around. A moot point doesn't matter, so it might as well be mute. Since chords produce music, why shouldn't we speak with vocal chords instead of vocal cords? The logic of the mistakes is why the mistakes occur.

Over time, some eggcorns become accepted variations or even replace the original word. For example, a chaise longue is a French type of chair, but generations of English speakers who know what a lounge is (but not a longue) have transformed the term into *chaise lounge*. The term *free rein* produced the eggcorn *free reign*, which makes sense because more people are familiar with a king's reign than a horse's reins. Both versions are found in print frequently, and *free reign* will probably be acceptable to everyone before long.

Language keeps changing, so make sure you consult a current dictionary to find the most accepted spelling of a word. It can also help to google a word. The spelling with the most hits isn't necessarily correct, but it will tell you something about how the word is being used.

DANGER ZONE

The following are 10 commonly confused groups of words that sound exactly or almost exactly alike. If you're not sure which one you mean, pull out your dictionary. It's better to look a word up now than (not *then*) look foolish later.

accept/except	presence/presents
advice/advise	than/then
affect/effect	there/their/they're
assure/ensure/insure	we're/were/where
conscience/conscious	you're/your

The Least You Need to Know

- Use a dictionary and thesaurus while writing to ensure you're using the appropriate words.
- Denotation is the strict meaning of a word, while connotation is the flavor or implication of a word.
- Be careful when using a thesaurus. This tool can lead to bizarre word choices if you don't use it alongside a dictionary.
- Slang is informal language that binds social groups, while jargon is the language of a profession. Both should be used with caution in your writing.
- Euphemisms hide or obscure meaning and should generally be avoided—except when you have a good reason to be vague.
- Eggcorns are spelling errors that make some sense.

Maintaining Parallel Structure

There are many ways to make your writing sound smooth and polished. You can read your work aloud. You can spend sufficient time editing. You can use appropriate word choices and strong verbs. As this chapter discusses, you can also use parallelism.

Parallelism is a way of structuring your sentences that makes them sound clean and clear. Notice that I didn't write, "Parallelism is a way of structuring your sentences that makes them sound clean and clearly." The combination "clean and clear" is parallel, since they are both the same type of word. Parallelism is all about using words with the same form and function to make the reading experience smooth and enjoyable.

Using parallel structure separates polished writers from casual writers. Once you learn the beauty of parallelism, you'll never want to write without it. You'll become addicted to writing strong sentences, pleasing phrases, and well-chosen words.

In This Chapter

- Making your writing clear with parallel structure
- How parallel structure helps you write a series
- Using parallelism to compare and contrast
- Using parallelism to make a memorable statement

Grasping the Concept of Parallel Structure

A good sentence should make sense, read well, and be clear. One way to accomplish this goal is by using parallel structure, which I did in the previous sentence.

In math, parallel lines go in the same direction and do not touch; they're next to each other but not intersecting. In grammar, a parallel sentence consists of phrases or words that have the same form, whether it's two halves of the sentence or the components of a series. Parallel structure is one of the easiest and most effective ways to make your writing sound clear and pleasant.

Writing a Series

One of the most frequent uses for parallelism is when writing a list or series. As discussed briefly in Chapter 1, all the items in a list should have the same form, like in these examples:

> I enjoy <u>swimming, boating, and camping</u>.

> Your father is <u>a saint and a gentleman</u>.

> My dog is <u>quick, smart, and short-haired</u>.

> The president has shown great wisdom in <u>foreign policy, environmental issues, and civil rights</u>.

> My favorite TV shows ever are <u>*Seinfeld, 30 Rock, The Shield,* and *Breaking Bad*</u>.

All those sentences sound smooth—or at least not jarring—because they use parallelism. The following are examples that lack parallelism:

> I enjoy <u>swimming, boating, and to eat fish.</u>

> Your father is <u>a saint and has great manners</u>.

> My dog is <u>quick, smart, and a rat terrier</u>.

> The president has shown great wisdom in <u>foreign policy, environmental issues, and debating issues</u>.

> My favorite TV shows ever are <u>*Seinfeld, 30 Rock, The Shield,* and reality shows</u>.

Those sentences sound a little off because the items are not all the same form. Good writers avoid this mistake.

Sometimes the forms may look very similar but aren't actually the same, which can fool you into thinking a nonparallel sentence is parallel. For example:

> Dan hates jogging, juggling, and going swimming.

The sentence should read:

Dan hates jogging, juggling, and swimming.

👉 **PRACTICAL POINT**

To write a parallel series, you need all the items to have the same form, but they don't need to be the same length. For example, the following is clearly parallel:

My uncle likes running, biking, and reading.

This sentence is also parallel:

My uncle likes running, biking, and reading mysteries.

It's not as perfectly parallel as the first example, but it still sounds much better than a nonparallel series. If you wanted to even out the phrases, you could write something like the following:

My uncle likes running long distances, biking competitively, and reading mysteries.

How parallel you like your parallelism is up to you.

Parallelism and Prepositional Phrases

Watch out for prepositions when writing a series. Sometimes the preposition can carry over the whole list, like this:

Today I need to go to the beach, the hairdresser, and the bank.

You could also write that in the following slightly more dramatic-sounding sentence:

Today I need to go to the beach, to the hairdresser, and to the bank.

Just make sure that whatever you do, you keep it consistent. The following would be a bad example:

Today I need to go to the beach, the hairdresser, and to the bank.

Although prepositions can trip you up, prepositional phrases are also commonly used in parallel sentences.

I went <u>to the store</u> and <u>for a walk</u>.

My cat likes to sit <u>on the couch</u>, <u>on the bed</u>, and <u>in a box</u>.

Have you looked <u>under the bed</u> and <u>in the drawer</u> for your keys?

I enjoy swimming <u>in the river</u> and <u>in pools</u>.

My favorite times of day are <u>after lunch</u> and <u>before bedtime</u>.

As with other examples, those sentences would sound terrible if the parallelism were removed, as in these poor examples:

I went <u>to the store</u> and <u>walking</u>.

My cat likes to sit <u>on the couch</u>, <u>on the bed</u>, and <u>Indian style</u>.

Have you looked <u>under the bed</u> and <u>northwest</u> for your keys?

I enjoy swimming <u>in the river</u> and <u>the backstroke</u>.

My favorite times of day are <u>after lunch</u> and <u>10:00 p.m.</u>

Parallelism is one of the easiest ways to make your sentences smooth and easy to read. Use it.

Practice

Look at the following sentences are indicate which ones use parallel construction. If they're not parallel, revise them accordingly.

1. This chimpanzee is good at grooming, making tools, and looking cute.

2. Reading comics and listening to music are fun.

3. The thief robs liquor stores, banks, and mugs people.

4. Most hairdressers will also trim eyebrows, shave beards, and validate parking.

5. The senator's duties include fundraising, legislating, and serving on committees.

6. I like coffee because it's hot, roasty, and wakes me up.

7. My rich aunt left me a gazebo, a tennis court, and warned me in her will never to travel to Australia.

8. People say you should never work with children, animals, or in a circus.

9. Al, Joe, and Brent are my friends.

10. Have you looked under the table, in the drawer, and on the floor?

Answers:

1. This chimpanzee is good at <u>grooming, making tools, and looking cute</u>. (Parallel: all three items are gerunds.)

2. <u>Reading comics and listening to music</u> are fun. (Parallel: both items are gerunds.)

3. The thief robs <u>liquor stores, banks, and mugs people</u>. (Not parallel: "mugs people" is a verb phrase while the other items are nouns.)

   Correct: The thief robs liquor stores, banks, and people.

4. Most hairdressers will also <u>trim eyebrows, shave beards, and validate parking</u>. (Parallel: all three items are verbs.)

5. The senator's duties include <u>fundraising, legislating, and serving on committees</u>. (Parallel: all three items are gerunds.)

6. I like coffee because it's <u>hot, roasty, and wakes me up</u>. (Not parallel: "wakes me up" is a verb phrase while the other items are adjectives.)

   Correct: I like coffee because it's hot, roasty, and stimulating.

7. My rich aunt left me <u>a gazebo, a tennis court, and warned me in her will never to travel to Australia</u>. (Not parallel: "warned me in her will never to travel to Australia" is a verb phrase while the other items are nouns.)

   Correct: My rich aunt left me a gazebo, a tennis court, and a warning never to travel to Australia.

8. They say you should never work with <u>children, animals, or in a circus</u>. (Not parallel: "in a circus" is a prepositional phrase while the other items are nouns.)

   Correct: They say you should never work with children, animals, or a circus.

9. <u>Al, Joe, and Brent</u> are my friends. (Parallel: all three items are nouns.)

10. Have you looked <u>under the table, in the drawer, and on the floor</u>? (Parallel: all three items are prepositional phrases.)

Parallelism and Résumés

Parallelism does more than make your sentences sound smoother: it can help you get a job.

On a résumé, you will usually have to list a serious of duties performed at a job, and it's important to use parallelism. Here's a bad example:

Summer Camp Counselor 1998–2004

- Led activities
- Cared for disabled children
- I was a supervisor
- Arts and crafts

Here's a better example, using parallelism:

Summer Camp Counselor 1998–2004

- Led activities
- Cared for disabled children
- Supervised other counselors
- Taught arts and crafts

By putting your duties in parallel form, you make them easier to read. When you're applying for a job, you need every edge you can get, so don't forget this basic of writing.

Using Coordinating Conjunctions

Parallelism helps you make a series sound smooth and clear, but it is also very useful when writing all sorts of sentences. Like a list, these examples use the coordinating conjunction *and:*

Eating and drinking are popular.

Ted and Nancy are my friends.

Spring and autumn are the mildest seasons.

Star Trek and *Star Wars* are both popular.

My mom and dad are nice people.

All of those sentences would sound weird if the material joined by *and* weren't parallel, as in these examples:

<u>Eating and beer</u> are popular.

<u>Ted and that woman</u> are my friends.

<u>Spring and September</u> are the mildest times of year.

<u>*Star Trek* and the movies of George Lucas</u> are both popular.

<u>My mom and Frank</u> are nice people.

Comparing and Contrasting Items

When you're comparing and contrasting two things, parallel construction is very handy—and easy—to use. The following examples all make comparisons while using parallelism:

Cat people are quirky; dog people are not.

Summer is blazing hot; winter is freezing cold.

Chickens are beautiful creatures. Turkeys are disgusting beasts.

Coffee wakes you up; beer puts you to sleep.

Friends come and go. Family stays and helps.

A famous book used this exact type of phrasing: *Men Are from Mars, Women Are from Venus.*

Using Correlative Conjunctions

Parallel structure gets a little trickier when it comes to correlative conjunctions. These involve words pairs such as:

both … and

either … or

neither … nor

not only … but also

Since correlative conjunctions are used to compare and contrast, you should use parallelism to make sure the items are in the same form. The following examples use parallelism:

> Summer makes me <u>both happy and sweaty</u>.

> My family is <u>neither rich nor famous</u>.

> I am <u>not only a bounty hunter, but also an interior decorator</u>.

> I would like <u>either the steak or the chicken</u>.

If the items were not the same form, these sentences would sound weird. Read the following examples that don't use parallelism:

> Summer makes me <u>both happy and I feel sweaty</u>.

> My family is <u>neither rich nor celebrities</u>.

> I am <u>not only a bounty hunter, but also I decorate homes</u>.

> I would like <u>either the steak or I'll try the chicken</u>.

Those sentences sound odd, right? They are jarring and distracting to readers. Avoid making your own readers uncomfortable by using parallelism whenever possible.

Practice

Identify which of the following sentences use or do not use parallelism correctly along with correlative conjunctions.

1. *Seinfeld* was neither funny nor about nothing.

2. Being a standup comic is neither easy nor rewarding.

3. I hate both people who yell on their cell phones and being hungry.

4. My brother is rich and famous.

5. My dog will roll either on grass or on the sidewalk.

6. I enjoy both math and writing essays.

7. My cat is neither friendly nor a calico.

8. Coffee is not only delicious, but also energizing.

9. Politics is neither fair nor pleasant.

10. In the morning, I enjoy both pancakes and waffles.

Answers:

1. *Seinfeld* was neither funny nor about nothing.

   (Not parallel: *funny* is an adjective and *about nothing* is a prepositional phrase.)

2. Being a standup comic is neither easy nor rewarding.

   (Parallel: *easy* and *rewarding* are both adjectives.)

3. I hate both people who yell on their cell phones and being hungry.

   (Not parallel: "people who yell on their cell phones" is a noun phase and "about being hungry" is a verb phrase.)

4. My brother is rich and famous.

   (Parallel: *rich* and *famous* are both adjectives.)

5. My dog will roll either on grass or on the sidewalk.

   (Parallel: "on grass" and "on the sidewalk" are both prepositional phrases.)

6. I enjoy both math and writing essays.

   (Not parallel: *math* is a noun and *writing essays* is a verb phrase.)

7. My cat is neither friendly nor a calico.

   (Not parallel: *friendly* is an adjective and *a calico* is a noun.)

8. Coffee is not only delicious, but also energizing.

   (Parallel: *delicious* and *energizing* are both adjectives.)

9. Politics is neither fair nor pleasant.

   (Parallel: *fair* and *pleasant* are both adjectives.)

10. In the morning, I enjoy both pancakes and waffles.

    (Parallel: *pancakes* and *waffles* are both nouns.)

The Least You Need to Know

- Parallelism helps you write clear, readable sentences.
- When writing a list or series, use parallelism; in other words, make the items all the same form.
- Parallelism can help you phrase many sentences; it is particularly effective in crafting memorable statements.
- Parallelism should be used when listing jobs and duties on a résumé.
- Parallelism is useful when comparing things. Use parallelism along with correlative conjunctions such as *both ... and.*

CHAPTER 14

Varying Sentence Structure

Obviously, grammar is important. If it wasn't important, this book and other grammar books wouldn't exist. If grammar didn't matter, you could throw down words in any order at all.

But here's a little secret: grammatically perfect writing can still be terrible. Grammar is an essential element of good writing, but it's only the first step. You could even think of it as a prerequisite for good writing. Your writing won't be good if you have grammar problems, but you can't be satisfied with your writing being grammatical and doing nothing else.

Why? Because good grammar will make your writing readable, but it won't make it interesting. Beyond grammar lies style. Good writers do more than make their nouns and verbs agree: they write intriguing sentences, flowing paragraphs, and crisp prose that make you want to keep reading. This chapter will share some tips on how to make your writing more stylish and enjoyable to read.

In This Chapter

- Why and how to vary your sentences
- The virtues of sentence variety
- Using conjunctions and punctuation to join choppy sentences
- Breaking up lengthy sentences with independent clauses

Rearranging Words and Phrases: Syntax

Syntax is the arrangement of words in a language. There are many, many ways you can rearrange a sentence. For example, here's a simple thought:

My dog has a Napoleon complex.

Here are several other ways you could say about the same thing:

My dog Wrigley has a Napoleon complex.

A Napoleon complex is something my dog has.

My dog has a Napoleon complex, so he's often barking at bigger dogs.

My dog is a feisty little guy.

You know who has a Napoleon complex? My dog.

My dog, who has a Napoleon complex, is often barking at bigger dogs.

I should've named my dog Napoleon instead of Wrigley.

Wrigley, why are you barking at that big dog?

Some of those sentences add information, such as the name of the dog, specific dog behaviors, or details of the Napoleon complex. Some of them move information around the sentence. Some use commas to set off information. The last example turns the sentence into a question.

This is a small sample of the options you have for rearranging sentences. As you learn the possibilities of English syntax, you'll get better at exploiting its infinite, Lego-like possibilities. Like Legos, the elements of English syntax are flexible, combinable, and sturdy; you can make many sentences out of the same building blocks.

 DEFINITION

In grammar, **syntax** refers to the way words, phrases, and clauses are arranged to form sentences.

Combining Short Sentences

Writers who are new to a language—or just a little inexperienced—often write a lot of short sentences. There's nothing wrong with short sentences per se, but too many of them can make your writing choppy. Read these sentences aloud and you might notice something wrong:

The sky is dark. It looks like rain. Can you feel the humidity? It's cloudy. That's a bummer.

Those sentences are fine from a grammatical standpoint, but from a style standpoint, there's a problem. All those short sentences are causing a lack of flow. In the following section, you'll learn some ways of combining sentences.

Using a Conjunction

One of the easiest ways to combine sentences is with a conjunction. Take the following:

> The sky is dark. It looks like rain.

To combine them, add a comma and conjunction:

> The sky is dark, and it looks like rain.

When two sentences—also known, grammatically, as independent clauses—are joined with a conjunction, a comma should precede the conjunction. Here are some other examples.

> I like cats. I'm allergic to them.

> I like cats, but I'm allergic to them.

> The con man sold bridges. The police were on his trail.

> The con man sold bridges, so the police were on his trail.

> I want to go on a date. I'm so nervous.

> I want to go on a date, but I'm so nervous.

Using a Semicolon

Instead of a comma and a conjunction, you can join sentences with a semicolon.

> The detective had a hunch. The killer was the bartender.

> The detective had a hunch; the killer was the bartender.

> The Buffalo Bills lost four Super Bowls in a row. That's a record.

> The Buffalo Bills lost four Super Bowls in a row; that's a record.

> Everyone loves Johnny Cash. His music appeals to young and old.

> Everyone loves Johnny Cash; his music appeals to young and old.

For more on semicolons, see Chapter 17.

Using a Colon

A colon can also be used to bring together short sentences. When a colon is used, the second element is usually a response or follow-up to the first.

> I love robots. I want one that can do my laundry.

> I love robots: I want one that can do my laundry.

> The moon landing was a fake. It was staged by Hollywood.

> The moon landing was a fake: it was staged by Hollywood.

> My birthday is always fun. I eat my weight in cake.

> My birthday is always fun: I eat my weight in cake.

For more on colons, see Chapter 17.

Using a Pronoun

As you see, short sentences can be joined by punctuation. However, that's not always enough. Consider the following sentences, which have been combined by a semicolon:

> Jim is a jerk. Jim stole my motorcycle.

> Jim is a jerk; Jim stole my motorcycle.

Even after combining the sentences, the second example doesn't sound much better than the first. Why not? Well, the repetition of *Jim* is a bit annoying. Writing *Jim* twice in the first five words is just too much. Thankfully, pronouns can solve this problem.

> Jim is a jerk; he stole my motorcycle.

Pronouns are a useful way of avoiding repetition when joining sentences—or even if you're not joining them. Just by replacing a proper noun with a pronoun, your writing will sound better.

> When Jack visits, I go out. I try to avoid Jack.

> When Jack visits, I go out. I try to avoid <u>him</u>.

> Jennifer bought me lunch. I think Jennifer likes me.

> Jennifer bought me lunch. I think <u>she</u> likes me.

> My dad is an astronaut. Once, my dad traveled to Mars.

> My dad is an astronaut. Once, <u>he</u> traveled to Mars.

When working with pronouns, make sure it's clear who they're referring to at all times. The following is fine.

> Claudia likes cupcakes. She eats one every day.

The reverse doesn't work:

> She likes cupcakes. Claudia eats one every day.

After reading that first sentence, the reader will think "Who? Who likes cupcakes?" Even though they might be able to figure it out from the next sentence, don't risk creating even a moment's confusion in readers. Here's an even worse example:

> Claudia and Beth like cupcakes. She eats one every day.

It's unclear who the second sentence is referring to: Who is *she?* It could be Claudia or Beth. Your pronouns should always have clear referents; if they don't, your writing will be unclear. When there's a pronoun-reference problem, revise until the problem is fixed or simply replace the pronoun with a noun.

Giving Long Sentences a Break

There isn't anything inherently bad about a long sentence. There isn't anything inherently good, either. While long sentences—if well-constructed and clear—can take the reader on an enjoyable ride, they can also lose the reader in a confusing tangle of words. For example, read the following:

> Long sentences are a huge problem, I mean, a really huge problem that can befuddle and confuse readers because the sentence just keeps going on and on; make sure to keep your sentences to a decent length or your readers will have trouble keeping up with your thoughts: this is a very important rule, and it should never be broken unless you have a very good reason, like if you were trying to write a bad example (this sentence, in case you didn't notice, is an absolutely terrible example that you should not imitate, okay?).

That's an absurd example; you probably wouldn't write such an enormous sentence naturally, but sometimes you might end up writing sentences that are longer than they should be.

Why do people write sentences that are too long? Sometimes it just happens as you draft and try to get your thoughts on paper. That's not a big problem: you can fix it as you revise. Hint: reading your work aloud is a great way to spot lengthy sentences, and by hearing your sentences aloud, it can help you figure out where to trim them.

Other people just have a tendency to write long sentences. If this is one of your habits, make a mental (or real) note to break up sentences when you get to the editing stage of writing.

Unfortunately, sometimes people write long sentences for the same reason they think they should use long words: they're trying to sound smart. This is a terrible idea. Your goal should be to communicate, not make yourself look smart. Focus on communicating in the smoothest and most direct way possible.

Don't try to look smart. Just try to communicate clearly, which *is* smart.

Trimming the Fat

Just as you have many options for bringing short sentences together, you have many options for pulling long sentences apart. In fact, let's work with a slightly longer sentence you just read:

Just as you have many options for bringing short sentences together, you have many options for pulling long sentences apart.

You could make two sentences:

> You have many options for bringing short sentences together. You also have many options for pulling long sentences apart.

You could use different language that is also more concise:

> There are many ways to combine and separate sentences.

Often, you can trim sentences by identifying unnecessary words. How do you know which words are unnecessary? See if some are repeating the same information. Here's another example.

> I hate going to baseball games; they're so boring that I have a terrible time.

In that sentence, *hate* and *terrible time* are very similar ideas, since terrible times are hated by everyone. *Boring* is different information, since it's a reason why this person dislikes baseball. This sentence could be trimmed (or rewritten) in a few ways that eliminate redundant information:

> I hate going to baseball games; they're so boring.

> Baseball is so boring that I have a terrible time.

> I can't stand the boring game of baseball.

Varying Sentence Types

If you vary the length of sentences, your writing should have good sentence variety. However, there is a more technical way to look at this issue: you should vary the sentence types in your writing.

As discussed in Chapter 1, there are four basic sentence types: simple, compound, complex, and compound-complex.

The following are simple sentences, which consist of only independent clauses:

> The dog is sick.
>
> I love eating pizza.
>
> Politics is a snakepit.

Compound sentences have two independent clauses:

> The dog is sick; he barfed on the rug.
>
> I love eating pizza, but I hate eating mushrooms.
>
> Politics is a snakepit; it attracts sociopaths.

In complex sentences, there is one independent clause along with a dependent clause.

> The dog is sick, which has ruined my plans for the day.
>
> I love eating pizza with anybody except my sister.
>
> Politics is a snakepit that has ruined America.

To make a compound-complex sentence, you need two independent clauses and at least one subordinate clause.

> The dog is sick, which has ruined my plans for the day; I had to cancel everything.
>
> I love eating pizza with anybody except my sister; she is a terrible person.
>
> Politics is a snakepit that has ruined America, and there has to be a better way.

If your writing sounds repetitive, vary the types as well as the lengths of sentences.

Varying Sentence Beginnings

There's more to sentence variety than just length and type of sentence: how sentences begin is important, too. For example, take this paragraph about an author named Swinnea:

> Swinnea's work is a remarkable commentary on the chicken industry. Swinnea shows the inner workings of chicken farms, as well as the politics of chicken-based restaurants. Swinnea's writing style is humorous, though it always has a strong sense of purpose. Swinnea has become the leading authority on chickens and other barnyard fowl.

Notice anything wrong? Every sentence starts with Swinnea: Swinnea, Swinnea, Swinnea, Swinnea. Starting too many sentences the same way is sure to annoy readers. When you notice that too many sentences are beginning the same way, revise to add variety:

> Swinnea's work is a remarkable commentary on the chicken industry. He shows the inner workings of chicken farms, as well as the politics of chicken-based restaurants. In "Chicken-ology," Swinnea's writing style is humorous, though it always has a strong sense of purpose. Through his impressive work on the subject, Swinnea has become the leading authority on chickens and other barnyard fowl.

Swinnea is still a huge part of the paragraph, but his name isn't the beginning of every sentence like before. Now the paragraph is a better read.

> **DANGER ZONE**
>
> You should make sure that every paragraph of a paper doesn't start in the same way. Beginning every paragraph (or many paragraphs) with the same word or type of phrase shows a lack of creativity—and can drive your readers bonkers.

The Virtues of Variety

You may ask yourself: Why am I rearranging all these sentences anyway? Why can't I just write a sentence and leave it be?

Sorry, writing doesn't work like that. First drafts are rarely good enough: writing is mostly revising. Most elements of your work will change as you revise, edit, and proofread. The structure of your sentences is one of the aspects of writing that is easiest—and most important—to change.

Let's say you have a short paragraph about your cat.

> Mr. Pinkerton is a good cat. I got him at the pound.
>
> He is a calico. He sleeps with me. He hates my brother. The feeling is mutual. My brother is allergic.

Notice anything wrong? While the sentences are all grammatical, they're also painfully short. A short sentence is fine, but seven short sentences in a row is a style problem. You need to mix it up. Here's a second draft with some sentences combined:

> Mr. Pinkerton is a good cat. I got him at the pound.
>
> He is a calico who sleeps with me. He hates my brother, and the feeling is mutual. My brother is allergic to cats.

In that paragraph, some of the short sentences have been combined, and a little detail (about the cat allergy) has been added. Still, this is not a great paragraph. Most of the sentences are still very short and choppy. Let's try adding detail and length to more of the sentences:

> Mr. Pinkerton is a good cat—the best cat I've ever had. I got him at the pound six years ago, and my life hasn't been the same since. Mr. Pinkerton is a calico who sleeps with me. He hates my brother, and the feeling is mutual. My brother is allergic to cats.

The paragraph is starting to improve. There's more sentence variety, and only the last sentence is extremely short. Now that this tiny sentence follows some longer sentences, it's effective rather than repetitive.

However, the paragraph still jumps around. How did we get from this great cat to the conflict with the brother? That's an abrupt transition. This should probably be two paragraphs, since every paragraph should develop one idea and one idea only. It's time to revise again, adding details and depth:

> Mr. Pinkerton is a good cat—the best cat I've ever had. I got him at the pound six years ago, and my life hasn't been the same since. This beautiful calico sleeps with me and follows me around my apartment, almost like a dog. We're inseparable.

> There's only one problem—Mr. Pinkerton hates my brother. When my brother Jim stops by, Mr. Pinkerton hisses and tries to scratch him. Other times, Mr. Pinkerton hides until Jim goes away. Since Jim is allergic to cats, the dislike is mutual; this situation is straining my relationship with my brother.

Now we're getting somewhere. The separate ideas about the cat and the conflict have been given their own paragraphs and developed further. Both paragraphs have sentence variety: we're a long way from those teeny-weeny sentences.

This is just the beginning of the process for these paragraphs. If they're part of a personal essay, school paper, letter, or work of fiction, they could end up changing many more times, depending on what's appropriate for the larger piece of writing. They might also be cut if the writer realizes they're not necessary.

This is an important lesson for writers: don't get too attached to what you write. You'll always have to make changes, and you'll often have to cut. However, there is a bright side: words are cheap, and you can always write more.

The Least You Need to Know

- Too many short sentences will make your writing choppy and annoying to read; combine them with conjunctions, semicolons, and colons.
- Use pronouns to avoid repeating the name of the subject in sentences.
- Long sentences are also a problem: they can be difficult to read and can confuse readers. Communicate your ideas clearly.
- Your writing will have variety with a mix of sentence types: simple, compound, complex, and compound-complex.
- Revising sentences is a part of writing well, so leave yourself enough time to proofread and revise your work.

Avoiding and Fixing Common Errors

Nobody's perfect, especially when it comes to language. We all make mistakes when writing, and there are a lot of types of writing errors: spelling problems, agreement problems, improper capitalization, and so on. Fortunately, some mistakes happen a lot more often than others.

Why "fortunately"? Well, imagine if there were no consistency to writing errors. Imagine if the 200 most common errors all occurred with the same frequency. This would be a nightmare. How could you work on 200 problems that are all equally important? You can't.

The good news is that there are definitely writing errors that happen more often than others, and your writing will benefit from knowing them. Awareness of the most common errors will give you a better a chance of avoiding them.

Awareness is the first step to addressing any problem, and once you get a handle of these common writing problems, your writing will improve.

In This Chapter

- How to fix sentence fragments
- Repairing run-on sentences and comma splices
- Clarifying pronoun reference
- Avoiding dangling metaphors
- Keeping your subject and verb in agreement

Repairing Broken Sentences

There are many ways to write a good sentence. Unfortunately, there are also many ways a sentence can go wrong. In this chapter, I'll discuss a few of the most common grammatical mistakes and how to fix them.

Defragmenting a Fragmented Sentence

A complete sentence (or independent clause) has a subject and verb and expresses a complete thought. If a sentence doesn't have a subject and verb—and, therefore, doesn't convey a complete thought—it's a sentence fragment. The following are typical examples of sentence fragments that often appear in inexperienced writers' papers:

Which meant the movie was terrible.

The man who I saw in the alley.

Running across the tarmac.

In the dresser beside the fancy-looking bed.

Who I later learned was my father.

Some of those sentences are dependent clauses: for example, "Who I later learned was my father" has a subject and a verb—like all clauses—but it doesn't express a complete thought. Others, like—"Running across the tarmac"—don't have a subject and verb (it's a verb phrase). Either way, when you treat a phrase or dependent clause as a sentence, you end up with a sentence fragment.

The main problem with sentence fragments is that they leave the reader hanging in some way. They raise questions. Here are those fragments again, with some of the questions they raise:

Which meant the movie was terrible.

What exactly meant the movie was terrible?

The man who I saw in the alley.

What about him?

Running across the tarmac.

Who was running? Why?

In the dresser beside the fancy-looking bed.

What's in the dresser? Also, why should I care?

Who I later learned was my father.

Who is this man? Again, why should I care?

This is the opposite effect you want to have on your readers. Don't make your readers ask questions; make everything clear.

The Positive Side of Sentence Fragments

Writing is all about exceptions, and you'll probably notice that published writers use sentence fragments a lot. Quite a lot, actually. In fact, I just used one in the previous sentence.

There's no need to entirely avoid sentence fragments, but here are a couple things to remember about using them:

Always be aware of what's a sentence fragment. If you don't know you're using a fragment, chances are it will not work well in your writing.

Use fragments sparingly. Writers who are skilled enough to use a sentence fragment intentionally also know a little goes a long way. Don't get fragment-happy. Okay?

Make sure the fragment doesn't cause confusion. If the fragment puzzles readers, it's a mistake. Only use an intentional fragment if you're sure it will be clear and understandable to readers.

Practice

For the following examples, state whether each group of words is a fragment or a complete sentence/thought. Hint: don't be fooled by the length of the sentence or fragment.

1. The bird chirped.

2. Zebras ran.

3. Which went against everything he believed in since he was a boy.

4. The coffee shop is busy.

5. The restaurant by the side of the road, near the hotel.

6. Who is that dog?

7. In Las Vegas.

8. Who I'll never forget as long as I live.

9. A job for a man like you.

10. A book takes a long time to write.

Answers:

1. The bird chirped.

   (Complete sentence.)

2. Zebras ran.

   (Complete sentence.)

3. Which went against everything he believed in since he was a boy.

   (Fragment: this is only a dependent clause.)

4. The coffee shop is busy.

   (Complete sentence.)

5. The restaurant by the side of the road, near the hotel.

   (Fragment: this is only a noun phrase.)

6. Who is that dog?

   (Complete sentence.)

7. In Las Vegas.

   (Fragment: this is only a prepositional phrase.)

8. Whom I'll never forget as long as I live.

   (Fragment: this is only a noun clause.)

9. A job for a man like you.

   (Fragment: this is only a noun phrase.)

10. A book takes a long time to write.

    (Complete sentence.)

Repairing a Run-On Sentence

The run-on sentence is a common problem and a relatively easy one to fix. Here's an example of a run-on sentence:

   The dog barked the cat ran.

Are you surprised that such a short sentence is a run-on? Run-on sentences don't have to be long, even though many are. To be a run-on sentence, all you need are two or more independent clauses smashed together ungrammatically, without a conjunction or proper punctuation to connect them. Just as a fragment can be long, a run-on can be short.

Fixing a Comma Splice

The comma splice is another common error—and also a comma error. It happens when two independent clauses are linked with a comma, as in the following examples:

> I ran, the cops followed.

> The grass is green, the sky is blue.

> Weather is unpredictable, watching the Weather Channel is silly.

Those are all examples of comma splices. They can be fixed by replacing the commas with semicolons, like so:

> I ran; the cops followed.

> The grass is green; the sky is blue.

> Weather is unpredictable; watching the Weather Channel is silly.

They can also be fixed by making the independent clauses into separate sentences. Though this option could make your writing a little choppy, it can also give it a punchy, dramatic effect when used sparingly.

> I ran. The cops followed.

> The grass is green. The sky is blue.

> Weather is unpredictable. Watching the Weather Channel is silly.

You could also add a coordinating conjunction that makes sense in the sentence:

> I ran, and the cops followed.

> The grass is green, and the sky is blue.

> Weather is unpredictable, so watching the Weather Channel is silly.

Practice

For the following sentences, identify the comma splice or run-on sentence and then fix the problem. Watch out for sentences that have no grammatical problems.

1. Basketball is fun, especially the last few minutes.

2. Baseball is stupid, I hate it.

3. Concussions are a huge problem in football too many players are suffering.

4. Golf is difficult I don't know why anyone plays it.

5. Tennis is my favorite sport to watch.

6. Pro wrestling is fake, but it's still very dangerous.

7. Bowling is sometimes on TV can you believe that?

8. Soccer is the popular sport in the world, it's especially beloved in Europe.

9. Lacrosse is played with a stick.

10. Mixed martial arts is very popular, people love it.

11. Softball is a major summer sport my sister plays it.

12. There have been many great books about boxing.

13. Billiards is my favorite sport, I like that you can play it till you're old.

14. I'm terrible at ping pong I'm better at pinball.

15. My dad will watch any sports as long as there's a ball and/or some violence.

Answers:

1. Basketball is fun, especially the last few minutes.

   (No grammar problems.)

2. Baseball is stupid, I hate it.

   (Comma splice. Change to: "Baseball is stupid; I hate it.")

3. Concussions are a huge problem in football too many players are suffering.

   (Run-on sentence. Change to: "Concussions are a huge problem in football. Too many players are suffering.")

4. Golf is difficult I don't know why anyone plays it.

    (Run-on sentence. Change to: "Golf is difficult. I don't know why anyone plays it.")

5. Tennis is my favorite sport to watch.

    (No grammar problems.)

6. Pro wrestling is fake, but it's still very dangerous.

    (No grammar problems.)

7. Bowling is sometimes on TV can you believe that?

    (Run-on sentence. Change to: "Bowling is sometimes on TV. Can you believe that?")

8. Soccer is the popular sport in the world, it's especially beloved in Europe.

    (Comma splice. Change to "Soccer is the popular sport in the world—it's especially beloved in Europe.")

9. Lacrosse is played with a stick.

    (No grammar problems.)

10. Mixed martial arts is very popular, people love it.

    (Comma splice. Change to "Mixed martial arts is very popular; people love it.")

11. Softball is a major summer sport my sister plays it.

    (Run-on sentence. Change to: "Softball is a major summer sport. My sister plays it.")

12. There have been many great books about boxing.

    (No grammar problems.)

13. Billiards is my favorite sport, I like that you can play it till you're old.

    (Comma splice. Change to: "Billiards is my favorite sport. I like that you can play it till you're old.")

14. I'm terrible at ping pong I'm better at pinball.

    (Run-on sentence. Change to: "I'm terrible at ping pong. I'm better at pinball.")

15. My dad will watch any sports as long as there's a ball and/or some violence.

    (No grammar problems.)

Clarifying the Relationship Between Ideas

There are two main ways that ideas are linked in writing: coordination and subordination. You can think of coordination as a marriage of equals and subordination as a boss and an employee. It's important not to confuse the two.

Coordination

Coordination involves linking two things together in a sentence. Coordination usually involves a coordinating conjunction, and it often occurs with the word *and:* one of the most useful, common words in English. Coordination can also occur with punctuation such as the semicolon or colon. The following are examples of coordination:

> The lady wept, and the gentleman bowed.
>
> I'm tired; I need a nap.
>
> Hold my hand; I'm depressed.
>
> The sky is overcast, and there's a chill in the air.
>
> I'm having a bad day, but I think it will get better.

You should also note that coordination links independent clauses. Coordination brings together grammatical equals who could stand on their own.

Subordination

In *subordination,* there are not two grammatical equals: there are an independent clause and a subordinate clause. The following sentences, which use subordination, consist of one dependent clause and one independent clause. The dependent clauses are underlined:

> <u>When I was younger</u>, I was quite an athlete.
>
> I hate <u>that I get nervous when driving</u>.
>
> <u>Because it's raining</u>, the baseball game is canceled.
>
> I respect the man <u>who I thought was my father</u>.

See how what's not underlined is still a complete thought? The combination of that independent clause plus a dependent clause is what makes subordination work.

> **DEFINITION**
>
> **Coordination** brings together two independent clauses to make a sentence.
> **Subordination** brings together an independent clause and a dependent clause to make a sentence.

Practice

In the following sentences, note whether coordination or subordination is used.

1. When hitchhiking in the country, you should carry a gun.

2. There's no one I love more than the girl I met in 1986.

3. Because of various circumstances, I have decided to resign as CEO.

4. In spring, I go hiking, and in fall, I go hiking, too.

5. No one knows what I've gone through.

6. I like ice cream; I also like gelato.

7. Though many are fighting it, America is becoming an obese nation.

8. I'm not sure when I realized that my own brother is a thief.

9. I have to tell you one thing: unfortunately, I forgot what that thing is.

10. You disgust me because of the crimes you have committed.

11. I sprained my ankle, and I scraped my knee.

12. I'm very patriotic; I love this country so much.

13. I'd like to go to the party, but I don't have time.

14. When I get a chance, I will go see your play.

15. I overheard your mom; she was talking about my mom.

Answers:

1. When hitchhiking in the country, you should carry a gun. (Subordination.)

2. There's no one I love more than the girl I met in 1986. (Subordination.)

3. Because of various circumstances, I have decided to resign as CEO. (Subordination.)

4. In spring, I go hiking, and in fall, I go hiking, too. (Coordination.)

5. No one knows what I've gone through. (Subordination.)

6. I like ice cream; I also like gelato. (Coordination.)

7. Though many are fighting it, America is becoming an obese nation. (Subordination.)

8. I'm not sure when I realized that my own brother is an organ thief. (Subordination.)

9. I have to tell you one thing: unfortunately, I forgot what that thing is. (Coordination.)

10. You disgust me because of the crimes you have committed. (Subordination.)

11. I sprained my ankle, and I scraped my knee. (Coordination.)

12. I'm very patriotic; I love this country so much. (Coordination.)

13. I'd like to go to the party, but I don't have time. (Coordination.)

14. When I get a chance, I will go see your play. (Subordination.)

15. I overheard your mom; she was talking about my mom. (Coordination.)

Clarifying Pronoun References

As mentioned in Chapter 5, pronoun antecedents are an important part of writing. Always make sure your pronouns have clear antecedents.

Incorrect: He is a banker. He makes a lot of money.

Correct: Mike is my friend. He's a banker.

In the incorrect example, it's unclear who *he* is. You have to make this clear through revision. Here's another pair:

Incorrect: Jill is funny. Jane is serious. She is also an actor.

Correct: Jill is funny. Jane is serious. Jane is also an actor.

In the incorrect example, you might guess that Jane is the actor, because *Jane* is closer to *she* than *Jill*, but this isn't totally clear.

Don't make your reader wonder, "Who does the pronoun refer to?" Make it obvious.

Fixing Misplaced and Dangling Modifiers

A dangling modifier is a phrase that begins a sentence but does not clearly refer to the subject of the sentence. Dangling modifiers create confusion. These are some examples:

> Slowly cooling off, I took a sip of the coffee.

> Trudging through the snow, the weather got worse and worse.

> Cowering behind the couch, the fireworks terrified my dog.

See the problem? In the second example, the sentence starts with "Trudging through the snow," which must refer to a person. However, the subject of the sentence is "the weather." This mismatch is a classic dangling modifier. The following are revisions of those sentences that are clearer:

> As the coffee slowly cooled off, I took a sip.

> The weather got worse and worse as I trudged through the snow.

> Cowering behind the couch, my dog was terrified of the fireworks.

As you can see, you have many options for how to rearrange a sentence. Look at Chapter 9 for more information on phrases and how they can be moved around grammatically.

Avoiding Shifts in Subject and Verb Forms

Remember the seven Cs? Consistency was one of them. A common inconsistency in writing is when the subject or verb shifts in a piece of writing.

As discussed in Chapter 1, it's very important for verbs to stay consistent, particularly in terms of tense. If you're writing about the past, stay in the past. Don't be a time traveler when writing unless absolutely necessary.

It's also important for your subjects to remain consistent. For instance, you need to use two hands when shooting a basketball. If you don't use two hands, your shot will miss the mark.

See how confusing that was? After pages and pages of giving writing advice, I suddenly gave advice on how to shoot a basketball. That's jarring and off-putting.

You also need to be aware of smaller, subtler shifts in your subject that can startle readers. Often this has to do with the purpose of a piece of writing. If you're supposed to be analyzing a topic and suddenly start giving the reader advice, that's a problem. You need to stay on point and maintain a consistent point of view and purpose.

The Least You Need to Know

- Sentence fragments are not complete sentences; they are either incomplete thoughts or they lack a subject and/or verb.

- A run-on sentence is two or more independent clauses jammed together improperly, with no conjunction or appropriate punctuation connecting them.

- A comma splice is two independent clauses linked with a comma instead of a period, a semicolon, or a comma and conjunction.

- Make sure your pronouns have clear antecedents—don't make the reader struggle to figure them out.

- Keep your subjects and verbs in agreement, and keep your verb tenses consistent.

CHAPTER 16

Avoiding Sexism, Bias, and Other No-No's

There are many different types of people in this world, and it's important to address them respectfully. Since language is always changing, and terms for different groups of people also change, it's important to be careful and vigilant when referring to someone's gender, race, religion, or other status.

If you can remember a time when someone insulted you, deliberately or accidentally, you'll get a sense for how people feel when they're described with offensive language. The offense is much greater when someone is part of a group that has been discriminated against for years.

You must choose your words carefully when writing about a controversial topic or referring to specific groups of people. You don't want to inadvertently offend a reader by describing them in language that's out-of-date or insensitive.

In other words, you need to write in a way that's inoffensive. In this chapter, you'll learn how to write without bias.

In This Chapter

- Promoting gender equality in language
- Choosing the right racial and ethnic terms
- Remaining sensitive to labels
- Avoiding the temptation to overgeneralize

Maintaining Sex and Gender Equality

Women have long fought for equality, and this ongoing battle isn't restricted to achieving equal opportunities, equal pay, and mutual respect in the real world. Understandably, women also demand equal treatment in language. After all, how we talk about men and women influences how we treat them, and we want to treat everyone with respect.

Unfortunately, the English language provides no quick and easy solution for formulating sex- and gender-neutral expressions, especially when it comes to choosing pronouns. The old-school approach of using the pronoun *he* exclusively to refer back to a noun that has no specific sex or gender, such as *customer* or *technician*, is sexist. However, using *he or she* and *him or her* throughout a passage is tedious and annoys the reader. So what's a writer to do?

The goal is to maintain sex and gender equality without calling attention to the fact that you're doing so. To achieve this goal, you need to think creatively and employ a mix of several different strategies, as explained in the following sections.

> **DEFINITION**
>
> What's the difference between sex and gender? **Sex** refers to biology—whether an individual is physically a man or a woman. **Gender**, on the other hand, refers to certain traits commonly associated with one of the sexes. Think of the difference in terms of woman/man (sex) versus feminine/masculine (gender).

Choosing Sexless Nouns

The first and most obvious way to maintain sex and gender neutrality in your writing is to choose nouns that convey no sex or gender identity; for example, instead of using *policeman*, use *police officer*. The following table provides a list of gender-specific terms followed by their non-gender-specific alternatives.

Nonsexist Noun Substitutes

Sexist Noun	Nonsexist Substitute
actress	actor
businessman or businesswoman	business person/people, executive, manager, merchant, entrepreneur, people in business
cameraman, camerawoman	photographer or videographer
chairman, chairwoman	chairperson or chair
congressman, congresswoman	representative, congressional representative, member of congress, or congressperson

Sexist Noun	Nonsexist Substitute
craftsman	craftsperson or artisan
fireman	firefighter
hostess	host
manmade	synthetic
newsman, newswoman	newscaster; reporter
policeman, policewoman	police officer or law enforcement officer
salesman or saleswoman	salesperson or sales representative
stewardess	flight attendant
waiter, waitress	server
weatherman	weather forecaster

USAGE TIDBIT

If you're having trouble coming up with a suitable substitute, consult a thesaurus. You can find one online at thesaurus.com.

Dealing with the He/She Dilemma

One of the most frustrating issues writers deal with on a daily basis involves covering the two sexes fairly when using the pronouns *he, she, her, him,* and so on. Writing something like "A doctor generally prescribes what he believes is the most effective medication" is sexist. After all, the medical profession has plenty of female doctors.

So what's the solution? Well, you have several options. One option, not necessarily the most attractive one, is to use both the masculine and feminine pronouns:

> A doctor often chooses what <u>he or she</u> believes is the most effective medication.

This solution has two drawbacks:

Wordiness: The repetition of *he or she* results in extra words that burden the reader, especially if dual pronouns are used frequently.

Favoritism: Whichever gender you mention first gets preferential treatment. To counter this, you must flip the order of the pronouns half the time.

To overcome these issues, someone came up with the notion of dividing the two pronouns with a slash (*he/she*) or using the unisex pronoun *s/he*. Neither of these solutions has caught on, thank goodness.

One of the easiest ways around the sexist pronoun dilemma is to make everyone plural:

> <u>Doctors</u> generally prescribe what <u>they</u> believe are the most effective <u>medications</u>.

By making everyone plural, you can then refer to them using the gender-neutral pronouns *they, them,* and *their.* Problem solved. Unfortunately, this isn't always a viable option.

Sometimes, you can simply drop the pronoun:

> A doctor generally prescribes ~~what he believes is~~ the most effective medication.

In this particular example, dropping the pronoun also results in dropping the verb *believes,* which alters the meaning. Here's an example in which dropping the pronoun doesn't change the meaning:

> **Sexist:** Every student determines the most efficient way <u>she can</u> study.

> **Neutral:** Every student determines the most efficient way <u>to</u> study.

Another way to avoid sexism in pronoun use is to replace the pronoun with an article. Here are a couple examples:

> **Sexist:** A police officer may choose whether to arrest <u>his</u> suspect.

> **Neutral:** A police officer may choose whether to arrest <u>the</u> suspect.

> **Sexist:** Every weather forecaster knows to check <u>her</u> current weather map prior to broadcast.

> **Neutral:** Every weather forecaster knows to check <u>a</u> current weather map prior to broadcast.

Sometimes, writers simply repeat the noun, which, by definition, gets repetitive; for example:

> A <u>doctor</u> generally prescribes what the <u>doctor</u> believes is the most effective medication.

Keep repeating that noun over and over again, and you'll need that medicine yourself.

A quick and easy way to avoid gender-specific pronouns is to address the reader as *you*. Here's an example:

> **Sexist:** A police officer may choose whether to arrest <u>his</u> suspect.

> **Neutral:** As a police officer, <u>you</u> may choose whether to arrest a suspect.

Of course, this approach is rarely an option. If you're writing a how-to manual for police officers, addressing the reader directly is appropriate. However, if you're writing an article about police procedures for a general audience, you need to explore other options.

Sometimes, you can revise your way out of a potentially sexist statement, usually with the use of a relative pronoun. Here's an example:

> **Sexist:** When an employee passes the certification test, <u>he</u> is eligible for a promotion.

> **Neutral:** An employee <u>who passes the certification test </u>is eligible for a promotion.

One relatively common practice is to alternate the use of pronouns. If you're writing a nonfiction book, for example, you could use *he* and *she* in alternating chapters or in alternating sections within each chapter. This approach has two drawbacks:

You must keep score. The goal is to include equal coverage, so ideally, your text should include an equal number of references to male and female roles. Achieving this goal is pretty easy in a paragraph, but when you're dealing with long articles or book-length works, it is nearly impossible.

You must still avoid bias. If you end up referring to most managers as *he* and most employees as *she* or to most police officers as *she* and most criminals as *he*, you have a problem. You need to provide balanced coverage.

Fortunately, there's a better solution to English's gender pronoun problems: *they*. Though *they* is most commonly used as a plural pronoun, it can also be used as a gender-neutral pronoun. Here's an example:

> **Sexist:** When an employee passes the certification test, <u>he</u> is eligible for a promotion.

> **Neutral:** When an employee passes the certification test, <u>they</u> are eligible for a promotion.

Some people dislike this usage, since it takes a plural pronoun and makes it singular. However, using *they* as singular is nothing new. The *Oxford English Dictionary* has examples of *they* used as a singular pronoun going back to the 1500s. Since this usage is established in the language and solves a huge problem, you should go ahead and use *they, them,* and *their* as singular. I suspect the voices of people who dislike it will get quieter with time.

PRACTICAL POINT

Grammar rules are like laws: if enough people break the rule for good reason, the rule eventually changes to accommodate popular sentiment. For example, too many people drank alcohol for its prohibition to work. If masses of people ignore or alter a grammar rule, that rule will eventually change or disappear, too.

Practice

Revise the following sentences, using the specified approach along with choosing sexless nouns, when necessary, to make each statement gender neutral:

1. Each stewardess must wash her hands before serving drinks to passengers. (pluralize pronoun)

   _____

2. Every policeman should alternate his time between desk work and patrol. (drop pronoun)

   _____

3. Whenever a student misses class, she should obtain makeup work from her teachers. (use both)

   _____

4. Whenever a driver receives three moving violations, she must complete the operator retraining program. (rewrite)

   _____

5. Each manager should treat his employees with respect. (address reader)

   _____

6. A student should always respect his elders. (use plural pronoun as singular)

   _____

Answers:

1. Flight attendants must wash their hands before serving drinks to passengers.

2. Every police officer should alternate time between desk work and patrol.

3. Whenever a student misses class, he or she should obtain makeup work from his or her teachers.

4. A (or Any) driver who receives three moving violations must complete the operator retraining program.

5. As a manager, you should treat your employees with respect.

6. A student should always respect their elders.

Calling People What They Want to Be Called

Few people would want to use ethnic or racial slurs to intentionally demean individuals or groups. But if you're not very careful, you could write in an offensive way by choosing the wrong terminology to describe an individual or a group. Referring to someone over 65 as *elderly*, for example, might offend that person even if you meant no harm.

The five most important rules to follow to avoid biased language are these:

Make distinctions only when necessary. If you can convey the same meaning without mentioning that the person was a gay male, a Japanese businessman, or one of the older managers, omit such details.

Call people what they want to be called. If you're unsure what the preferred term is, look it up. If you're still unsure, ask a few members of the group you're describing which terms they deem most acceptable.

Be specific. Specificity keeps you out of trouble. For example, you're better off describing someone from Japan as *Japanese* than using the more general term *Asian*. Likewise, indicating a specific age or range is preferable to using a general term, such as *adolescent* or *older person*.

Avoid inaccurate generalizations … and almost all generalizations are inaccurate. Don't ascribe certain traits or behaviors to certain groups unless *every single person* in the group exhibits those traits and behaviors. See "Avoiding Generalizations and Absolutes" later in this chapter for details.

Be careful when grouping people. Here's a dangerous sentence: "We need to keep guns out of the hands of dangerous people, including convicted felons and people with severe mental illness." That sentence implies that all people with severe mental illness are dangerous, which clearly isn't the case. Don't let a sloppy sentence slander a whole group of people; revise till your writing is fair.

In the following sections, I go into a little more detail on how to avoid bias when you have to distinguish people by race, ethnicity, age, sexual identity or orientation, or medical or physical conditions.

 DANGER ZONE

The term *politically correct* (PC) is often used to describe language that likely won't offend anyone; language that isn't loaded. Ironically, the term *politically correct* has become loaded itself. It's often used insultingly for terms that go too far in softening language: many see the term as encouraging euphemistic, dishonest language. It's fine to abandon the term politically correct altogether and stick with more specific terms, such as fair and unbiased. If you're fair and unbiased, you don't have to worry about political correctness at all.

Avoiding Racial and Ethnic Bias

Choosing the best terms to describe people by race and ethnicity is difficult, especially given the fact that so many people, especially in the United States, are of more than one race and/or ethnicity. Here are a few guidelines to follow:

If you mention one person's race or ethnicity, mention everyone's. For example, instead of writing "Of the 250 students, only 25 were black," you might write, "Of the 250 students, 25 were black, 175 were white, and 50 were Latino."

The terms *black* and *African American* are both generally acceptable, with the preference varying depending on your audience.

The term *people of color* is acceptable in most circles to describe all people who aren't Caucasian.

People of Latin American descent may prefer to think of themselves as Hispanic, Latina/Latino, or Chicana/Chicano, depending on where they live. Using *Latino* to describe all people who hail from Latin America is usually acceptable unless you're addressing or describing members of a specific community. Again, the more specific you can be, the better: for example, *Cuban* or *Argentinian*.

Asian or *Asian American* is preferred over *Oriental*. Better yet, use labels based on the country of origin, such as *Korean* or *Chinese*.

The terms *American Indian* and *Native American* both have their detractors. If possible, use the name of the specific tribe, preferably in the group's native tongue, such as *Diné* instead of *Navajo* and *Lenape* instead of *Delaware*. Many of the native people of Canada and Alaska prefer the term *Inuit* over *Eskimo*.

Use parallel terms when describing different groups; for example, *blacks and whites* and *Asian Americans and African Americans* are acceptable phrases. Don't describe one group using color and the other using a country or region. For example, don't describe one group as *Caucasians* and the other as *blacks*.

Steering Clear of Ageism

Ageism is any prejudice or discrimination against a person based on the person's age, regardless of whether the person is young or old. In other words, don't depict young people as being irresponsible or foolish or old people as feeble or uncool. Don't put people in boxes. Here are a few guidelines to follow:

Be careful with the terms *boy* and *girl*. Although some grammarians advise to restrict those terms to high-school-age people and younger, I recommend grade school or younger (specifically 12 years old and younger).

You're usually safe referring to a teenager as *young man* or *adolescent male* and *young woman* or *adolescent female*. Refer to people 18 years and older as *men* and *women*.

When referring to older people, avoid terms such as *the elderly* and *old geezers*. *Senior citizens* and *seniors* are usually acceptable, but you're better off with something specific, such as *people over 65*, *septuagenarians*, or an individual's actual age.

 DANGER ZONE

> When people chat, they often refer to men and women as guys and girls. There isn't any problem with the word *guy* (from a bias point of view anyway) but *girl* can be a controversial word. If you refer to a grown woman as a girl, it could easily be construed as insulting and patronizing. The solution is simple: when you're writing about a woman, call her a woman.

The Right Words for Gender Identity and Sexual Orientation

Some people are uncomfortable talking about sex, but if you find yourself in a situation in which you need to discuss gender identity and sexual orientation, knowing which words to use and how to string them together can boost your confidence and keep you out of trouble. Here are a few things to keep in mind:

The term *gender identity* refers to whether a person sees himself or herself as a male or female, regardless of the person's biological sex at birth.

Sexual orientation refers to a person's preference in sexual partners—*homosexual* (attracted to members of the same sex), *heterosexual* (attracted to members of the opposite sex), and *bisexual* (attracted to members of both sexes).

The word *transgender* is an adjective used to describe people born one sex who identify themselves as being of the other sex; for example, someone who describes herself as "a woman in the body of a man." Even though this person is biologically a man, she sees herself as a woman, and you should refer to her as *she*. Always use *transgender* as an adjective and never as a noun.

The word *transsexual* describes individuals who live or want to live as members of the other sex; for example, a person who is biologically a man but is living or wants to live as a woman. Transsexuals may undergo *sex reassignment* (don't call it a *sex change*), through surgery and hormone treatments, to become members of the other sex.

Use the term *sexual orientation* instead of *sexual preference*, which implies that people are free to choose whether they're sexually attracted to members of the same or the other sex.

Avoid referring to people as *homosexuals* or *bisexuals*. The preferred terms are *lesbians, gay men, bisexual men,* and *bisexual women.* Also keep in mind that *gay* refers to both males and females in the homosexual community, so if you're talking about men, use *gay men,* and if you're talking about women, use *lesbians* or *gay women.*

Remember to use parallel terms; for example *homosexual and heterosexual couples.* Using nonparallel terminology, such as *married and same-sex couples* implies that marriage is suitable only for a biological man and woman. While that may be what the law says or what some people think, try to accommodate different beliefs and values.

In some circles and in certain publications, referring to homosexual people as *queers* is acceptable, but be careful; you usually need to be a member of the community in order to use terms traditionally considered offensive.

Gender identities and sexual orientations don't necessarily fall into neat little either/or categories. Gender identity can be hazy and flexible. People who identify themselves as heterosexual may have times when they're sexually attracted to members of the same sex. This is one reason why avoiding labels is usually best.

> **USAGE TIDBIT**
>
> Unless you absolutely must mention a person's gender identity or sexual orientation, ditch the labels. Whether a person is transgender or transsexual, for example, doesn't really matter. What matters is only what that person thinks. If a person who's biologically a woman identifies himself as a man, treat him and refer to him as a man, not as a *female-to-male transgender person* even though that particular phrase is considered acceptable. Of course, if you're publishing a study on transgender men and women, that might be an important detail to mention.

Avoiding Bias Against People with Medical Conditions and Disabilities

People with medical conditions and disabilities have enough problems to deal with without having to carry the added burden of stigma. One way you can help fight stigma is to use the right words and phrases when you have to mention a particular condition or disability. Here are some guidelines to follow:

Put people first. Instead of saying *autistic children,* for example, say *children with autism.* Putting people first avoids reducing people to a condition.

Use *has* and *have* instead of *is* and *are.* Nobody *is* a condition, such as bipolar disorder or dementia, but people can have such conditions.

Put people before conditions. Calling someone an AIDS victim or saying that the person suffers from mental illness implies that the medical condition has power over that person. It's better to prioritize the person over the disease. For example, instead of referring to someone as an *AIDS victim,* you might consider using the phrase *person with AIDS.* Instead of saying that a person *suffers from depression,* you might say that the person is *living with depression.*

Avoid the terms *patient* and *case*. Unless you're referring to a patient in a hospital, refer to people by their names or as *people* or *participants* (in a study).

Steer clear of euphemisms. Euphemisms, such as *differently challenged* and *handicapable,* are condescending. See more on euphemisms in Chapter 12.

> **USAGE TIDBIT**
>
> For additional details on bias-free expressions, consult the *Publication Manual of the American Psychological Association* or visit apastyle.org.

Practice

Rewrite the following sentences to eliminate bias. Don't worry: there is usually more than one acceptable answer.

1. We polled 150 homosexuals to find out more about their sexual preferences.

   _____

2. People who suffer with depression tend to need considerably more sleep than do normal people.

   _____

3. Native Americans and Orientals comprise about 75 percent of the town's population.

   _____

4. The man and his wife watched an educational video about the mentally ill.

   _____

5. Despite their age, senior citizens descended on Washington to protest the plan to raise the retirement age.

   _____

Answers:

1. We polled 150 <u>gay men and women</u> to find out more about their sexual <u>orientation</u>.

2. People <u>with</u> depression tend to need considerably more sleep than do <u>others</u> (or <u>than do people without depression</u>).

3. Native Americans and <u>Asians</u> comprise about 75 percent of the town's population.

4. The <u>husband</u> and his <u>wife</u> watched an educational video about <u>people with mental illness</u>.

5. <u>Citizens</u> descended on Washington to protest the plan to raise the retirement age.

Sticking with Facts, Figures, and Specifics

A few years ago I had a student who wrote something like the following in a paper: "During his rookie year with the Chicago Bulls, Michael Jordan was not a very good player and was almost cut from the team."

This immediately struck me as bizarre. Michael Jordan is widely regarded as one of the best basketball players of all time. Could he really have been almost cut as an NBA rookie? That seemed impossible. Before confronting the student, I did a little fact-checking of my own, with an appropriate source for this topic: NBA.com.

It turns out Michael Jordan's rookie season was extraordinary. He made the all-star team. He was rookie of the year. He was second-team All-NBA. He scored over 28 points a game. In short, his first year was better than the best year of most players in NBA history. There's no way he was almost cut.

I went back to the student, saying, "I don't think your facts about Michael Jordan are correct. Can you clarify where this information came from?"

It turns out there was a little truth to this story about Jordan: he struggled as a player and was almost cut from his *high school* basketball team. My student heard this anecdote, forgot the details, and then repeated it without double-checking the facts.

Don't let this happen to you. You'll get in trouble if you rely on common knowledge because common knowledge is often wrong. Look up your facts before you write.

Maintaining an Objective Viewpoint

Maintaining an objective viewpoint and avoiding bias aren't only about choosing the right nouns, pronouns, and adjectives. You also need to think logically, express yourself clearly, and support with evidence any claims you make. In the following sections, I offer some guidance in how to write more objectively.

Never Say *Never:* Avoiding Generalizations and Absolutes

Even if it happens to be fiction, good writing is honest and reveals what is true. Bad writing, on the other hand, obscures the truth and misleads people. For example, claiming that all politicians are corrupt probably isn't true. At least a few politicians, somewhere in the world, are doing what they believe is best and do not allow money to influence their decisions. An easy way to avoid the most blatant overgeneralizations is to proceed with caution whenever one of these absolute terms pops into your head:

all	must	nothing
always	never	only
everybody	nobody	should
everyone	no one	
everything	none	

The trouble with claims that begin with absolutes is that they're rarely correct and they make the claim vulnerable to an easy rebuttal. Someone needs to provide only a single piece of evidence that counters your claim in order to prove you wrong. For example, if I ask my son, "Why do I always have to remind you to take out the trash?" and he points out correctly that three months ago, on May 13, he did, in fact, take out the trash without my reminding him, he wins, and I have to backpedal.

Unfortunately, absolute statements don't always begin with a word that makes them easy to identify. For example, a statement that "Conservatives support a pro-life platform" implies that all conservatives support a pro-life platform, which I know isn't true. I know several people who consider themselves conservatives but pro-choice.

When you see the words *always* or *never,* you should be a little suspicious. Writing rarely works that way and neither does the world.

To avoid making overgeneralizations, qualify statements with words such as *most, many, almost, rarely,* and *nearly.* Better yet, be specific; for example, instead of saying *several,* give an exact number, such as *3* or *7* or *258.* Instead of saying "most people favor …," give a percentage; for example, "53 percent of the 3,025 people polled favor the proposed school voucher program." Instead of saying, "In the past …," specify the exact time; for example, "Fifty years ago, researchers believed …." Specifics make writing strong.

> **DANGER ZONE**
>
> While qualifications are important, avoid the temptation to qualify everything you write. Too many qualifications can drain the vigor from your writing. Find a balance between saying too much and too little.

Support Any Claims with Evidence

Whenever you state something as fact, back it up with evidence from a reliable source. For example, instead of merely claiming that "the number of children with food allergies has risen dramatically in just the past few years," add the facts and figures and cite your source:

> According to the Centers for Disease Control and Prevention (CDC), food allergy prevalence among children younger than 18 rose from 3.4 to 5.1 percent between 1997 and 2011.

As you can see, the evidence not only cites a reliable source, but it also clears up a lot of ambiguity. It explains what is meant by *children* (younger than 18), *dramatic increase* (from 3.4 to 5.1 percent), and past few years (1997 to 2011). By adding specific evidence, you make you make your argument stronger and more credible.

Be Careful When Making Value Judgments

A value judgment is a subjective assessment of the value, quality, or goodness of someone or something. Whenever you make a value judgment, you're sizing up someone or something based on your own standards. For example, you may consider someone who doesn't mow and edge his or her lawn twice a week lazy or someone whose home is impeccably clean an overachiever. However, not everyone shares your standards and beliefs.

Instead of using subjective assessments to describe people, places, and things, you should objectively describe characteristics or behaviors and let the audience draw its own conclusions. Instead of describing a manager as overbearing, for example, you might mention that the manager demanded daily progress reports from everyone in the department and visited every employee's cubicle twice a day to observe. If you do go ahead and make the value judgment, be sure to back it up with specifics to define more precisely the standard you're using to make that judgment.

Practice

Choose the more objective sentence in each of the following sentence pairs:

❑ Life, as we know it, does not exist on any planet outside of our solar system.

❑ Scientists have yet to discover signs of life on planets other than Earth.

❑ Several people at the party mentioned that the cheese dip was particularly delicious.

❑ Everyone at the party enjoyed the cheese dip.

❑ According to the CDC, 51.5 percent of adults 18 years and older have had at least 12 alcoholic drinks over the course of the past year.

❑ Most adults 18 years and older report that they are regular drinkers; that is, they drink at least 12 alcoholic beverages annually.

❑ Public opinion has little influence over gun control legislation.

❑ Although a recent poll showed 83 percent of the electorate favoring stricter gun control laws, the Senate voted against expanding background checks.

❑ Researchers concluded that chronic stress impairs a person's problem-solving performance, because they had no time to engage in self-affirmation activities.

❑ Participants who were operating under high levels of chronic stress solved half as many problems as the unstressed participants.

Answers:

✓ Scientists have yet to discover signs of life on planets other than Earth.

✓ Several people at the party mentioned that the cheese dip was particularly delicious.

✓ According to the CDC, 51.5 percent of adults 18 years and older have had at least 12 drinks over the course of the past year.

✓ Although a recent poll showed 83 percent of the electorate favoring stricter gun control laws, the Senate voted against expanding background checks.

✓ Participants who were operating under high levels of chronic stress solved half as many problems as the unstressed participants.

The Least You Need to Know

- To avoid gender bias, choose gender-neutral nouns and try to work around using the pronouns *he* and *she*.
- Don't make distinctions based on gender, race, ethnicity, medical conditions, or disabilities unless such information is relevant.
- Avoid terms such as *elderly* and *senior citizen* to describe older people; a specific age or range is preferable.
- The word *gay* refers to both males and females; to draw a distinction, use *gay men and women*.
- When referring to people with medical conditions or disabilities, use person-first language; for example, *children with ADHD* instead of *ADHD children*.

PART 5

Fine-Tuning the Mechanics

Now that you've spent some time on the big-picture aspects of writing, it's time to get small again, and take a look at those tiny tools of writing called punctuation marks.

Some little things have big jobs, and that's certainly true of the punctuation marks that end sentences: periods, question marks, and exclamation marks. I'll also discuss some punctuation marks that are often misused: commas, colons, and semicolons.

Don't feel bad if you've misused a comma or two in your day; commas have so many jobs that it's no wonder people get confused. On the other hand, semicolons don't have many jobs at all—just two—so you have no excuse not to learn those jobs by heart. I'll cover less frustrating punctuation marks as well: quotation marks, hyphens, dashes, parentheses, and brackets.

This part will also include tips for capitalizing words and navigating the minefield that is English spelling. I'll mention many of the general rules for English spelling, as well as the numerous exceptions.

Punctuation, spelling, and capitalization may seem like small issues, but they make a big impression on readers. If you use them correctly, you'll look like a smart, careful writer. If you misuse them, you'll look inexperienced or sloppy. In writing, there really are no little things.

CHAPTER 17

Basic Punctuation

In writing, the little things matter—especially the little things known as punctuation marks. Without punctuation, sentences would be confusing messes. With improperly used punctuation, sentences are hard to understand and annoying to readers who know the rules.

Every punctuation mark has its own use or uses. Some have only one use (the question mark) or two uses (the semicolon), making them fairly easy to learn. Others, such as the comma, have many uses. Even worse, some of the uses are judgment calls rather than hard rules. That makes the comma particularly challenging to use.

It's worth taking some time to focus on punctuation, which is connected to grammar and style but really its own category. Sometimes punctuation is the difference between a grammatical sentence and an ungrammatical sentence. Sometimes punctuation is the difference between a boring sentence and an interesting sentence.

This chapter will help you get a handle on all of the above and more.

Putting an End to Your Sentences

Like all good things, sentences have to end. Following are the three punctuation marks you can use to end a sentence.

The End, Period.

The most common way to end a sentence—as you can see in the sentence you're reading right now—is the period. This tiny dot is powerful: it says, "You're done." Long and short sentences can both be ended by a period.

The mailman wept.

There's a bug in your hair.

I like to play pinball with my friend Neil.

When summer comes, it fills me with longing for the days when my beloved Valerie used to throw peanuts to squirrels in the park.

The vast majority of sentences in English end with a period.

> **PRACTICAL POINT**
>
> How many spaces go after a period? One or two? Back in the days of typewriters, it was common to skip two spaces after a period. These days, skipping one space is far more common. You're better off in almost every situation allowing just one space. However, there are exceptions. The most recent edition of the APA manual brought back the practice of skipping two spaces. For some reason, this out-of-date practice just won't die.

Ending with a Question Mark?

The question mark is probably the best-named punctuation mark, since it only has one function: ending a question. Questions come in many sizes and types in English.

Where's the train station?

What do you think of the philosophy of Wittgenstein?

Huh?

Have you ever been in love, so deeply in love, that you feel like you're losing your mind?

When you use a question mark, make sure the sentence really is a question. The best tip-off is a word such as *who, what, where, when, why,* or *how. Did* and *do* also begin many questions. It can help you recognize a question if you read it aloud and feel your voice inflecting upward at the end of the sentence.

Don't forget the question mark when you write a question. Some writers accidentally write sentences like this:

> How do we know vampires don't exist.

Since that sentence is asking something, it's a question and needs a question mark:

> How do we know vampires don't exist?

If you really don't want to write a question, rephrase the idea as a statement:

> We don't know for sure whether or not vampires exist.

That's not a question because it states something rather than asks something.

End Already! The Exclamation Point

The third way to end a sentence ends with a bang! The exclamation point is used for sentences that end with strong emphasis. This punctuation mark brings high energy: you could think of it as raising your voice or banging your fist on the table.

> There's a fire in the kitchen!
>
> I can't believe you forgot my birthday!
>
> I lost my keys!
>
> Ow!

You have disappointed your parents and disgraced your ancestors!

As you can tell from these examples, the exclamation mark is best used in situations that are informal. Using exclamation marks in an email, tweet, or text message is fine. An exclamation mark could also be acceptable in a personal essay, if used sparingly. If you're writing fiction, exclamation marks could be helpful in writing dialogue. Many advertisements use exclamation marks to convey energy and enthusiasm.

However, in formal writing situations, you should avoid exclamation marks. If you're writing a résumé, cover letter, research paper, or anything with a serious purpose, don't use exclamation marks. They set the wrong tone, and they'll make you sound silly (and loud).

Practice

Add final punctuation to the following sentences:

1. How many times do I have to tell you I hate pea soup

2. My name is Henry; I eat a lot of plums

3. I am so angry right now

4. When I watch *Mad Men,* I'm glad I wasn't around in the 1960s

5. Where the heck are my keys

Answers:

1. How many times do I have to tell you I hate pea soup?

2. My name is Henry; I eat a lot of plums.

3. I am so angry right now! (This sentence could also end with a period. In fact, a period often has better effect than an exclamation mark, which often feels forced and overblown.)

4. When I watch *Mad Men,* I'm glad I wasn't around in the 1960s. (Despite starting with *when,* this is a statement, not a question, so it ends with a period.)

5. Where the heck are my keys?

Knowing When to Use Commas

Commas are one of the most helpful punctuation marks—and one of the most confusing. This situation is ironic, since the main purpose of the comma is to avoid confusion.

Why are commas an issue for many writers? Well, some comma rules are strict and universally accepted; other rules are flexible and extremely subjective. You have a lot of company if you've ever misplaced a comma, but with a review of the types of comma use, you should be ready to use commas like a pro.

Separating Items in a Series

A politician, a nun, and a sailor walk into a bar. I'm not sure what they did there, but it would be hard to tell jokes like that—or write any kind of list—without commas. Separating items in a list is one of the main uses of the comma. For example:

> Cupcakes, brownies, potato chips, and pizza ruined my diet.

Without commas, this would be a smooshed-together mess that's difficult to read:

> Cupcakes brownies potato chips and pizza ruined my diet.

Not everyone agrees on whether there should be a comma after the second-to-last item in a list. Some publications (especially newspapers) omit that final comma—called a *serial comma*—like so:

> The politician kissed a baby, told a lie and ate a hamburger.

DEFINITION

The comma that comes after the second-to-last item in a series is often referred to as a **serial comma** or Oxford comma, so-named because it's preferred by Oxford University Press. Many—including the author of this book—prefer using the Oxford comma, since it doesn't hurt and does sometimes help eliminate ambiguity in sentences.

Separating Two or More Adjectives

If you're writing about a dapper, classy, well-dressed dude, you need commas to separate the adjectives. This rule applies even when dealing with only two adjectives:

> My dog is a well-behaved, fluffy poodle.

Don't get comma-happy, though: resist the temptation to put a comma between *fluffy* and *poodle;* that is, don't separate the last adjective in the series from the noun it modifies. The commas should only separate adjectives; a comma before the noun will create confusion.

Joining Two Independent Clauses

An independent clause is a complete thought that could be a grammatical sentence. Independent clauses can be very short, as in these examples:

> Cats ran.
>
> Dogs howled.

When joining independent clauses, you have a few options. You can join them using a semicolon:

> Cats ran; dogs howled.

You can join them using a comma and a conjunction:

> Cats ran, and dogs howled.

That comma is needed only if the sentence joins two independent clauses. The following sentence doesn't need a comma:

> The bird sang and fluttered around the apartment.

Why no comma after *and?* Because you only have one subject (the bird) performing two actions (singing and fluttering). You're not joining two separate, complete sentences.

 DANGER ZONE

A common mistake—the comma splice—occurs when two independent clauses are joined by a comma with no conjunction, like so:

> My dad is an astronaut, my mom is a teacher.

Fortunately, this is an easy mistake to fix:

> My dad is an astronaut, and my mom is a teacher.

You can also fix the problem with a semicolon:

> My dad is an astronaut; my mom is a teacher.

For more on joining independent clauses, see Chapter 4.

Setting Off Nonessential Clauses and Phrases

In language and in life, some things are essential and others are nonessential. Commas are used to set off nonessential clauses and phrases from the rest of a sentence.

For example, here's an essential element:

> The president asked for an advisor who is an expert in foreign affairs.

That whole phrase—"an advisor who is an expert in foreign affairs"—is essential. An advisor who doesn't know foreign affairs from Foghorn Leghorn wouldn't do. Here's a similar sentence with a nonessential element:

> The president summoned Congressman Wilson, who is a football fan.

The sentence structure is almost exactly the same, but the meaning is different. The fact that Congressman Wilson is a football fan is probably not the reason for the president's summons, so the information is nonessential. For this kind of nonessential clause, use a comma.

Sometimes these clauses or phrases appear in the middle of the sentence:

> The book, written three years ago, won six awards.

Often, determining whether a clause or phrase is essential or nonessential is a tough call. Depending on the rest of the paragraph, this punctuation might be fine, too:

> The book written three years ago won six awards.

Pausing After an Introductory Element

After getting a good night's sleep, you'll probably write better. You'll also remember comma rules better, as in that sentence about sleeping and writing. Introductory words and phrases are usually followed by commas, especially when a comma makes the sentence easier to read, as in these examples:

> Last winter, I lost my toboggan.
>
> Usually, my cousin works out at the gym.
>
> When I get bored and restless, I walk on the beach.
>
> After contemplating the events of that fateful Thursday afternoon, I napped.

If those introductory elements were removed, you'd still have grammatical sentences:

> I lost my toboggan.
>
> My cousin works out at the gym.
>
> I walk on the beach.
>
> I napped.

Introductory elements modify the sentence in some way, adding information that tells you where, when, or how the actions of the sentence are happening. These introductory elements act as adverbs, and single adverbs are often introductory elements themselves, as in the following sentences:

> Gradually, I learned how to speak Russian.
>
> Politically, the scandal is a minefield for the president.
>
> Brazenly, my cousin asked to borrow money.
>
> Lately, I've been getting weird pains in my side.

Sometimes an introductory word or phrase can exist without a comma, and it's up to you as a writer to decide if the comma is necessary or not. For example, in this sentence, the comma after "For example" is helpful, but in the previous sentence, a comma after "Sometimes" isn't really needed.

> **PRACTICAL POINT**
>
> *Hopefully* is one of the most controversial words in English. It has long been used in sentences like, "The puppy gazed hopefully at his owner's dinner plate." However, many writers object to *hopefully* being used as a modifier for an entire sentence, meaning "it is hoped." The following are examples of the controversial usage:
>
> Hopefully, the Cubs will win the World Series someday.
>
> Hopefully, I'll find true love.
>
> Hopefully, the sun won't blow up anytime soon.
>
> Despite the dislike some feel for this usage, it's very common in speech, and it's becoming more commonly accepted in writing. Use *hopefully* to modify sentences in informal writing, but avoid it in formal writing. When in doubt, it's better to err on the side of not annoying people.

Pausing for Interruptions in a Sentence

Sometimes you use a comma just because it sounds right, you know?

For example, in the preceding sentence, placing a comma right before addressing the reader makes the sentence easier to read and understand. Other times, a comma might be used to create a pause, as in this headline from *Entertainment Weekly:*

"Networks Embrace the Miniseries, Again"

That comma puts extra emphasis on the last word. This type of comma is closely related to how we speak, and it's most appropriate in writing that's a little informal.

Hey, commas can be complex.

Other Uses for Commas

If that's not enough, commas have even more uses. You need them to write dates, places, addresses, and numbers:

I was born on April 4, 2009.

My mom is from Memphis, Tennessee.

My friend Joe lives at 14 Blake St., Apt. 765.

My brother says he scored 144,500 points at Ms. Pac-Man.

You also use commas to introduce direct quotations:

My brother said, "I scored 144,500 points at Ms. Pac-Man!"

You don't need a comma for a similar sentence that doesn't include a direct quote:

My brother said he scored a lot of points at Ms. Pac-Man.

No wonder so many people make comma mistakes—no other punctuation mark is so versatile. Despite the potential for confusion and mistakes, though, don't let commas discourage you. As you write and read more, you'll get a handle on the problems commas can and can't solve. You'll also get better at using them properly.

Well-placed commas will make your writing clear, smooth, and flowing—in other words, enjoyable to read.

Using a Semicolon to Join Items

After the comma, the semicolon might be the most commonly misused punctuation mark. Even native English speakers frequently make semicolon mistakes. Yet the semicolon is a useful weapon in a writer's arsenal, and you can avoid confusion if you remember that it only has two uses.

Joining Independent Clauses

The first use of the semicolon is to join two independent clauses; I used it for that purpose in this sentence. As we learned earlier, an independent clause is a complete thought that could be a grammatical sentence in its own right. The following are examples of independent clauses joined by a semicolon:

Geese flew; ducks swam.

The king ordered an execution; the prince gasped in horror.

In spring, dogs play at the park; squirrels must be vigilant.

The semicolon is not the only option when dealing with two independent clauses. Sometimes, the best thing to do is let the independent clauses be separate sentences:

I have a crick in my neck. Do you know a good chiropractor?

Sometimes the independent clauses are best joined by a comma and coordinating conjunction.

> Cats are more independent than dogs, and that's why I love them.

When the flow and logic of the sentence suggest a quick sequence of thoughts, the semicolon is an elegant way of joining them.

> There's nothing I enjoy more than basketball; the players' athleticism is breathtaking.

The choice is up to you as a writer, based on your ear for language and your purpose for writing. Just make sure you don't throw in a semicolon when you need a colon. The following is a common mistake, but a mistake all the same:

> These are my favorite superheroes; Batman, Daredevil, and the Punisher.

A semicolon cannot introduce a list: that job belongs to the colon. The semicolon has two jobs; introducing lists isn't one of them.

Practice

For the following sentences, insert the proper punctuation:

1. I have a stomachache it feels like I ate a fireball.

2. There are two things I hate about tests studying and worrying.

3. I like to relax by listening to music jazz is especially soothing.

Answers:

1. I have a stomachache; it feels like I ate a fireball.

2. There are two things I hate about tests: studying and worrying.

3. I like to relax by listening to music: jazz is especially soothing. (For this sentence, a semicolon would also work.)

Separating Items in a Series

The other use of a semicolon involves items in a series. As discussed in the section on commas, a sentence containing a series should look like this:

> I'm on Facebook, Twitter, LinkedIn, and Pinterest.

That's easy enough. But what if one of the items in your list has a comma in it? The following would look odd because of comma overload:

> I've lived in Buffalo, New York, Chicago, Illinois, and Santa Fe, New Mexico.

> I like women with long, flowing hair, thriving, lucrative careers, and stylish, fashionable wardrobes.

> The keys to a good TV drama are a powerful, charismatic lead actor, a smart, adaptable showrunner, and a cool, interesting premise.

When an item in a series has a comma in it, separate the items using semicolons:

> I've lived in Buffalo, New York; Chicago, Illinois; and Santa Fe, New Mexico.

> I like women with long, flowing hair; thriving, lucrative careers; and stylish, fashionable wardrobes.

> The keys to a good TV drama are a powerful, charismatic lead actor; a smart, adaptable showrunner; and a cool, interesting premise.

Brushing Up on Colon Usage

Like a handshake, a colon is used for introductions. A colon tends to set up forthcoming information: read on and learn the types of language that can follow a colon.

Introducing a List

The most common use for the colon is in introducing a list.

> My dog likes four things: chasing, fetching, eating, and sleeping.

> These are the ingredients: flour, sugar, gluten, peanuts, and cilantro.

> The president has made progress in several areas: foreign policy, health care, and business growth.

You don't need a colon when there isn't a pause before introducing the list. With a little revision, those sentences no longer need a colon:

> My dog likes chasing, fetching, eating, and sleeping.

> The ingredients are flour, sugar, gluten, peanuts, and cilantro.

> The president has made progress in foreign policy, health care, and business growth.

Introducing a Formal Statement or Long Quotation

The colon is also used for introducing phrases or formal statements.

> The strange man had this to say to his critics: "I am not a bounty hunter."

> I hate going to the mall: it is a nightmare.

> Let me come right out and admit it: I've been having an affair.

Separating Independent Clauses

Remember the passage earlier about how semicolons separate independent clauses? Colons can do that job, too. When you have two independent clauses that are closely linked—too closely to make separate sentences—you can join them with a colon.

> The general had a plan: he would hide the chickens before his secretary came in.

> Too many dog owners forget something important: dogs are allergic to chocolate.

> Daniel Day-Lewis seems to win an Oscar for every movie he's in: it's that predictable.

Using a colon to separate independent clauses is a judgment call, but it's most appropriate when the first independent clause is asking a question that the second one answers. It's almost like a joke and a punch line: one follows the other.

More Uses for Colons

You can also use a colon in sentences that consist of an independent clause and a phrase. This use is very similar to the above cases where a colon joins two independent clauses.

> I've never been sure how to use *whom:* that pesky word.

> My dad is a postal worker: so was his dad.

> The robin's breast is red: a bright shade of red.

> I haven't used a pencil in years: not since college.

In all those cases, an em dash would also work pretty well.

> I've never been sure how to use whom—that pesky word.

> My dad is a postal worker—so was his dad.

> The robin's breast is red—a bright shade of red.

> I haven't used a pencil in years—not since college.

For more on em dashes, see Chapter 19.

Not only are colons like greetings, but they're used in greetings: especially formal greetings. If you're writing a business letter, a letter of application, or anything formal, a colon should follow the greeting.

> Dear sir:

> To whom it may concern:

> Dear Mr. Jenkins:

> Dear Dr. Thompson:

Colons are also used in writing times.

> I always take a nap at 3:30 in the afternoon.

> My son was born at 1:43 A.M.

> Football games usually start at 1:00.

> Be home by 5:30! That's when Mom's making supper.

You may have seen the colon used in math class, since they are used in writing ratios. If there are twice as many peaches as apples, there's a 2:1 (2 to 1) ratio of peaches to apples.

> In Congress, there's a 3:1 ratio of men to women.

> The proportion of dogs to cats in my house is 4:1.

> The ratio of water to other substances in your body is approximately 9:1.

> I bet on the Bulls to win the NBA title and got 5:1 odds.

Colons are also used in many book titles, to separate the title and the subtitle.

> *Eleven Rings: The Soul of Success* by Phil Jackson

> *Give and Take: A Revolutionary Approach to Success* by Adam M. Grant

> *The Paleo Solution: The Original Human Diet* by Robb Wolf and Loren Cordain

> *Running for Beginners: The Easiest Way to Start Running* by Simon Adams

That's the colon: a useful, versatile form of punctuation.

The Least You Need to Know

- A period is by far the most common way to end a sentence.
- Question marks end sentences that ask something; exclamation marks end sentences with a loud or emphatic point.
- Semicolons separate independent clauses or items in a list that contain commas. They only perform these two jobs.
- Colons introduce material, such as an independent clause, a phrase, or the body of a letter.
- Colons also appear in times (6:30), ratios (5:1), and many book and article titles.

CHAPTER 18

Quotation Marks and Apostrophes

Most punctuation is located or begins near the bottom of letters, like periods and commas. Quotation marks and apostrophes, on the other hand, appear near the tops of letters.

These punctuation marks aren't as versatile as the comma, but they have a few specific jobs you'll need to learn and understand.

The most important thing about quotation marks is that they allow you to use the words of other people while giving full credit. If you use quotation marks correctly, you'll never have to worry about accidentally plagiarizing.

The most important thing about apostrophes might be that they drive people crazy when improperly used. There are many webpages devoted to misused apostrophes, with pictures of mistakes from signs and other sources. If you don't want to be similarly embarrassed, you'll have to get a handle on the apostrophe and its uses, most of which have to do with possession.

In This Chapter

- Understanding and using quotation marks
- In or out? Placing punctuation with quotations
- The correct style for longer, block quotes
- Using apostrophes to form possessives and contractions
- Who says you can't use contractions?

Enclosing Text in Quotation Marks

Quotation marks are important because they allow you to report exactly what someone else said or wrote. Newspapers, novels, and academic papers are full of quotation marks because those genres frequently report what others said. Quotation marks are the tools that allow you to quote people accurately.

Quoting a Person's Exact Words

As my grandmother used to say, "You have to use quotation marks when reporting what someone said or wrote." The preceding sentence is an example of how to use quotation marks. Here are more examples:

> When I received the bad news, I said, "What? That can't be!"

> Shakespeare was the first writer to use the phrase "Something is rotten in the state of Denmark."

> On *Arrested Development,* Gob Bluth often says "I've made a huge mistake."

> Never say "I love you" just to be polite.

Quotation marks are used to document something that was said or written. Also—as in that last example about politeness—they can contain an example of something that might be said. Use quotation marks when the exact wording is important. Often, it's not. For example, sometimes you can be more general:

> My dad told me to always be respectful.

That sentence would be just fine in some situations. However, sometimes you might need to get more specific, like this:

> My dad told me, "Always respect your elders."

Punctuating Around Quotation Marks

There are a couple ways of punctuating around quotation marks: the logical way and the American way. In America, punctuation goes inside the quotation marks, as in the following examples:

> I hate when people use the word "passion."

> My brother said I was an "idiot."

> He said I should grab the "thingamajig," which I couldn't find anywhere.

In British English, punctuation goes outside the quotation marks, like so:

> I hate when people use the word "passion".

> My brother said I was an "idiot".

> He said I should grab the "thingamajig", which I couldn't find anywhere.

The British way is more logical because it excludes punctuation from the quotation marks if that punctuation is not part of the quotation. This makes more sense than the American way, but if you're writing for an American audience, put your punctuation before the quotation mark. The exception is when a quotation is part of a question:

> Why do you like the phrase "stuck in your craw"?

> Which president said the word "misunderestimate"?

> Which superhero has the catchphrase "It's clobberin' time!"?

However, if the question mark is part of the quotation rather than part of the sentence, the question mark goes inside the final quotation mark:

> Joe asked, "How did I get here?"

> I was confused and said, "Mom?" to my Aunt Nancy.

> "What is love?" asked the poet.

Formatting a Running Dialogue

If you're writing fiction, you'll need to use quotation marks a lot, since fiction usually includes a lot of dialogue. For the most part, you can punctuate the dialogue like quotations in other types of writing, but it's okay to leave out the "He said" or "She said" when it's obvious who is saying something. For example:

> "Do you like tennis?" Joe asked his mom.

> "Tennis?" his mom said incredulously.

> "Yes, tennis."

> "Why would I like tennis?"

> "I don't know."

> "Now shut up and eat your muffins."

> Joe sadly picked up a muffin.

Dealing with Long Quotations: Block Quotes

Sometimes you'll need to use a long quotation. If a quotation goes on for many sentences, it would look kind of ugly, and it could create confusion. The solution to this problem is the block quote.

The exact format for block quotes varies in different style manuals, but the general idea stays the same: you put the quotation in a big block of text and indent it a few times. The following is a quotation from earlier in this chapter:

> Quotation marks are important because they allow you to report exactly what someone else said or wrote. Newspapers, novels, and academic papers are full of quotation marks because those genres frequently report what others said. Quotation marks are the tools that allow you to quote people accurately.

In Modern Language Association (MLA) style, you should use a block if the quotation takes up more than four lines. In American Psychological Association (APA) style, you use a block quote if the quotation is at least 40 words. *The Chicago Manual of Style* (CMS) guidelines are looser, suggesting a block quote for quotations 4 or 5 lines long but demanding it for quotations 10 lines long. Since formats change with new editions, always check the latest edition of the style guide you're using.

In all formats, you don't need quotation marks for a block quote. The fact that the text is formatted as a block quote is enough to let readers know it's a quotation.

Dealing with Quotations Inside Quotations

What if you're quoting someone who is also quoting someone? How do you handle a quote within a quote? First, here's how not to handle it:

> The president said, "I met a woman today who said, "I hate taxes.""

Doesn't that look weird? Fortunately, there's a workaround. For quotes within quotes, switch to single quotes:

> The president said, "I met a woman today who said, 'I hate taxes.'"

This is the only use for single quotes, so remember to use them for this reason alone.

Enclosing Titles in Quotes

Titles of artworks often go in quotation marks, especially when you're talking about a part of a longer work. For example:

"Teenage Riot" is the best song from the album *Daydream Nation.*

My favorite *Seinfeld* episode is "The Yada Yada."

The short story "Cousins from Hell" is part of the longer collection *Terrifying Families.*

As you can see from those examples, you should put longer or complete works—such as albums, TV shows, movies, and books—in italics.

Flagging Slang and Technical Terms

Sometimes quotation marks are used to highlight a term that is unusual for some reason. This could be a technical term, a slang term, or any word or phrase that is new or unusual.

The businessman kept speaking about "synergistic paradigms."

The senior citizens did not know what the teenager meant by "crunk."

I can't stand the word "staycation."

When a word is discussed as a word, it can also be put in italics, which is the style used in this book. Follow the rules required by your format, teacher, or editor, but if you have a choice, italics look cleaner and less obtrusive:

The businessman kept speaking about *synergistic paradigms.*

The senior citizens did not know what the teenager meant by *crunk.*

I can't stand the word *staycation.*

 DANGER ZONE

Inexperienced writers often forget quotation marks. For example, let's say a student wrote the following:

According to Miller, high school football should be outlawed.

That's fine if this is a paraphrase of Miller, meaning the student put Miller's ideas into new words. However, if Miller wrote the exact words "High school football should be outlawed," then those words need quotation marks around them. By forgetting the quotation marks, the writer accidently plagiarized. Don't let this happen to you. Be very careful about using other people's words. Stealing words and ideas is as unethical as stealing physical property.

Using Apostrophes

The main job of the apostrophe is to create possessive words: words that establish that certain things, beings, or qualities belong to other things, beings, or qualities.

Forming Possessives

The following examples show nouns linked by apostrophes to create possessive words:

> The president's children were adorable.
>
> Have you seen my dog's toy?
>
> That coffee shop's mochas are delicious.
>
> My uncle's personality is depressing.
>
> France's best food is crêpes.

The apostrophe establishes the possessive relationship. These sentences could all be reworded in ways that read awkwardly but can help you remember the meaning.

> The children of the president were adorable.
>
> Have you seen the toy that belongs to my dog?
>
> The mochas made by that coffee shop are delicious.
>
> The personality of my uncle is depressing.
>
> The best food from France is crêpes.

Plural Nouns Ending in s

A tricky case occurs when you have a noun that ends in *s*. There are two ways to make that kind of word possessive, and you should check with the format or style guide you're using. The first way is simply to add an apostrophe.

> Jesus' apostles are mentioned in the Gospels.
>
> Where are my cats' toys?
>
> My parents' house is old.
>
> Is this Dennis' hat?
>
> That isn't my job. It's Congress' job.

Those words can also become plural by adding *'s*.

> Jesus's apostles are mentioned in the Gospels.

> Where are my cats's toys?

> My parents's house is old.

> Is this Dennis's hat?

> That isn't my job. It's Congress's job.

If you have a choice, skip the extra *s*. Adding only an apostrophe looks a lot cleaner.

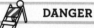 **DANGER ZONE**

> Adding apostrophes to plural words is a common mistake. The following examples are all mistakes because the apostrophes are not needed:
>
> > The siblings' lost their cat.
> >
> > Most presidents' see their hair go gray while in office.
> >
> > Have you seen my guinea pigs'?
>
> When using an apostrophe—or any punctuation mark—you should make sure you have a reason for using it. If you're not creating a possessive word or contraction, you likely don't need an apostrophe.

Indefinite Pronouns

Indefinite pronouns are pronouns that are general, not referring to a specific entity. You also need an apostrophe when making these words possessive.

> It's <u>anyone's</u> guess where my mom put it.

> <u>Someone's</u> coat is sitting on the chair.

> I respect <u>everyone's</u> human rights.

Dual Possession

In some sentences, you need to discuss two people or things that possess something. This can be punctuated two different ways, depending on the meaning of the sentences.

In some cases, the two entities equally possess something:

> Joe and Jenny's house is stylish.
>
> Gary and Stan's poker games are off the hook.
>
> I hate going to Jill and Joanne's knitting club.
>
> Michael Jordan and Scottie Pippen's teams were impressive.
>
> My mom and dad's car was broken down a lot.

In all these cases, the possession is truly a joint effort. For example, in the last sentence, the mom and dad equally owned the car. In the second-to-last example, Jordan and Pippen were part of the same teams, which won six championships. In cases like this, only the second item needs an apostrophe and *s*. Just as the two entities share whatever is in the rest of the sentence, they share the same punctuation.

On the other hand, sometimes you may need to write similar-looking sentences that have a different meaning because the two beings possess similar things that are not exactly the same. These examples need different punctuation:

> Jordan's and Pippen's styles were different.
>
> My mom's and dad's childhoods were difficult.
>
> What's the difference between the quarterback's and linebacker's leadership roles?
>
> How did the Bills' and Sabres' seasons go?

In these cases, the nouns each get their own *'s* because they possess distinctive, separate things. The Bills and Sabres may have both finished seasons, but they weren't the same season. Jordan and Pippen may have been on the same team, but their playing styles weren't identical. A mom and dad might have both had difficult childhoods, but they weren't the same difficult childhoods. They possess different things, so they get their own possessive punctuation.

Using apostrophes correctly allows readers to grasp your exact meaning so you can communicate effectively.

Practice

Punctuate the following sentences:

1. Have you seen my dog and sons toys?

2. Do your parents have a van?

3. How do the president and vice-presidents roles differ?

4. Are Catholicism and Judaisms prayers similar?

5. Did Sally and Saras house—the one they grew up in—burn down?

Answers:

1. Have you seen my dog's and son's toys? (Both get apostrophes, since they are probably not the same toys.)

2. Do your parents have a van? (No apostrophes, since *parents* is not possessive.)

3. How do the president's and vice-president's roles differ? (Both *president* and *vice-president* get their own apostrophe and *s,* since they have separate roles.)

4. Are Catholicism's and Judaism's prayers similar? (Both *Catholicism* and *Judaism* get their own apostrophe and *s,* since they are separate religions.)

5. Did Sally and Sara's house—the one they grew up in—burn down? (Only *Sara* gets an apostrophe and *s,* since Sally and Sara grew up in the same house, so they have joint possession.)

Time- and Money-Related Words

Sometimes you'll need to write about time or money in a way that requires an apostrophe, as in the following examples:

I have two weeks' vacation coming to me.

Can I buy one hundred dollars' worth of parakeets?

In a month's time, you can get a lot of work done.

Converting Some Singulars into Plurals

Occasionally, you might see an apostrophe used to make a plural, like if you were talking about the 1700's or the 1960's.

Resist this usage. You never need to use an apostrophe to make a plural word. Writing *1700s* and *1960s* is correct.

One of the most common mistakes in English is mixing up *its* and *it's*. That little apostrophe confuses many writers, partly due to an inconsistency in English.

Here's the inconsistency: remember when we said apostrophes are for possessive words? Surprise! The exact opposite is true for *its* and *it's*. All the following sentences include possessive *its*—with no apostrophe—and they're all possessive.

> The building lost its awning in the storm.
>
> Freedom is its own reward.
>
> Your baby dropped its rattle.

The following sentences—all correct—have it's with an apostrophe, and they're not possessive.

> It's raining today.
>
> This color is bright. It's my sister's favorite.
>
> Getting older: it's not easy.

This can be confusing because *it's* does not use an apostrophe to make a possessive word; it uses an apostrophe to make a contraction. To find out which form is correct, see how the sentences sound with *it is*. The following examples sound pretty odd:

> The building lost it is awning in the storm.
>
> Freedom is it is own reward.
>
> Your baby dropped it is rattle.

Since that doesn't work, they were all correct with its. Now let's double-check the second batch.

> It is raining today.
>
> This color is bright. It is my sister's favorite.
>
> Getting older: it is not easy.

Those all make sense, so *it's* is correct.

Forming Contractions

Some words can be combined into one word with the help of an apostrophe, and these are called contractions. The following sentences all include a contraction:

<u>Don't</u> touch that!

I <u>can't</u> lift 500 pounds.

My father <u>didn't</u> take me to the circus.

My dog <u>won't</u> fetch my slippers.

There <u>isn't</u> anything wrong with wearing a hat.

<u>Wouldn't</u> you like some cake?

I <u>hadn't</u> planned to go to the party.

I <u>shouldn't</u> steal paper clips from work.

There <u>wasn't</u> anything I could say to make my mother happy.

<u>Let's</u> get some coffee.

Here's a look at those sentences with the contractions removed and the missing words spelled out.

<u>Do not</u> touch that!

I <u>cannot</u> lift 500 pounds.

My father <u>did not</u> take me to the circus.

My dog <u>will not</u> fetch my slippers.

There <u>is not</u> anything wrong with wearing a hat.

<u>Would not</u> you like some cake?

I <u>had not</u> planned to go to the party.

I <u>should not</u> steal paper clips from work.

There <u>was not</u> anything I could say to make my mother happy.

<u>Let us</u> get some coffee.

Some contractions are easier to remember than others. *Shouldn't* is close to *should not* and therefore easy to figure out. You'll have to memorize others. For example, *won't* is a contraction of *will not*.

Contractions are very common in speech and writing. However, in very formal types of writing, you should avoid contractions, which are considered too colloquial. When in doubt, ask the teacher or editor for their preference. As with most aspects of writing, there are different views on contractions, depending on your audience and purpose.

The Least You Need to Know

- Quotation marks are used to distinguish someone else's exact words from your own.
- Apostrophes are used mainly for making words possessive, like if you were talking about a dog's dish: the dish that belongs to the dog.
- Apostrophes are also used to make contractions, as in changing *do not* to *don't*.
- *Its* is possessive and *it's* is a contraction: this is a distinction you'll have to memorize.
- Contractions aren't welcome in very formal writing—fortunately, this book isn't that formal.

CHAPTER 19

Hyphens, Dashes, Parentheses, and Brackets

This chapter deals with punctuation marks that cleave, which is an interesting word: it is its own antonym (opposite). To cleave is to bring together, and to cleave is also to separate.

The punctuation marks in this chapter cleave in both senses: hyphens, dashes, parentheses, and brackets bring together some elements of words or sentences while separating others. They are very useful in writing clear, flowing prose.

These marks are especially helpful in bringing some of the qualities of speech to writing. When you talk, it's easy to raise your voice, whisper, or dramatically pause to make a point. In writing, these punctuation marks can help readers hear your writing the way you want them to hear it: the way you hear it in your head.

This chapter is very important to style, since every writer has his or her own preferences when it comes to dashes, parentheses, and so on.

In This Chapter

- The hyphen: a joiner of words
- The em and en dash: two similar marks with different purposes
- How (and why) to use parentheses
- Where [and when] to use brackets

Putting Hyphens to Good Use

Hyphens are punctuation marks that connect words or parts of words. They are shorter than dashes, and they have totally different jobs. Don't confuse a hyphen (-) with a dash (—).

Breaking a Word at the End of a Line

Back in the days of typewriters, hyphens were used to break works at the end of lines, like so:

> I've had enough. When will you ever stop com-
> plaining about the weather?

Now that word processing programs wrap around text, this use of hyphens is very rare. You're only likely to see it in something quite old.

Hyphenating Compound Numbers

When spelling out numbers, hyphens help readers remember that the number is a single entity. The following is clear:

> I have eighty-one Batman action figures.

If you forget the hyphen, it's a little less clear:

> I have eighty one Batman action figures.

For just a second, the reader will think the number you're talking about is eighty, not eighty-one. Help your readers out by remembering those hyphens in numbers.

You only need to hyphenate numbers from 21 to 99. If you're writing out a longer number, you should still hyphenate the part that includes a number from 21-99, as in the following examples:

> four hundred ninety-six
>
> one thousand twenty-nine
>
> one million, eighty thousand, forty-three

Practice

Write out the following numbers, hyphenating where necessary:

1. 306

2. 87

3. 102

4. 9,000

5. 37

6. 190

7. 62

8. 23

9. 11

10. 456

Answers:

1. three hundred six

2. eighty-seven

3. one hundred two

4. nine thousand

5. thirty-seven

6. one hundred ninety

7. sixty-two

8. twenty-three

9. eleven

10. four hundred fifty-six

Setting Off a Prefix ... or Not

Prefixes are those little word parts that go on the front of words: like *pre–*, *mega–*, and *hyper–*. Do prefixed words need hyphens? Sometimes.

Language changes over time, and one of the most consistent changes is the disappearance of hyphens. For example, consider the word *email*. When electronic mail was new, it was consistently abbreviated as e-mail—the *e–* prefix standing for *electronic*. As time passed—and electronic mail became a commonplace, normal part of life—more and more people dropped the hyphen and spelled it *email*. Eventually, *email* became the norm.

Check a current dictionary if you're unsure whether or not a word should be hyphenated. It can also help to Google both versions of a word to see which version is most popular. As mentioned elsewhere, if the masses make a change in English, the change will eventually stick.

See Chapter 20 for more on prefixes, suffixes, and infixes.

Hyphenating Compound Adjectives

One of the most helpful uses of hyphens is to link compound adjectives. All of the following examples hyphenate adjectives for the sake of clarity.

> I am a public-relations intern.
>
> My uncle is a free-wheeling traveler.
>
> Be careful of that spring-loaded bear trap.
>
> This voice-activated computer is nifty.
>
> That battery-operated light is cheap.

All these examples use hyphens to make the sentences read more smoothly and clearly. Here's the alternative without hyphens:

> I am a public relations intern.
>
> My uncle is a free wheeling traveler.
>
> Be careful of that spring loaded bear trap.
>
> This voice activated computer is nifty.
>
> That battery operated light is cheap.

Though these sentences look about the same, they're not as clear as the hyphenated batch. For example, take a closer look at this sentence:

> Be careful of that spring loaded bear trap.

As you start reading it, it seems as though the sentence is about some kind of spring: "Be careful of that spring …" Since *spring* and *loaded* are unattached, a reader can get tripped up. That hyphen lets readers know that *spring-loaded* is a single lexical item. Similar problems occur without the hyphen here:

> My uncle is a free wheeling traveler.

If you read this quickly, you might think *free* and *wheeling* have totally separate meanings in the sentence. You might wonder exactly how this uncle is free, and in what way he might be wheeling. You don't want to cause confusion in your readers, not even for a second. By hyphenating *free-wheeling*, you've made your meaning crystal clear.

The exception to this rule happens in the case of compound adjectives that are very established as words. For example, you can mention a *major league player* rather than a *major-league player*, since *major league* is so commonly used. When to use or omit a hyphen in a compound adjective is definitely a judgment call. Just make it an informed judgment.

Making Good Use of the Dash

The hyphen's longer friend is the dash. There are two kinds of dashes, and both are important to know.

Choosing an Em or En Dash

The em dash and the en dash are the two types of dashes. The en and em dashes are about the length of the letters for which they are named. Read on to learn their uses.

Indicating a Range of Numbers

Though the en dash is occasionally used like a hyphen in making compound words, its main use involves writing a range of numbers:

> The students' ages range from 18–55.

> I have somewhere between 3–5 close friends.

> Someday I think I'd like 2–3 children.

> That family is so rich I think they own 2–3 mansions.

> This toy is designed for ages 5–8.

You also need to use an en dash when writing a range of years:

> The original *Star Wars* movies came out from 1972–1983.

> My uncle lived from 1934–1989.

> The best years of my life were from about 1990–1994.

> I wonder what TV will be like in the years 2050–2100.

> Picasso's blue period lasted from 1900–1904.

The en dash looks so much like a hyphen that it is very difficult to tell the two apart at a glance. In fact, hyphens are often used for the same jobs as the en dash. Since the em dash is more commonly used, when I mention a dash from this point on, assume it's an em dash.

Introducing a Clarifying Statement

I like action movies—especially superhero movies.

Fall is the best season—the weather is just perfect.

Batman is the best superhero—he's heroic and relatable.

I need coffee in the morning—it gets me going.

I feel cranky—everything is getting on my nerves.

Enclosing Incidental (Nonessential) Text in Parentheses

The main job of parentheses is to set off nonessential text from the rest of the sentence. Parentheses aren't the only punctuation mark to do this job, so we need to talk again about dashes and commas.

Commas, Dashes, or Parentheses?

Here's one of the biggest judgment calls in writing: Should you set off a phrase with commas, dashes, or parentheses?

In some cases, this is pretty clear. When the phrase is nonessential, as mentioned in the comma chapter, use commas.

My uncle, the highest-ranked unicyclist in North Dakota, is coming for dinner.

Then again, using dashes in that sentence wouldn't exactly be wrong.

My uncle—the highest-ranked unicyclist in North Dakota—is coming for dinner.

In that case, I would lean toward commas, since the information feels particularly trivial. Dashes create more emphasis than commas: they make the information stand out. Dashes are the best choice when you have information you'd like to highlight.

The novelist—who has won the Pulitzer Prize—will be speaking at the university.

Small dogs—no matter how well behaved at home—may run into trouble with big dogs at the park.

The scandal—which involved drugs and prostitution—brought the administration to its knees.

Other times, parentheses would be a better choice:

I like big dogs (mastiffs, Great Danes, etc.) more than little dogs.

My great-aunt (my mom's aunt) is a designer of dresses.

I love painting (usually with watercolors) on the weekends.

Think of what's in parentheses as almost a whispered aside. The material in parentheses adds a tiny bit of color or information to the sentence. These details help flesh out a thought, often by giving examples.

Ultimately, the choice between commas, dashes, or parentheses is a matter of taste. For example, some writers love dashes, while others hardly ever use them. As you read and write more, your style will emerge. Look at how other writers compose their sentences and you'll see ways you can improve your own prose.

USAGE TIDBIT

When deciding if commas, dashes, or parentheses would work best, see which most enhance the meaning of your sentence. After that, consider variety. If a page of your writing has a half-dozen sentences with dashes, it might be time to start mixing it up with commas and parentheses. As in life, variety is a good thing.

Periods: In or Out?

One question that confuses even experienced writers is whether or not a period should go inside or outside the parentheses if the parentheses come at the end of the sentence. For some reason, this is a hard one to remember.

Here's the rule of thumb: If the material inside the parentheses is an independent clause, put the period inside the closing parenthesis, as in the following examples:

I hate math. (It's the worst subject.)

My uncle is a creep. (He's currently in jail.)

Summer is the best. (I love swimming and boating.)

My dog is fast. (He's won many races.)

I feel sick. (My nose is running.)

If the material in parentheses is not an independent clause, put the period after the closing parenthesis, as in these examples:

I love science fiction (especially Isaac Asimov).

I have some strange symptoms (dizziness, odd pains).

My doctor is handsome (and tall).

I like to swim in the lake (and ocean, when possible).

Bikers never seem to pay attention to traffic rules (especially stop signs).

Practice

In the following sentences, add the appropriate punctuation and capitalization if necessary:

1. I like tennis (it's so much fun to play)

2. My foot feels weird (and itchy)

3. My cat won't let me sleep (she always meows in the middle of the night)

4. Batman has awesome gadgets (like his batarangs)

5. The scandal was huge (it took down a president)

6. Spring is coming soon (hopefully)

7. It's raining out (it's been pouring all day)

8. Holidays are stressful (there's too much to do)

9. I enjoy jazz (especially John Coltrane)

10. My neighborhood has a lot of restaurants (especially sushi)

Answers:

1. I like tennis. (It's so much fun to play.)

   The period goes inside the closing parenthesis because "it's so much fun to play" is an independent clause.

2. My foot feels weird (and itchy).

   The period goes outside the closing parenthesis because "and itchy" is not an independent clause.

3. My cat won't let me sleep. (She always meows in the middle of the night.)

   The period goes inside the parenthesis because "she always meows in the middle of the night" is an independent clause.

4. Batman has awesome gadgets (like his batarangs).

   The period goes outside the parenthesis because "like his batarangs" is not an independent clause.

5. The scandal was huge. (It took down a president.)

   The period goes inside the parenthesis because "it took down a president" is an independent clause.

6. Spring is coming soon (hopefully).

   The period goes outside the parenthesis because *hopefully* is not an independent clause.

7. It's raining out. (It's been pouring all day.)

   The period goes inside the parenthesis because "it's been pouring all day" is an independent clause.

8. Holidays are stressful. (There's too much to do.)

   The period goes inside the parenthesis because "there's too much to do" is an independent clause.

9. I enjoy jazz (especially John Coltrane).

   The period goes outside the parenthesis because "especially John Coltrane" is not an independent clause.

10. My neighborhood has a lot of restaurants (especially sushi).

    The period goes outside the parenthesis because "especially sushi" is not an independent clause.

Making Sure the Text Is Incidental

Now you know how to deal with incidental material, but how do you know if it really is incidental (in other words, nonessential)? There's an easy way to tell: pull it out of the sentence and see if you still have a complete thought.

My laptop—which is two years old—is getting slow.

My son (who is 10) has developed an annoying habit of whistling constantly.

If I had more money—much more money—I'd take a trip to Vegas.

Now let's take the material out.

> My laptop is getting slow.

> My son has developed an annoying habit of whistling constantly.

> If I had more money, I'd take a trip to Vegas.

In those cases, you're fine. The incidental material proved to be nonessential because its removal didn't result in an incomplete thought.

Using Brackets [Rarely, If Ever]

These aren't the kind of brackets that are so popular in March during the NCAA men's basketball tournament. Rather, brackets are a square friend of parentheses that are not used nearly as often.

One use of brackets is when you quote someone but need to add words for clarity. In the following examples, the material in brackets was not part of the original quotation:

> Jones wrote, "I hate it [basketball] so much. It's the worst sport."

> As the president said to the American people, "We're doomed. They [killer robots from the future] are on their way, and they're angry."

> His suicide note said, "It [starting a Ponzi scheme] was the beginning of my downfall."

The brackets are a clear signal to readers that you're clarifying what's in the quotation but not changing the quotation.

Brackets help you find a middle way between two rules of thumb: you should always quote accurately, and you should always be clear. When an exact quotation is unclear, you're in a pickle. Using brackets to add clarifying material allows you to quote accurately while helping the reader understand what the author meant.

A word of caution: make sure the clarifying material you add is true to the source. It's dishonest to add material that changes or distorts the meaning. Only add bracketed material that will help readers understand what the writer intended.

> **USAGE TIDBIT**
>
> When it comes to quotations, using brackets is the opposite of using an ellipsis. Brackets are used to add information, like this:
>
> Frank said, "That so-and-so [Dave] is an evil, diabolical, demented, twisted maniac!"
>
> An ellipsis subtracts material from a quotation:
>
> Frank said, "That so-and-so is an evil … maniac!"
>
> Use both of these methods of quoting sparingly, since it's better to quote exactly what was said.

The Least You Need to Know

- Hyphens are used to make compound words such as *pre-board* and *battery-operated*.
- En dashes are used to indicate a range of numbers (like 2001–2005) and sometimes make compound words, like hyphens.
- Dashes are longer than hyphens and separate elements of a sentence—like this.
- Parentheses separate nonessential information from the rest of the sentence.
- Brackets are rarely used, but they help add information to a quotation that can make the meaning clearer.

Spelling Rules, Tips, and Tricks

We can all sympathize with the terror of being in a spelling bee. "Spell that!" can feel like an impossible task, especially in a language with as many influences and ancestors as English.

Spelling is one of many areas where other people will judge you for mistakes. If you send an email application for a job and don't catch the spelling errors, you're not likely to get the job. Even in situations like dating, many people want nothing to do with someone who can't bother to spell words correctly. Spelling is a huge part of creating a positive impression in readers. Good spelling shows you're detail-oriented, careful, and respectful of your audience.

While spellcheckers solve a lot of spelling problems, you need a basic knowledge of the spelling rules and patterns in English. No one is a perfect speller, but with a little work and practice, you'll find spelling isn't as daunting as it seems.

In This Chapter

- The difficulty of phonetic spelling in English
- Learning different vowel and consonant sounds
- Spelling rules and exceptions you must learn
- Making words plural and other suffix-related issues

Spelling Phonetically: A Challenge in English

Some languages—such as Spanish—have very consistent rules for spelling in which you can see a new word and immediately have a pretty good idea of how to pronounce it. In those languages, you can also hear a new word and have a pretty good idea how to spell it.

English isn't like that. Phonetic spelling will take you only so far: in other words, not far at all. Because English has a tangled history—and more sounds than letters in the alphabet—English spelling is challenging, even to native speakers.

Buckle your seatbelts. It's time to take a closer look at English spelling.

Brushing Up on Spelling Rules

English is a tricky language to spell because for every rule, there's an exception—and usually more than one exception. However, there are some general rules you should know.

Vowel Sounds

There are two types of vowel sounds in English: long and short. The short sounds can be heard in *bat, bet, bit, bought,* and *but.* The long sounds can be heard in *bait, beet, bite, boat,* and *beaut.*

Often, a short vowel sound becomes long with the addition of a final *e:*

short	long
bit	bite
cut	cute
din	dine
fad	fade
kit	kite
mat	mate
mop	mope
sat	sate
ton	tone
trip	tripe

Another way to spot long vowel sounds is to look out for double consonants. Double consonants are almost always long:

beep

boom

creep

feed

flee

moon

noon

vacuum

Of course, there are always exceptions. For example, the rare *aa* in aardvark is short, not long.

The "i before e except after c" Rule

One of the most well-known English spelling rules is "i before e except after c." These words follow that rule:

brief

chief

grief

perceive

receive

These words break the rule:

beige

conscience

Keith

science

their

There are plenty of other words that break the rule, too. At this point, you may be asking yourself: "If there are so many exceptions, how is this a rule?"

I would say it's really not. However, since "i before e except after c" is so commonly taught, it's something you should know about. Just make sure you double-check the spelling before blindly applying this rule: in fact, that's a good lesson for all rules.

Doubling a Consonant

There's a special spelling rule for one-syllable words that end in a consonant: the final consonant gets doubled when adding a suffix.

I stop.	He's stopping.
He's fat.	I'm fatter.
She's hip.	He's hipper.

This rule does not apply to one-syllable words that end in a consonant blend:

He blends.	I blended.
You're fast.	I'm faster.
I grasp.	He grasped.

Practice

Put the following verbs in their present participle form by adding *–ing* and adjusting the spelling as needed:

1. clasp
2. coast
3. flip
4. hit
5. flinch
6. moon
7. row
8. squat
9. stall

10. stomp

11. stop

12. task

13. trip

14. wade

15. wet

Answers:

1. clasping

2. coasting

3. flipping

4. hitting

5. flinching

6. mooning (Do not double the final consonant if it follows two vowels.)

7. rowing

8. squatting

9. stalling (Do not double the final consonant if it is doubled.)

10. stomping

11. stopping

12. tasking

13. tripping

14. wading (If the final consonant is followed by *e*, drop the *e*.)

15. wetting

Hard and Soft Consonants

Just as vowels can be short or long, many consonants can be soft or hard. While *b, m,* and others always sound the same, some consonants have two different sounds. For example, these are examples of a soft *c* sound, which sounds like an *s:*

> cent
>
> certain
>
> cinch
>
> sentence
>
> since

The following words feature the hard *c* sound, which is the same sound as a hard *k:*

> apricot
>
> attic
>
> caterpillar
>
> cork
>
> corn

G is another letter with a soft and hard sound. These words feature the soft sound:

> genealogy
>
> general
>
> giant
>
> gym
>
> gypsum

These words include the hard *g* sound:

> again
>
> aghast
>
> goodness
>
> gothic
>
> great

The N Sound

The letter *n* has only one sound, but that sound can be made by a few other sound blends. The following words all start with the same sound that begins *nun, nope, ninja,* and *noon:*

gnat

gnostic

knife

knight

know

In fact, *night* and *knight* are pronounced exactly the same way, though their meanings are pretty different. The opposite of day (*night*) is pretty different from a medieval warrior (*knight*).

Plurals

When making a word plural—like *words,* the plural of word—simply add an *s.* This is how you make the vast majority of words plural.

airplane	airplanes
basket	baskets
cat	cats
coffee	coffees
computer	computers
fire	fires
muffin	muffins
pumpkin	pumpkins
senator	senators
tangerine	tangerines

For words ending with the letters *–ch*, *–sh*, or *–s*, you need *–es* to make a plural word.

ax	axes
bass	basses
brush	brushes
crash	crashes
fax	faxes
glass	glasses
hatch	hatches
hex	hexes
latch	latches
stash	stashes

Words Ending in Y

When you make a word ending in *–y* plural, you have to change the spelling to *–ie* in some cases:

dinghy	dinghies
puppy	puppies
symphony	symphonies
tragedy	tragedies
trophy	trophies

This rule does not apply to words that have a vowel before the final *y*. For example: the plural of *holiday* is *holidays*.

Practice

Make the following words plural:

1. arm
2. bass
3. belch
4. bench
5. boy
6. chair
7. comedy
8. face
9. hitch
10. house
11. kitty
12. lamp
13. latch
14. light
15. number
16. rutabaga
17. table
18. tax
19. thatch
20. thingy

Answers:

1. arms
2. basses
3. belches
4. benches
5. boys
6. chairs
7. comedies
8. faces
9. hitches
10. houses
11. kitties
12. lamps
13. latches
14. lights
15. numbers
16. rutabagas
17. tables
18. taxes
19. thatches
20. thingies

Irregular Plural Words

Many English words have an irregular plural form, which you'll have to memorize. These are some of the most common irregular plural words:

child	children
foot	feet
goose	geese

man	men
matrix	matrices
mouse	mice
person	people
stratum	strata
tooth	teeth
woman	women

When Plural and Singular Are the Same

For some English words, the singular form doubles as the plural form. For example, while you could say the pond is full of fishes, you could also say the pond is full of fish. The following words have the same singular and plural forms:

aircraft

barracks

deep

moose

pants

salmon

scissors

sheep

species

swine

When F Becomes V

In the case of nouns that end with an *f* sound, turn the *f* into a *v* to make the plural:

elf	elves
knife	knives
life	lives
shelf	shelves
wife	wives

> ☞ **PRACTICAL POINT**
>
> There's no exception to the rule that there are always exceptions to the rules of English spelling. This creates challenges for anyone writing in English. You can learn every rule in the book, but there will always be words that don't fit the rules. These have to be memorized. For example, take the consonant blend *tw*. It's not that common in English, but it's used in the following examples:
>
> | | |
> |---|---|
> | twaddle | twine |
> | tweet | twist |
> | twerp | twitter |
>
> So what about the word *two*? The spelling of the number 2 looks like it should be pronounced with the *tw* sound, but it's not: *two* sounds exactly like *too* and *to*. You just have to learn and memorize these exceptions. As you read, write, hear, and speak more English, it will get easier—even if it never makes total sense.

Attaching Prefixes and Suffixes

Affixes are lexical items that are attached to roots. They change the meaning of the word in some way. For example, if you add *–s* to *book,* you have *books*: more than one book.

Prefixes

Prefixes are attached to the beginning of a word. For example, the words kilometer and nanometer have the prefixes *kilo–* and *nano–*. There are many prefixes in English. For example:

I'm <u>super</u>-excited for this movie.

I prefer <u>low</u>-fat yogurt.

Don't forget to <u>pre</u>-heat the oven.

Stay tuned for the <u>post</u>-game show.

Joe Biden is the <u>vice</u>-president of the United States.

My <u>ex</u>-husband is a jerk.

Did you send an <u>inter</u>-office memo?

I can't draw a <u>semi</u>-circle.

Make sure to <u>de</u>-ice the car.

In the movie, the hero fought the <u>robo</u>-monster.

As you can see, many prefixes are attached with a hyphen. Look at Chapter 19 for more on hyphens.

However, this isn't always the case. Sometimes a word becomes so commonly accepted that the hyphen is no longer necessary. The prefixes in the following words all do their job without the help of a hyphen.

> The Peace Corp helps many <u>under</u>developed countries.
>
> Have you heard this band? They're <u>in</u>sane!
>
> I am an <u>a</u>theist.
>
> I'm sick. I need <u>anti</u>biotics.
>
> Coat hangers often <u>be</u>come <u>en</u>tangled.
>
> The United States is in the Western <u>Hemi</u>sphere.
>
> Have you seen my <u>over</u>coat?
>
> That singer is <u>be</u>witching.
>
> I'm often <u>un</u>sure what to do.
>
> I enjoy many <u>extra</u>curricular activities.

Suffixes

Suffixes go on the end of words. As with prefixes, they often are attached to a word with the help of a hyphen.

> Many people are eating only gluten-<u>free</u> food.
>
> I believe all teaching should be student-<u>centric</u>.
>
> The toy is battery-<u>operated</u>.
>
> Make sure the whole house is child-<u>proof</u>.
>
> Is this restaurant family-<u>friendly</u>?

Even more than prefixes, it's very common for suffixes to not use a hyphen. Many of these are adjectives:

> I feel a little flu<u>ish</u>.
>
> The couch is large and cumber<u>some</u>.
>
> Hang the picture of length<u>wise</u>.

Puppies are usually excit<u>able</u>.

My sister has a theat<u>rical</u> background.

Others are nouns:

My Uncle Jimmy is an alco<u>holic</u>.

Free<u>dom</u> is important to me.

America is a dem<u>ocracy</u>.

In college, I studied bio<u>logy</u>.

Do you believe in commun<u>ism?</u>

Suffixes are also attached to the back of verbs:

I start<u>ed</u> Spanish classes today.

Listen to the birds sing<u>ing</u>.

Basketball players are good at runn<u>ing</u> and jump<u>ing</u>.

My dog chas<u>ed</u> the squirrel into the tree.

I learn<u>ed</u> to juggle in France.

Infixes

There's a far less common cousin of the prefix and suffix: the infix. While prefixes go on the front of the word, and suffixes go on the end, infixes are sandwiched in the middle. Infixes nearly always intensify the meaning of a word without adding additional meaning. Nothing intensifies like an obscenity, and many infixes are obscene, but there are a few examples we can list here.

That movie was un-<u>freaking</u>-believable.

My shirt is brand-<u>spanking</u>-new.

I can't do that. It's im-<u>bloody</u>-possible!

> **USAGE TIDBIT**
>
> Read, read, read. The best way to become a better speller is by becoming a better reader. The more you read, the more familiar you'll get with English spelling and quirky words. Read this book in particular: David Crystal's *Spell It Out: The Singular Story of English Spelling* is a remarkable look at the history of English spelling. Crystal puts the tangled history of spelling in context and shows the logic behind spelling that seems arbitrary. This book will help you become a better speller and more informed person about English in general.

The Least You Need to Know

- Phonetic spelling will only take you so far in English, due to the many languages that have influenced English spelling.

- Get to know patterns in English, such as doubling the final consonant after a one-syllable word that attaches a suffix (stopping, getting).

- Take some time to study irregular forms of words, such as *people*, a plural form of *person*.

- Prefixes are word parts that go on the front of the word, and suffixes go on the end.

- Suffixes and prefixes often, but not always, are linked to a word with hyphens.

CHAPTER 21

Capitalization, Abbreviations, and Numbers

There are many choices available to writers in terms of sentence style, grammar, word choice, and punctuation. There is one final choice too: how to write a letter.

There are two ways to write letters in English: uppercase (ABC) and lowercase (abc). Uppercase letters are also called capital letters, and when you start a word with a capital letter, you're capitalizing it. There are many situations in English that demand capitalization, such as the beginning of a sentence or a proper noun, like *English*. There are also many ways to improperly capitalize.

FOR EXAMPLE, DOES THIS LOOK WEIRD?

how about this?

NoTice anyTHing oUt of wHacK heRe?

Using too many or not enough capital letters can cause confusion or annoyance in readers. Therefore, it's important to get a handle on the rules of capitalization, which are one of the most consistent areas of English. Once you get to know when and why to capitalize, you'll be prepared for most writing situations.

In This Chapter

- When to use capital letters
- The dangers of inconsistent capitalization
- The different types of abbreviations
- How to write numbers, dates, and times

Capitalization

There are two ways to write letters in English: uppercase (ABC) and lowercase (abc). Uppercase letters are also called capital letters, and when you start a word with a capital letter, you capitalize it. There are many situations in English that demand capitalization.

Capitalizing the First Word of Sentences and Quotations

One of the primary uses of capital letters is for the beginning of sentences. As you'll notice when looking at sentences—including this sentence—the first letter of the first word is capitalized. This is a signal to readers that a new sentence (and new thought) is beginning.

Also, the first word of a quotation is capitalized if the original was capitalized.

> Shakespeare wrote, "Something is rotten in the state of Denmark."

An Independent Clause Following a Colon

An independent clause that follows a colon is also often capitalized, as here:

> There are two kinds of people: The kind who use colons correctly and the kind who don't.

This is a judgment call, and you could punctuate the same sentence without capitalizing after the colon:

> There are two kinds of people: the kind who use colons correctly and the kind who don't.

Capitalizing Proper Nouns and Adjectives

Another of the main uses of capital letters is for proper names. Capitalization distinguishes a proper noun (like *Joe*) from other nouns that are more general (like *guy*). Proper nouns can be people, places, or things.

> My brother's name is Albert.

> Susan and Jen went to dinner.

> I am from Buffalo, New York.

> Man, I would love to visit Australia.

> My computer is an Apple.

This includes the names of businesses and organizations:

> I work for Pepsi.

> Mark Zuckerberg founded Facebook.

> I am an ambassador to the United Nations.

> The legislative body of the United States is Congress.

> I'm a member of the Lakeview Book Club.

Even if the company or group uses all lowercase letters in their official name or logo, you should capitalize their name when you write it.

Nationalities, Races, and Religions

There are many kinds of proper nouns besides people and places. Religion and nationality give us many words that must be capitalized, such as *Canada, Muslim,* and *New Zealand.* Always capitalize the names of religions, races, and nationalities.

> My teacher was Jewish.

> The Pope is the leader of the Catholic Church.

> I think Mexican food is delicious.

> My teacher is African American.

Specific Places, Things, or Events

Some events are so historically important that they are capitalized:

> There are several museums dedicated to the Holocaust.

> The French Revolution changed world history.

> Brewing went underground in the United States during Prohibition.

Capitalizing *I*

One of the conventions of English spelling is that *I* is capitalized when it's used as a first-person pronoun.

>   I hate when you show up late!

>   Did you remember what I told you?

>   I fell off the porch and broke my collarbone.

>   What do I look like?

>   I'm going to get you!

Sometimes when writing emails, texts, or tweets, people don't capitalize *I* and write like this.

>   i like you!

>   where should i go?

>   i'm sleepy.

This may be acceptable in extremely informal messages to friends—and sometimes in poetry—but you should never forget to capitalize *I* in any writing that is public or written for anyone you might to impress. Using lowercase *i* is the writing equivalent of coming to a business meeting wearing ripped jeans and a shirt with mustard stains on it. It sends the wrong message and will make people think you're sloppy, ignorant, or just not smart.

Other First-Person Pronouns Are Not Capitalized

Though *me* and *myself* mean the same thing as *I,* they should not be capitalized:

>   Don't you recognize me?

>   Do I have to do everything myself?

>   Kids today are always thinking, "me me me …."

>   Sometimes I hate myself.

>   You make me proud.

Also, note that the opposite of I—the word *you*—is not capitalized.

> 👉 (**PRACTICAL POINT**)
>
> Another, rarer case is the interjection *O*. O my! This gets capitalized as well, though it's possible you may never use it. *O* has pretty much been replaced by *oh*, which is not capitalized.

Capitalizing Titles

Titles are capitalized, too. This includes the titles of movies, TV shows, books, record albums, and other creations.

> I loved *Iron Man 3* and *Star Trek: Into Darkness.*
>
> Have you read *To Kill a Mockingbird?*
>
> The best Sonic Youth album is *Daydream Nation.*
>
> I once saw Kenneth Branagh play the lead in *Hamlet* in London.
>
> *The Book of Mormon* is a musical by the creators of *South Park.*

Also, headlines and titles of articles are capitalized, though there are several ways to do it. The format varies, as you'll see in different magazines, journals, newspapers, and internet publications.

In some formats, only the very first word of the title is capitalized.

> The mayor is caught embezzling
>
> Study shows coffee cures the common cold
>
> Dog rescues his owner

Other formats capitalize every single word.

> The Mayor Is Caught Embezzling
>
> Study Shows Coffee Cures The Common Cold
>
> Dog Rescues His Owner

Many formats capitalize every important word, neglecting only the shortest and least significant words.

> The Mayor is Caught Embezzling
>
> Study Shows Coffee Cures the Common Cold
>
> Dog Rescues his Owner

One of the trickiest elements of capitalizing is when different rules seem to contradict each other. You can resolve possible conflicts by following the rule that's most powerful, either overall or in that situation.

For example, names are always capitalized. So even if you're following a format where only the first word of a headline is capitalized, you still need to capitalize a name.

> President meets Madonna
>
> Fans mob Tim Duncan
>
> Who really wrote Shakespeare's plays?
>
> Was Emily Dickinson a vampire?

The personal pronoun *I* is always capitalized, but *myself* is not capitalized. However, *myself* would be capitalized in the title of a book, for example.

> *I Did It Myself: A Selfish Story*
>
> *From Myself to Yourself: Making a Connection*
>
> *Drinking Myself to Death: A Drunkard's Tale*
>
> *Myself, Me, and I: Pronouns of the Self*

In writing, there are very few rules that are followed 100 percent of the time. You have to examine the situation, think about your audience and purpose, and decide what makes sense. The more you read and write, the better your judgment will be.

Personal Titles Are Sometimes Capitalized

A person's title is capitalized if it's part of their name, as in these examples:

> I'd love to meet President Barack Obama.
>
> Where is Congressman Wilson?
>
> Is Mayor Bloomberg vegan?
>
> Editor-in-Chief Jameson is a jerk.

In those cases, the titles are part of the person's name. Since names are always capitalized, you should capitalize the titles, too. You don't need to capitalize a title that comes after the name:

> Jameson, the editor-in-chief, is a jerk.
>
> Bloomberg, the mayor, is in the gazebo.

Wilson, a congressman, has no morals.

Barack Obama was elected president in 2008.

You can capitalize some familial words if they're being used as proper nouns. The following are correct:

Hey Dad, what are you doing?

I need to get off the phone, Mom.

Where's Uncle Fred?

These are also correct:

My mom likes to leave voicemails.

I wish my dad had more money.

Is my aunt around?

This is the rule: if you refer to your mom or dad as a mom or dad (almost like you'd refer to a banker, quarterback, or editor) then you don't capitalize them. If you refer to them directly—using *Mom* or *Dad* as a name—then you should capitalize them.

Words Referring to God

Names that refer to God or any other deity are capitalized, too:

I've been praying to God for a new car.

Please help me, Jesus.

The Scandinavian people used to worship Odin.

By the beard of Zeus, my head hurts!

You don't capitalize *god* if you're simply referring to a god or gods, as in the following examples:

The ancient Greeks worshipped many gods, such as Apollo.

Thor is the only god who became a major superhero.

Christians consider Jesus half-human, half-god.

Athena was a goddess.

Abbreviations

An abbreviation is a shortening of a word or group of words, either by removing letters or using only the first initials of all or some of the words. Abbreviations are used when it would look or sound clumsy to write something long over and over.

Many types of abbreviations are not capitalized. For example, if you wrote *dept.* to abbreviate *department,* you don't need to capitalize it. (Unless it's part of a proper name, like the Arts Dept.)

These are a few common abbreviations:

Ave.	Avenue
Dr.	doctor
E.	East
fridge	refrigerator
plane	airplane
pres.	president
prof	professor
sec	second
U.S.	United States
W.	West

An acronym is a type of abbreviation that is capitalized; in fact, acronyms use all capital letters. Acronyms are also pronounced like a regular word. The following are some common acronyms:

AIDS	acquired immune deficiency syndrome
FEMA	Federal Emergency Management Agency
NASA	National Aeronautics and Space Administration
POTUS	President of the United States
SIDS	sudden infant death syndrome

Other acronyms abbreviate phrases:

ASAP	as soon as possible
FAQ	frequently asked questions
FOMO	fear of missing out

NIMBY	not in my backyard
YOLO	you only live once

Acronyms have a close relation: the initialism. Initialisms also use all capital letters, but they have one difference: initialisms are not pronounced like a regular word. You have to spell initialisms out when you say them. You have to say every initial.

CEO	chief executive officer
CIA	Central Intelligence Agency
IED	improvised explosive device
MRI	magnetic resonance imaging
NFL	National Football League

Like acronyms, some initialisms abbreviate phrases, like the following:

BYOB	bring your own booze
MIA	missing in action
OMG	oh my God
PDA	public display of affection
RIP	rest in peace

Practice

Identify which of the following are acronyms, initialisms, or just plain abbreviations?

1. I enjoy TV, movies, etc.

2. Are you a fan of the NHL?

3. Want to go scuba diving?

4. I'm filming a PSA.

5. I was born Jan. 11, 1981.

6. I have a drinking problem. I think I need to go to AA.

7. Could you send me that file as a gif?

8. Is Gov. Roberts around?

9. I donated to UNICEF.

Answers:

1. I enjoy TV, movies, etc.

   Abbreviation: *Etc.* is a shortening of *etcetera,* and TV is a shortening of *television.*

2. Are you a fan of the NHL?

   Initialism: NHL stands for National Hockey League and is pronounced one letter at a time.

3. Want to go scuba diving?

   Acronym: Scuba stands for self-contained underwater breathing apparatus and is pronounced as a regular word.

4. I'm filming a PSA.

   Initialism: PSA stands for public service announcement and is pronounced one letter at a time.

5. I was born Jan. 11, 1981.

   Abbreviation: *Jan.* is a shortening of *January.*

6. I have a drinking problem. I think I need to go to AA.

   Initialism: AA stands for Alcoholics Anonymous and is pronounced one letter at a time.

7. Could you send me that file as a gif?

   Acronym: gif stands for graphics interchange format and is pronounced as a regular word.

8. Is Gov. Roberts around?

   Abbreviation: *Gov.* is a shortening of *Governor.*

9. I donated to UNICEF.

   Acronym: UNICEF stands for United Nations International Children's Emergency Fund and is pronounced as a regular word.

Numbers, Dates, and Time

Even if you prefer English class to math class, you're still going to have to deal with numbers. Fortunately, there are only a few ways of writing numbers.

For the first nine numbers and zero, write them out as a word:

zero

one

two

three

four

five

six

seven

eight

nine

For larger numbers, use the numerals:

10

15

67

114

879

When writing numbers that are four digits or more, add a comma every three digits starting from the right-hand side:

1,000

2,000

5,000

10,000

100,000

400,000,000

300,800,567,021

481,878,231,000,000

1,567,222,317,908,234

32,000,000,000,000,000

There will often be exceptions to these rules, depending on the style guide you're using. You might sometimes have to write ten thousand instead of 10,000. As always, follow the appropriate rules for your writing situation.

When writing a date, you need to use commas on both sides of the year:

> On January 14, 1987, I was married.
>
> Is August 5, 1971, your birthday?
>
> December 18, 1999, was the worst day of my life.

Times are written with a colon, and often followed by *A.M.* or *P.M.*:

> Where were you at 3:00 P.M.?
>
> I keep waking up at 2:30 in the morning.
>
> 9:00 A.M. is the starting time for my job.

 DANGER ZONE

Watch for redundancy when speaking or writing times. You should say "10 A.M." or "10 in the morning," not "10 A.M. in the morning." That would be as bad as saying "ATM machine"—since the *M* already stands for machine, there's no reason to say it twice.

The Least You Need to Know

- Capitalize proper names: the names of specific people, places, religions, and works of art.
- Abbreviations are a type of shorthand, like writing Dr. Miller instead of Doctor Miller.
- Acronyms like POTUS are pronounced as a word; initialisms like CIA are pronounced by spelling letter by letter.
- In general, write out single-digit numbers such as nine and use numerals for numbers of two or more digits such as 17 and 861.

Glossary

adjective   A word that modifies nouns.

adverb   A word that modifies verbs, adjectives, and other adverbs.

affix   An element attached to the beginning, middle, or end of a root or word that modifies its meaning. Affixes include prefixes, infixes, and suffixes.

agreement   The condition when parts of a sentence have the same case, gender, number, or person.

analogy   A comparison between two different entities or processes, usually based on a similarity between the two.

antecedent   The referent of a pronoun—the noun to which it refers.

appositive   A grammatical construction that puts a subject or object in different words. Appositives rename.

auxiliary verb   These include forms of *be, do,* and *has.* Auxiliary verbs add meaning to other verbs in some forms, such as "I had been studying." In that sentence, *had* and *been* are auxiliary verbs.

bias-free language   Language that is offensive or insensitive to any gender, race, religion, or sexuality.

case   How a noun or pronoun functions in a sentence. The case is different if a noun or pronoun is used as subject, object, or appositive.

clause   A group of words with a subject and a predicate.

cliché   A worn-out, overused word or expression that has become almost meaningless.

collective noun   A singular noun that also functions as a plural, such as *people.*

comparative   A word such as *better, bigger, faster,* or *taller.*

complete sentence   A group of words that has a subject and predicate and expresses a complete thought.

complex sentence   A sentence with an independent clause and a dependent clause.

compound sentence   A sentence with two independent clauses.

compound-complex sentence   A sentence with two independent clauses and at least one dependent clause.

conjugate   To show or produce the different forms of a verb.

conjunction   A word used to connect other clauses, phrases, or words—two common conjunctions are *and* and *but.*

connotation   The flavor or undertones of a word—the associations of a word. Connotation isn't the explicit meaning, which is denotation.

contraction   A shortened version of a word or words, like *don't* (do not) and *can't* (cannot).

dangling modifier   A word or phrase that modifies an entity other than the subject of the sentence. This error causes confusion.

demonstrative   A word that points to or stands for another. In English, the demonstratives are *this, that, these,* and *those.* Demonstratives can act as either adjectives or pronouns.

denotation   The literal meaning of a word, as opposed to the connotation, which consists of the associations of a word.

dependent clause   A group of words that has a subject and predicate but cannot stand on its own as a sentence.

diction   Word choice. This is why a word book is called a dictionary.

direct object   The entity acted upon by the subject of a sentence.

elliptical clause   A clause with some words eliminated for the sake of the sentence's sound. An elliptical clause is acceptable if it makes sense to readers.

euphemism   A softer, vaguer word for something, like saying employees were downsized instead of fired.

exclamation   A word or sentence with great emphasis, usually punctuated with an exclamation mark, such as "Hey!" or "My foot hurts!"

gerund   The *–ing* form of a verb used as a noun, as in "Swimming is fun."

grammar   The total structure of a language, including syntax and morphology.

imperative   A command, such as "Give me that!" or "Help me move this couch." The implied subject of an imperative is *you*.

imperfect   The verb form for an action that's still happening but isn't finished.

indefinite pronoun   A pronoun without a specific antecedent, such as *who, whom,* and *that*.

independent clause   A group of words with a subject and predicate that can stand on their own as a sentence. An independent clause is a complete thought.

indicative   A verb mood that states or declares something. "I am hungry" and "Squirrels are gross" are in the indicative mood.

indirect object   An entity affected by the action of the sentence. The indirect object is *Jim* in this sentence: "I threw the ball to Jim."

infinitive   The form of a word that includes *to,* such as *to eat* and *to defend*.

infix   An affix that is inserted into the middle of a word.

interjection   A word, usually short, that expresses an emotion. Interjections are often used as sentences in themselves. They include *mmm, ow, hey, uh,* and *yep*.

interrogative   A question or any form of a word related to questions.

interrogative pronoun   A pronoun such as *how, what, when, where, who,* and *why*. These pronouns are often used in questions.

intransitive verb   An intransitive verb can be used alone, with no object or complement, unlike a transitive verb, which must be done to someone or something. In "I stood," *stood* is an intransitive verb.

irony   A literary device that involves saying the opposite of what you mean, often for the sake of humor.

jargon   The language of a profession. This word can also refer to empty, pretentious language.

linking verb   A verb used to convey a state of being—the most common linking verb is *be*.

mechanics   The nuts and bolts of language, especially areas such as formatting and punctuation.

metaphor   A comparison that does not involve *like* or *as,* such as calling a crowd a swarm of people.

misplaced modifier   When a modifier is placed too far away from the word it should be modifying, creating confusion.

mixed metaphor   A metaphor that is inconsistent, like if you were comparing love to an ocean, and then suddenly the comparison shifted to a sandwich.

modifier   A word, phrase, or clause that changes the meaning of other words, often by describing them. Grammatically, modifiers are optional.

mood   A feature of verbs that signals the speaker's point of view or attitude. In English, the moods are indicative, imperative, and subjunctive.

noun   Not just persons, places, and things, nouns are also states of being and conditions. Nouns serve as subjects, objects, and direct objects in sentences.

object   The entity acted upon by the subject of the sentence.

parallel structure   When parts of a sentence have the same form, especially in a series.

participle   A verb used as an adjective, as in *screaming maniac* and *stalled car.*

phrase   A group of words with a specific function but lacking a subject and predicate.

possessive   The form of a word that indicates it belongs to another word. Many possessive words are created with the apostrophe and *s.*

possessive adjective   Adjectives such as *his, her, my, your our, their,* and *its.* These convey a relationship of ownership or belonging.

possessive pronoun   A pronoun that indicates what belongs to someone, such as *his, her,* or *their.*

predicate   The second half—and second essential part—of a sentence. (The first is the subject.) The predicate, which starts with a verb and sometimes only consists of a verb, tells what the subject does or is.

prefix   An affix that is attached to the beginning of a root.

preposition   A word signifying a relationship between other words, such as *between, of, on,* and *for.*

pronoun   A word used in place of another noun, such as referring to a man as *he* or a group of people as *them.*

punctuation   Marks such as commas, periods, and quotation marks that help convey meaning in writing.

redundancy   A repetitive quality in writing when the same information appears more than once while adding no additional meaning.

reflexive pronoun   A pronoun used when the subject performs an action on the subject—these include *myself, yourself, himself, herself, ourselves,* and *themselves.* For example, "I hurt myself."

relative clause   A dependent clause that modifies another element in a sentence. Also called an adjective clause.

relative pronoun   A pronoun such as *that, who, what, whatever, whom,* or *whomever.* Relative pronouns introduce relative clauses.

root   The smallest form of a word with meaning; *small* and *mean* are roots.

run-on sentence   An ungrammatical sentence in which two or more independent clauses are put together incorrectly.

sentence   A group of words that express a complete thought, usually consisting of a subject and predicate. A sentence can be a statement, question, or command (imperative).

sentence fragment   A group of words that does not comprise a complete thought. A sentence fragment is usually considered an error.

sexist language   Use of language that is insulting or unfair in some way toward women.

simile   A comparison using the words *like* or *as.*

simple sentence   A sentence consisting of one independent clause.

slang   Informal, humorous language that binds a social group.

split infinitive   When a word comes between the two parts of an infinitive, as in the famous example of *Star Trek*'s "To boldly go …"

style   A distinctive way of using language, such as the style of a magazine or an individual writer.

subject   The main actor of a sentence. The subject performs the action of a sentence.

subjunctive   A verb mood that expresses wishes and possibilities, such as "If I were you, I'd be careful," and "You should be home by 8:00."

subordinate clause   A clause that adds meaning to an independent clause but cannot stand on its own as a grammatical sentence. Also called a *dependent clause.*

suffix   An affix that is attached to the end of a word.

superlative   A word such as *fastest* or *greatest* that compares more than two things.

syntax   The way words, phases, and clauses are arranged in a language.

tense   The forms of a verb that indicate when an action occurs, such as past, present, or future. There are also several more complex tenses under the umbrellas of perfect and progressive.

tone   The level of emotion or formality in a piece of writing. Love letters have a romantic tone, while letters of application have a formal tone.

transitive verb   A verb that must have an object or complement to be used correctly. For example, you can't just schedule—you have to schedule a meeting.

usage   How a word is actually used in a language. This also refers to usage levels, which have different levels of formality.

verb   A word that conveys action or a state or being. Verbs make subjects active.

verbal   A word derived from a verb but used as another part of speech.

voice   Whether a sentence is active or passive. In active voice, the subject performs the action, and in passive voice, the subject is hidden or absent.

Resources

Books

Aarts, Bas. *Oxford Modern English Grammar.* New York: Oxford University Press, 2011.

Adams, Michael. *Slang: The People's Poetry.* New York: Oxford University Press, 2009.

Casagrande, June. *It Was the Best of Sentences, It Was the Worst of Sentences: A Writer's Guide to Crafting Killer Sentences.* New York: Ten Speed Press, 2010.

The Chicago Manual of Style, 16th Edition. Chicago: University of Chicago Press, 2010.

Clark, Roy Peter. *Writing Tools: 50 Essential Strategies for Every Writer.* New York: Little, Brown & Co., 2008.

Crystal, David. *Spell It Out: The Story of English Spelling.* London: Profile Books, 2013.

———. *The Story of English in 100 Words.* New York: Picador, 2013.

Fogarty, Mignon. *Grammar Girl's 101 Misused Words You'll Never Confuse Again.* New York: St. Martin's Griffin, 2011.

———. *Grammar Girl's Quick and Dirty Tips for Better Writing (Quick & Dirty Tips).* New York: Holt Paperbacks, 2008.

Goldberg, Natalie. *Writing Down the Bones: Freeing the Writer Within.* Boston: Shambhala, 2005.

Hacker, Diana, and Nancy Sommers. *A Writer's Reference with Writing in the Disciplines.* New York: Bedford/St. Martin's, 2011.

Hale, Constance. *Sin and Syntax: How to Craft Wickedly Effective Prose.* New York: Broadway Books, 2001.

King, Stephen. *On Writing: 10th Anniversary Edition: A Memoir of the Craft.* New York: Scribner, 2010.

Lammot, Anne. *Bird by Bird: Some Instructions on Writing and Life*. New York: Anchor, 1995.

Lanham, Richard A. *Revising Prose, Fifth Edition*. New York: Longman, 2006.

Liberman, Mark, and Geoffrey K. Pullum. *Far From the Madding Gerund and Other Dispatches from Language Log*. New York: William, James & Company, 2006.

Miller, Brenda. *Tell It Slant, Second Edition*. New York: McGraw-Hill, 2012.

MLA Handbook for Writers of Research Papers, Seventh Edition. New York: Modern Language Association, 2009.

Publication Manual of the American Psychological Association, Sixth Edition. Washington, D.C.: American Psychological Association, 2009.

Pullum, Geoffrey. *The Great Eskimo Vocabulary Hoax*. Chicago: University Of Chicago Press, 1991.

Strunk Jr., William, with E. B. White and Roger Angell. *The Elements of Style, Fourth Edition*. New York: Longman, 1999.

Thurman, Susan, and Larry Shea. *The Only Grammar Book You'll Ever Need: A One-Stop Source for Every Writing Assignment*. Avon, MA: Adams Media, 2003.

Trimble, John R. *Writing with Style: Conversations on the Art of Writing, 3rd Edition*. New York: Longman, 2010.

Walsh, Bill. *The Elephants of Style: A Trunkload of Tips on the Big Issues and Gray Areas of Contemporary American English*. New York: McGraw-Hill, 2004.

———. *Yes, I Could Care Less: How to Be a Language Snob Without Being a Jerk*. New York: St. Martin's Griffin, 2013.

Williams, Joseph M., and Gregory G. Colomb. *Style: Lessons in Clarity and Grace, 10th Edition*. New York: Longman, 2010.

Yagoda, Ben. *How to Not Write Bad: The Most Common Writing Problems and the Best Ways to Avoid Them*. New York: Riverhead Trade, 2013.

Zinsser, William. *On Writing Well, 30th Anniversary Edition: The Classic Guide to Writing Nonfiction*. New York: HarperPerennial, 2006.

Websites

Dictionary of American Regional English

dare.wisc.edu

This website contains samples from and news on DARE, which collects Americanisms that are not used across the entire country.

Grammar Girl

quickanddirtytips.com/grammar-girl

This website contains helpful advice on grammar written in an accessible, enjoyable style.

Language Log

languagelog.ldc.upenn.edu/nll

Professional linguists discuss a variety of language-related topics.

OWL (Online Writing Lab)

owl.english.purdue.edu/owl

Though aimed at undergraduate students, there's help available for anyone on grammar, style, and citation formats.

Oxford English Dictionary

oed.com

The largest dictionary in the world, this is the ultimate authority on the history of the English language.

Index

J–K

L

M

N